Gloria Steinem

Recent Titles in Women Making History

Ruth Bader Ginsburg: A Life in American History
Nancy Hendricks

Gloria Steinem

A LIFE IN AMERICAN HISTORY

William H. Pruden III

Women Making History
Rosanne Welch and Peg A. Lamphier, Series Editors

BLOOMSBURY ACADEMIC
NEW YORK • LONDON • OXFORD • NEW DELHI • SYDNEY

BLOOMSBURY ACADEMIC
Bloomsbury Publishing Inc
1385 Broadway, New York, NY 10018, USA
50 Bedford Square, London, WC1B 3DP, UK
29 Earlsfort Terrace, Dublin 2, Ireland

BLOOMSBURY, BLOOMSBURY ACADEMIC and the Diana logo are trademarks
of Bloomsbury Publishing Plc

First published in the United States of America by ABC-CLIO 2021
Paperback edition published by Bloomsbury Academic 2025

Copyright © Bloomsbury Publishing Inc, 2025

For legal purposes the Acknowledgments on p. xiii constitute an extension
of this copyright page.

Cover design: Gloria Steinem at the UN, 1978.
(Science History Images/Alamy Stock Photo)

All rights reserved. No part of this publication may be reproduced or transmitted in any form or by any means, electronic or mechanical, including photocopying, recording, or any information storage or retrieval system, without prior permission in writing from the publishers.

Bloomsbury Publishing Inc does not have any control over, or responsibility for, any third-party websites referred to or in this book. All internet addresses given in this book were correct at the time of going to press. The author and publisher regret any inconvenience caused if addresses have changed or sites have ceased to exist, but can accept no responsibility for any such changes.

Library of Congress Cataloging-in-Publication Data
Names: Pruden, William H., III, author.
Title: Gloria Steinem : a life in American history / William H. Pruden III.
Description: Santa Barbara, California : ABC-CLIO, [2021] | Series: Women making history | Includes bibliographical references and index.
Identifiers: LCCN 2021008708 (print) | LCCN 2021008709 (ebook) | ISBN 9781440872709 (hardcover ; alk. paper) | ISBN 9781440872716 (ebook)
Subjects: LCSH: Steinem, Gloria. | Feminists—United States—Biography. | Women political activists—United States—Biography. | Women journalists—United States—Biography. | United States—Social conditions—1945-
Classification: LCC HQ1413.S675 P78 2021 (print) | LCC HQ1413.S675 (ebook) | DDC 305.42092 [B]—dc23
LC record available at https://lccn.loc.gov/2021008708
LC ebook record available at https://lccn.loc.gov/2021008709

ISBN: HB: 978-1-4408-7270-9
PB: 979-8-2161-9516-0
ePDF: 978-1-4408-7271-6
eBook: 979-8-2160-9087-8

Series: Women Making History

To find out more about our authors and books visit www.bloomsbury.com
and sign up for our newsletters.

Contents

Series Foreword vii

Preface ix

Acknowledgments xiii

Introduction: Why Gloria Steinem Matters xv

CHAPTER 1
Roots of Rebellion? Young Gloria and Challenges on the Home Front *1*

CHAPTER 2
An Inquiring Mind *19*

CHAPTER 3
Journalist, Activist, and Feminist *39*

CHAPTER 4
To the Barricades *63*

CHAPTER 5
The Activist Life *81*

CHAPTER 6
Ms. Magazine *99*

CHAPTER 7
The Personal Is Political *123*

CHAPTER 8
The Good Fight in a Conservative Age *143*

CHAPTER 9
An Eye on the Future *159*

Timeline 179

Primary Source Documents 185

Bibliography 217

Index 225

Series Foreword

We created this series because women today stand on the shoulders of those who came before them. They need to know the true power their foremothers had in shaping the world today and the obstacles those women overcame to achieve all that they have achieved and continue to achieve.

It is true that Gerda Lerner offered the first regular college course in women's history in 1963 and that, since then, women's history has become an academic discipline taught in nearly every American college and university. It is also true that women's history books number in the millions and cover a wealth of topics, time periods, and issues. Nonetheless, open any standard high school or college history textbook and you will find very few mentions of women's achievements or importance, and the few that do exist will be of the "exceptional woman" model, ghettoized to sidebars and footnotes.

With women missing from textbooks, students and citizens are allowed to believe that no woman ever meaningfully contributed to American history and that nothing women have ever done has had more than private, familial importance. In such books we do not learn that it was womens' petitioning efforts that brought the Thirteenth Amendment abolishing slavery to Abraham Lincoln's attention or that Social Security and child labor laws were the brainchild of Frances Perkins, the progressive female secretary of labor who was also the first woman appointed to a presidential cabinet.

Without this knowledge both female and male students are encouraged to think only men—primarily rich, white men—have ever done anything meaningful. This vision impedes our democracy in a nation that has finally become more aware of our beautiful diversity.

The National Bureau of Economic Research said women comprise the majority of college graduates in undergraduate institutions, law schools, and medical schools (56 percent in 2017). Still, women's high college attendance and graduation rates do not translate to equal pay or equal economic, political, or cultural power. There can be little argument that American women have made significant inroads *toward* equality in the last few decades, in spite of the ongoing dearth of women in normative approaches to American history teaching and writing. Hence, this series.

We want readers to know that we took the task of choosing the women to present seriously, adding new names to the list while looking to highlight new information about women we think we know. Many of these women have been written about in the past, but their lives were filtered through male or societal expectations. Here we hope the inclusion of the women's own words in the collection of primary documents we curated will finally allow them to speak for themselves about the issues that most mattered. The timeline will visually place them in history against events that hampered their efforts and alongside the events they created. Sidebars will give more detail on such events as the Triangle Shirtwaist Factory Fire. Finally, the chapter on Why She Matters will cement the reason such a woman deserves a new volume dedicated to her life.

Have we yet achieved parity? We'll let one of our subjects—the Honorable Ruth Bader Ginsburg—remind us that "when I'm sometimes asked when will there be enough [women on the supreme court]? And I say when there are nine, people are shocked. But there'd been nine men [for over 200 years], and nobody's ever raised a question about that."

Preface

Gloria Steinem: A Life in American History examines the life of an improbable but undisputed leader of the second-wave feminist movement. As an entry into ABC-CLIO's Women Making History series, the book chronicles Steinem's life against a backdrop of the social, political, and cultural change that swept the nation and of which she was both a catalyst and a reflection. In that way it shows readers Steinem's efforts and impact in the women's rights movement of the late twentieth and early twenty-first centuries. The strides toward equality made by the second wave are often unrecognized by succeeding generations, who take the altered landscape for granted, making this biography all the more significant.

GOAL

The goal of this book is to examine the life of activist and journalist Gloria Steinem and the changes occurring in the United States in which she lived. In doing so it seeks to demonstrate how those changes came about and the role she played in shifting American gender values.

APPROACH

The 1960s were a period of unprecedented upheaval and change in the United States, a decade that triggered a series of changes and responses that would characterize the nation through the end of the twentieth and into the twenty-first centuries. With the advent of the Black civil rights movement, the women's movement, the War on Poverty, the pledge to land a man on the moon, and the effort to end the war in Vietnam, the United States became a cauldron for change. The changes themselves and their subsequent responses made for a restless, conflicted nation that struggled with how to address shifting social rules while trying to come to grips with America's role in the world.

Add to the equation the way television changed the way Americans saw themselves. As a national medium, television news and entertainment programs helped break down the barriers that prevented the development of a national consciousness. As a result, the long-established social hierarchy of race and gender began to crack. Out of the struggle emerged a new nation, one that came closer to fulfilling the promise of equality for all. Where that equality was not achieved, activists planted the seeds for eventual success. Nothing reflected the ethos of expanding equality more than the women's movement. The study of Gloria Steinem's life and work in that movement provides a distinctive lens through which to view the changes of the times, because as a journalist and as an activist, she bridged the divide. Thus her story helps illuminate our understanding of what happened and why.

Using a narrative approach, the book traces the path by which Steinem arrived at her place as the iconic face of the women's movement and one of the leading reformers of the twentieth century. The introductory chapter examines why Gloria Steinem matters. Her place within the movement and the impact of the movement on the United States become clear, as well as the importance of her story to American history. The introduction will also lay out the lessons that can be taken from Steinem's half century of activism.

The biography begins with Steinem's distinctive, if star-crossed, youth, one in which, from the time she was eleven until she finished her junior year in high school, she was the primary caregiver for a mother who suffered from mental illness. The experience, coupled with her parents' divorce, clearly had an impact on much of her later life, and all of that will be evident to readers. Her college education and the early days of her career as a freelance journalist are presented in a straightforward narrative fashion while also providing the context of a country as it enters the height of the Cold War and faces the upheaval that would come to be considered characteristic of the 1960s. Steinem's work as a political journalist and her own political involvement place her squarely in the midst of this change. And after she has her feminist awakening, she experiences what proves to be a life-altering turn of events—at the same time that the developing women's movement is poised to hit its stride.

The meshing of the movement and her life is at the heart of the book's story. Whether it be her work with the creation of *Ms.* magazine or the divisions within the movement of which she is, however, unwillingly, a part, Steinem's life and actions serve as an effective lens through which to view both her and the movement, as well as other changes in journalism, in politics, and in the nature of leadership that are central to the United States of this era. In looking at Gloria's life and in observing her decades-long efforts, one gets a course in political activism and organizing. It is just one of the many ways in which, however unconsciously, her leadership stems from the way her life is a reflection of the changes that occurred. In fact, part of her importance, as well as her prominence, stems from the fact that she embodies so much of what she advocates. All of these aspects, as well as her evolution from late-blooming feminist to cultural icon, are explored.

Given Steinem's extensive network, both social and professional, the journey through her life also serves as a survey of much of the political and social history of the period. In addition, where she is not at the center of the activism, her writing generally reflects the times, offering insightful commentary on the issues of the day and thereby also serving as an effective lens through which to view American politics and society.

Steinem's centrality and longevity, as well as an overriding vision and distinctive approach, served to connect not only the variety of movements—civil rights, women's, and antiwar—but also the different trends that characterized the changing politics of the 1960s and beyond. Whether it was a matter of being in the vanguard of sixties liberalism or serving as a foil of the resurgent conservatism of the 1980s, Gloria was at the heart of the changing times, so a look at her life and actions allow for one to get a picture of the broader tableau. All of this is presented in a way that connects Steinem to the life and times in which she lived, worked, and advocated.

The narrative approach is abandoned in two chapters, each of which focuses on a particular aspect of Steinem's life and career. One is devoted to her work with *Ms.* magazine, a central element of both her life and legacy as well as of the women's movement. The other chapter addresses her high-profile personal life, something that was no small part of the celebrity status that fueled her reform efforts. At the same time, a look at that part of her life offers greater insight into the human side of the advocate and activist.

Throughout the book, sidebars shine a spotlight on a person, event, or object that helps the reader more fully understand Steinem, the movement, or the era. Each sidebar is intended to help expand the reader's understanding and appreciation for both Steinem and this distinctive and tumultuous period. To help put Steinem and the women's movement into a clearer historical context, the book also includes a timeline, a series of historical highlights over the course of her lifetime, which helps provide a better sense of her place and role in the ever-changing American landscape.

SOURCES AND USAGE

Along with the parenthetical citations throughout the book, there is an extensive bibliography of print and electronic media. These items represent a combination of items central to the creation of the narrative as well as additional items that provide for an expanded understanding of people and events central to Steinem's life and the women's movement. Of particular value were previous works on Steinem, especially Stern's *Gloria Steinem: Her Passions, Politics, and Mystique,* Heilbrun's *Education of a Woman: The Life of Gloria Steinem,* and Marcello's *Gloria Steinem: A Biography.* Cohen's *The Sisterhood: The True Story of the Women Who Changed the World* and Thom's *Inside Ms.: 25 Years of the Magazine and the Feminist Movement* were also very valuable. Given her early work as a journalist and her never-ending writing efforts, be they books, freelance articles, or items in *Ms.,* Steinem's own writing is an invaluable resource for anyone seeking to better understand who she is and what she did. The accompanying bibliography includes all her books, but offers only a representative sample of her articles, including the best known and most influential. Of these books, *Outrageous Acts and Everyday Rebellions* and *My Life on the Road* are the most valuable.

Readers would be well served to further pursue these works as well as looking at some of the various media offerings now available, including the HBO special, *Gloria: In Her Own Words,* and ABC News's *Nightline: UpClose with Gloria Steinem* (2007, DVD).

Acknowledgments

The author wishes to thank Dr. Peg Lamphier and Dr. Rosanne Welch of California State Polytechnic University, Pomona, for the opportunity to write this book. They had the faith that I could make the transition from encyclopedia entry writer to book author, and I hope I have done them justice. I owe Peg a special debt of gratitude. Her support and encouragement were invaluable as she patiently oversaw my efforts. I want also to thank Dr. Guy Lancaster, editor of the *Encyclopedia of Arkansas*. It was Guy who first opened the door to substantive historical writing for this high school history teacher and aspiring historian, providing a chance that has proven to be rewarding beyond my wildest dreams.

Introduction: Why Gloria Steinem Matters

When the modern women's movement, spurred by the publication of *The Feminine Mystique* in 1963 and the founding of NOW in 1966, began to take shape in the late 1960s, the United States was a very different place from what it would become. The existing limitations, formal and informal, on the opportunities available to women would be unimaginable to the women of the 2020s who have benefited from the movement's efforts.

Consider that when the U.S. House of Representatives convened in January 1971, there were 12 women members, but when the House convened in 2019, the number of women members had climbed to 102, with a woman, Representative Nancy Pelosi, of California, wielding the gavel as Speaker of the House. Similarly, the 1971 U.S. Senate included only one female member: Margaret Chase Smith, of Maine. By 2019, 25 Senate seats were occupied by women. As of 1971, the United States had had only had three women governors, all of whom had followed their spouses into the job. The first woman elected governor on her own merits was Connecticut congresswoman Ella Grasso, in 1974. There were nine as of January 2019, and in the intervening forty-five years, over thirty additional women have served as their state's chief executive. That same period also saw an explosion in the number of women who won election to offices at the state and local level (and Gloria Steinem campaigned for more than a few of them).

Meanwhile, in 1984 a woman, Geraldine Ferraro, was chosen as the Democratic nominee for vice president. Women also broke through to serve as campaign managers for major party nominees in 1988 and 2016. In the latter year, the United States finally saw a major party nominate a woman for president, when the Democrats selected Hillary Clinton as their standard-bearer. Fewer than four years later, the ranks of aspirants for the 2020 Democratic nomination included four female senators, including the ultimate vice presidential nominee, Kamala Harris.

The same period also saw unprecedented increases in the number of women serving as college and university presidents, and the number of female corporate CEOs has also reached unprecedented heights. In 1960 women made up less than 4 percent of the nation's lawyers, but by 2018 the number of American lawyers who were women was up to 38 percent. And lest anyone think that was an aberration, in 2017, for the first time, there were more female students in the nation's law schools than there were men. Similarly, in 1950 women made up approximately 6 percent of the nation's doctors. By 1990 that percentage had risen to 17, and in 2000 it was just under 23. By 2015 the percentage of American physicians who were women was up to 39 percent.

The last fifty years have seen a sea change in the status of women in the United States, and while no one would pretend that any single person was responsible for that change, much that occurred can be traced to Gloria Steinem's unceasing efforts to reshape American culture so that women would be not just accepted but embraced in such positions of power and influence. No one has been a more continuing presence, a more consistent cheerleader, or a more determined and dedicated advocate for the cause of women during that time than Steinem has been.

In 1963, when Betty Friedan's *The Feminine Mystique* was published, Gloria was a struggling writer, and in NOW's early years she regularly rebuffed its efforts to get her to join the group. While the challenges she faced as a single working woman typified those faced by women across the country, the developing feminist revolution was, at that point, the furthest thing from Gloria's mind. Yet by the early 1980s, when Ronald Reagan's ascension to the presidency and the failure to ratify the Equal Rights Amendment (ERA) signaled a slowing of the women's movement, Gloria Steinem had become the undisputed public face of the movement. Her image, her personal story, and her efforts were inextricably intertwined with and representative of the movement that sought to empower over half of the nation's population. While many factors and actors combined to change the landscape of American society, no individual has achieved a higher public profile, made more important contributions, or come to more fully symbolize the second-wave feminist movement than Gloria Steinem has done.

The movement and the changes it brought were multifaceted, and so, too, were Steinem's involvement and impact. She was no mere symbol. She acted as an engine, moving from issue to issue, past countless challenges. While she would eventually move in lofty social circles, ones that belied her roots, her status reflected the fact that given the same opportunities as men (particularly white, upper-class men) enjoyed, women could flourish. That fact enabled her to make a distinct connection—both in fact and symbolically—with the nation's women. She became an inspiration to a generation of women who wanted to be Gloria Steinem. Her intelligence was a rebuke to the stereotype that equated beauty to stupidity. Her attractiveness, as well as her social cachet, while sometimes a cause for envy, was no less a rebuke to the naysayers who argued that the women's movement was made up of old maids and angry dykes—women who could not "get a man." Gloria embodied the movement's promise that if the doors of opportunity were opened, the freedom to choose was secured, and the right to define success was made real, women could be anything and anyone they wanted.

Gloria's emergence as the face of the women's movement stemmed in no small part from her being at the center of a convergence of forces and changes that characterized the United States during her lifetime. She grew up at a time when the American dream, the ability to do better than one's parents, was alive and well. It was a time when establishment-approved credentials, such as a Seven Sisters degree, carried a certain cachet that could propel a working-class young woman through the doors of American opportunity. At the same time, the civil rights movement, and later the women's movement, sought to upend the established order. And the establishment itself saw a massive increase in democracy in the aftermath of the Voting Rights Act and the Democratic Party's response to the Chicago convention. The world was changing, and Gloria personified that change. Then as the years passed, Gloria also served as the public representative of the ever-dwindling group of activist veterans who harked back to the movement's heyday in the 1960s and 1970s. At the same time, she became tired, if not resentful, of questions about why the women's movement died, arguing that the question itself was a testament to the movement's success, a reflection of the fact that rather than being a separate cause, its continuing concerns were an integrated part of a changed American society.

Through it all, while glamorous Gloria had left a trail of high-profile lovers in her wake, she had also wrestled with the generations-old societal expectations that said that she should settle down, get married, and have children. In continuing on a single, career-oriented path, she embodied a central tenet of the movement: a woman's right to make choices, one of which was to establish herself as an independent entity with accomplishments and status unrelated to a relationship or a man. And as she has aged, Gloria has embodied the timeless issues connected with the changes that aging brings to women. Gloria has never been able to avoid the issue of her beauty, but she has also never been comfortable with it. In her later years, though, she has attacked perceptions of beauty as they relate to aging and in doing so has again become a pioneer.

In fact, autonomy, not independence, has been Gloria's touchstone, and it has impacted her approach to life and work. She has always sought collegial and supportive working environments. Whether in her early efforts as a lecturer crisscrossing the country, always teamed up with a partner, or in her work as an organizer, she consistently sought to work with others to develop a team or organization that could further the cause. She did not put herself front and center; any impression to that effect was a product of a celebrity-focused media that anointed her the face of the movement. Not surprisingly, Gloria the writer professed that the "only . . . kind of power I want . . . is the power to persuade," asserting, "I do not want the power to tell other people what to do" (Shriver 2011). Indeed, her work as a writer and grassroots organizer has offered clear evidence of that preference. Like many other female leaders, she has preferred nonhierarchical, collaborative work, and, as she did at *Ms.*, she has created systems of decentralized authority whenever possible. All of it reflected her belief that "revolutions that last don't happen from the top down. They happen from the bottom up" (Shriver 2011).

At the same time, befitting both her roots as a political reporter and the lesson long ago imparted by her mother that "democracy is just something you must do every day, like brushing your teeth," for five decades she consistently and continually worked for change through the electoral process (Steinem 2015). From her role as one of the founders of the National Women's Political Caucus (NWPC) to her continuing efforts on behalf of candidates running for large and small offices alike, she has demonstrated an unceasing commitment to increasing the involvement and influence of women in politics. Yet for all her high-profile appearances, it was the appearances she made on behalf of candidates, to whom she offered support simply because she believed their election would enhance the humanity she sought that meant the most to her. Year after year she made countless appearances, often unheralded, on behalf of candidates seeking offices at all levels in towns and cities from coast to coast. For them, an appearance by Gloria and the local buzz it could create or the added funds it could raise could change the whole tenor of the campaign. Those appearances were also the more comfortable and rewarding efforts for Gloria, especially since she disliked being overly tied to a party line. Consequently, appearing on behalf of candidates running in local races where she could take a more personal approach was far more appealing, and such events came to increasingly dominate her calendar. In many ways her greatest political contributions were made behind the scenes as an organizer and fundraiser—or as a mediator, such as when the organization of the NWPC threatened to break down amid a battle between Betty Friedan and Bella Abzug. Gloria Steinem authored the organization's mission statement, secured compromises on some key issues, and then traveled the country to help organize and fund local chapters. It was the same role she later filled at the National Houston Conference.

The fact that Hillary Clinton not only won the Democratic nomination for president in 2016 but also won more popular votes than Donald Trump was not just a product of the effort made in that campaign. It was also the product of over fifty years of consciousness-raising, fundraising, and persuading; of countless talking circles and auditorium speeches; of marches and countless other means that were used to help shift and shape people's perspectives and to help women realize what they could do, what opportunities they could pursue, and what rights they were entitled to. And Gloria was involved every step of the way. Indeed, in the same way that Barack Obama's election in 2008 was, at least to some degree, a culmination of some of the efforts of Martin Luther King Jr. and his generation of civil rights activists, so, too, was Hillary Clinton's near miss a product of the efforts that Gloria and others expended over the last five decades. An article in the *New York Times* titled "2019 Belongs to Shirley Chisholm" noted that fifty years earlier, in 1969, Chisholm, the first African American woman to hold a seat in Congress, had emerged, and that five decades later she was beginning to be recognized in a whole different way by a new generation. Steinem's efforts not only helped fuel Chisholm's political rise in the 1970s but also have recently helped keep people like Chisholm and Bella Abzug alive in the minds of an American populace that suffers from a dangerous case of historical amnesia that undermines the cause of women.

From the beginning, Gloria had a broader vision of the women's movement, one that never changed and that others eventually came to embrace. Tied to that vision was the distinctive place that she occupied in the women's movement and, indeed, in the reform community at large. She was a self-described radical, and when she articulates her vision of the global society of the twenty-first century, the label fits. And yet, unlike most radicals, she was not an outsider, although she always tried to understand those who were. Through it all, she built relationships and made connections that could ultimately help further the cause. When she came to the movement, she was recognized as a journalist and activist, but she seemed to have tentacles in countless other areas. Her past political efforts, her political ties, and her ongoing campaign activity were well known and gave her easy access to political figures like George McGovern and countless others for whom she had campaigned, media figures she had worked with stretching back to the Youth Festivals, and countless other figures from the arts and society at large who were active supporters of the movement toward equality. In addition, she counted among her friends the pioneering attorney, later judge and justice, Ruth Bader Ginsburg, as well as Brenda Feigen Fasteau, who had served alongside Ginsburg in the early days of the American Civil Liberties Union's (ACLU) influential Women's Rights Project. All of this extended Gloria Steinem's reach and influence, but more importantly, it allowed her to see the big picture in a movement she hoped would ultimately impact the biggest of audiences: the world.

Having been partially involved with the civil rights movement, and understanding poverty from her own life and what she saw in India, Gloria's feminist ideology was founded in the quest for human equality. And, of course, her first article after her feminist awakening, "After Black Power Comes Women's Liberation," connected the two movements in terms of common roots and goals. Building upon that philosophical base, Gloria performed an important role as the media-created, singular leader of a movement that changed the country. Yet as her view on passing the torch has made clear, she understands she was never the real face of the movement. Indeed, she knew, even if it sometimes seemed that others did not, that no single person could be the face of a movement and no movement worth its salt could be encapsulated in one person or one symbol. Instead, all movements, but in particular the women's rights movement, reflect a broader group and must be diverse in ways that no single person could be. Rather, as she made her own path, she was vigilant in her efforts to expand the field of those who played important roles and to be sure they were recognized for it. From her partners on her speaking tours to her NWPC colleagues to the writers and readers whose voices she showcased in *Ms.* to the important role of Black civil rights pioneers in the women's movement, she consistently sought to spread the credit and highlight the other leaders and human resources the movement had to offer. Equally telling is the fact that when asked, as she often has been, whether there should be another Gloria Steinem to continue the effort, she has replied simply but emphatically, "I don't think there should have been a first one" (Hepola 2012).

No small part of Gloria's influence has stemmed from her distinctive style and a middle-of-the-road interpersonal approach that helped bridge the many divisions that marked the movement. No one could accuse her of being anything less than tenacious in her pursuit of equality and the other goals high on the movement's agenda. However, unlike the bombastic Bella or the caustic Betty, Gloria was able to discuss and present issues in reasonable and human—and no less committed—ways. This allowed her to make real connections with the broader populace who made up the feminist constituency. No less valuable was her willingness to do the things behind the scenes that were so necessary and important. Yes, she was front and center in most of the various organizational photo ops, but that was less by desire than by design and in some cases was little more than a grudging recognition that Gloria was a media magnet for the movement they all cared about.

In fact, in the early going, as she began to travel and speak with her partners, her journalism bent cut both ways. The diligent researcher part of her made her fully prepared, while after some prompting, the storytelling journalist came to realize the value of hearing and then sharing the stories of the women she met. She came to realize that central to advancing the cause of women's rights was helping women understand that their pain, their frustration, their fear of loneliness was not theirs alone but was instead something they shared with many others. There was strength in numbers, and this realization helped countless women come around and begin to address their situation. Her road show and countless appearances across the country provided a forum for those women while also serving as a classroom for them and for her. Her ability to bridge this divide was unique to her and represented a singular part of her influence.

All of this reflected her approach to activism. Author Susan Brownmiller, one of the many feminists who have alternately challenged and been in awe of Gloria's status over the many years of their shared involvement in the movement, noted that part of Gloria's enduring influence comes from her calm, low-key approach. While a highly visible presence for decades, she was never the boisterous one like her friend Bella Abzug or the acerbic one like Betty Friedan. Instead, because Gloria Steinem sported an appealing sense of humor, a way with words, and a calm tone and presence that reflected her impressive listening skills, people saw in her, at least in Brownmiller's view, a calm figure who helped them feel comfortable with the women's movement she represented. She made clear that it was not the emasculating effort that opponents tried to make it. And over the years, Steinem's approach has never really changed. Whenever she appears at an event, she is, as befits her celebrity status, always drawing crowds. But Brownmiller further observes that what makes Steinem different is that even while she is at the center of a crowd, she is inevitably listening, always trying to learn, always trying to empower women with stories to share (Leland 2016).

Part of Gloria's influence and impact is based in her writing, which she has used both to further the movement and shape the culture. Whether in her articles or books, all of which, at their best, shine a probing and insightful spotlight on important issues, she helps raise public awareness and consciousness. In addition, the attention her writing has gotten has often been an offshoot of her other efforts. Indeed, given her high public profile, if Gloria says something, it gets more attention than that same statement or insight offered by a lesser-known advocate. Similarly, the author's name plays no small role in at least an initial interest in a book or article, and while it is impossible to read readers' minds, there can be little doubt that it has impacted the circulation and readership of her work. In general, her works have been thoughtful, if sometimes forced, especially in her efforts to relate them to women's issues—*Marilyn* and *Revolution from Within: A Book of Self-Esteem*, despite Gloria's own avowals of the importance of self-esteem to all people, but particularly to women's well-being, fit into that category. At the same time their lack of any great insight does not detract from the fact that they still added substantively to the important ongoing dialogue and debate that the country had to engage in if any of the goals that she has long discussed were to be achieved. So, too, did her later work, *Doing Sixty and Seventy*, which offered a road map to the challenges of aging for a generation—her own—that had never navigated those later years in the changed climate. It was not something from which they could draw on their mother's experiences, so Gloria tried to fill the void.

No less important an element of her writing efforts was her work with *Ms*. The pioneering feminist magazine served as a forum for the movement, for American women writers, and for the countless women who had felt they had no voice but, through the pages of the magazine, were now given one. *Ms.* combined investigative pieces with ones that both highlighted women's accomplishments as well as the previously ignored women who did them. The magazine's own operations also served to showcase a new kind of cooperative workplace while illuminating the tangled relationship between journalism and corporate marketing. And it helped raise awareness about the role—the ever-growing role—of women in the American consumer culture. Few things are more central to Gloria's legacy than *Ms.* is.

In addition to her unrivaled reach, one that was reflected in the impact and influence of *Ms.*, part of Gloria's power and influence was simply a product of her enduring involvement with the women's movement. Back at the beginning, she had planned to be involved in the movement for a few years before moving on with her life. Instead, it became her life. The idealistic, self-proclaimed "hopeaholic" came to believe that if the movement could just explain to people how unjust the situation was and how unfair the laws were, then they would accept equality for women. To do just that, Gloria set out to spread that message, one gymnasium, auditorium, community center, and college cafeteria at a time—and she never stopped. She has seen it all. She has been in the forefront of the battles and the primary target of the backlash. But through it all, she has remained dedicated to a cause that she has articulated as long and as passionately as anyone can.

Central to that longevity is the fact that Gloria has never lost her ability to connect. While her core beliefs have never changed, she has responded to societal changes and the context in which events took place in a manner that has allowed her to continue to make an impact. Unlike some pioneers, she has adapted to the changes in the world, the issues that matter, and the political landscape. From the start, Gloria's involvement with the movement was multifaceted and wide ranging, and during those times when she might have sought to limit her involvement, others pulled her back in. Her unparalleled ability to inspire activity and gain media attention for whatever cause they were seeking to highlight made her an unrivaled asset. There are those who will someday say that when Gloria was well into her eighties, the nation was almost two full decades into the twenty-first century, and some saw her as a veritable dinosaur, out of touch with and irrelevant to the feminists of the time, but no one could afford to dismiss her. For whether they realized it or not, virtually everything upon which they were basing their ongoing efforts were things to which she could point and take some credit for having turned into their new reality. The very things that were taken for granted in 2020 were almost without exception the fruits of the labors of the many women who had devotedly marched with Gloria in pursuit of a revolution, and it remained important for her to keep that history alive and to make sure, in the midst of another period of retrenchment under President Trump, that women understood how far they had come and how precious and hard earned that progress was.

Critics have accused Gloria of being mired in the 1960s and 1970s, unable or unwilling to adapt to changing times and the diversity demands of global, third-wave feminism. She has generally responded by noting that the issues she addresses and the causes she advocates—equality, respect, freedom to choose—reflect eternal truths, not ones that change with the times. Her aviator glasses may have been replaced by modern rimless frames and her skirts are not the minis of generations ago, but for Gloria equality has never been a fad, and on more than a few issues, especially on the global front, she can rightfully say she was there all along.

Indeed, after over fifty years of working for female equality, she has a clear vision of what twenty-first-century feminism should look like, and it is very much in line with the humanist agenda she has long extolled. For Gloria, feminism is the right and the opportunity for every woman, everywhere, to define herself. After five decades of activism, she believes many people have come to accept the idea that women can do what men can, and the inverse, that men can do what women can, though much progress remains to be made in accepting the full personhood of all women.

One reason Gloria chose to continue her activism into her seventies and eighties was that she recognized no one else could do what she does; she became an icon, whether she sought that status or not. She bridles at critics who suggest she should pass the torch, instead explaining, "No, I'm keeping my torch, thank you very much. And I'm using it to light the torches of others. Because the truth is that the old image of one person with a torch is part of the problem, not the solution. We each need a torch if we are to see where we're going. And together, we create so much more light" (Steinem 1983). And recognizing the number of still unlit torches that remain, Gloria believes that as long as she can make a difference, she intends to keep doing so. Of course, she is the repository of as much institutional and movement history as anyone in the United States could be, as well as the feminist who could most quickly get the media to pay attention to an issue or event. At the same time, her historical perspective leaves her knowing that all the change she had seen, all the progress that American women have made, did not happen by accident and could be undone. And so Gloria continues to lead in the way she always has—by effort and example.

For all her accomplishments and her high public profile, Gloria has remained something of an enigma and was sometimes a contradiction in terms. She was determined to create a world based on merit and accomplishment, but she was not above developing relationships that could help her climb the career ladder. But in that way, she reminded us that heroes and heroines are people too. Gloria endured the vagaries of being a public person in a changing political and cultural landscape, and she kept issues important to American society on the national agenda. She has sometimes seemed like the national nag, but while not always right, she has never failed to contribute to the dialogue that is central to democracy. Indeed, her view of utopia is based in the freedom to choose for all.

Never forgetting the lesson she learned in her geology class at Smith—"ask the turtle"—or the talking circles she discovered in India, she listened to what not just women but all people wanted, and in responding she expanded our view of what we—women and men—can do. In opening those doors, she has enriched our possibilities. At the same time, those same efforts have also brought forth new challenges, but she also helped strengthen the nation's ability to respond to them. And in the end, those new challenges are a reflection of the way she has altered a national culture: its politics, its economy, and its cultural norms. The women's movement changed the way people thought about their roles. It changed peoples' dreams and altered their views of what was possible. For five decades, Gloria has worked in numerous ways to alter that dynamic and make those changes real. Before live and large audiences, in one-on-one conversations, in talk circles across the nation, through the pages of her books and articles, and on countless television appearances, she has helped shape the nation's culture—political and social—so that it did not just allow for previously unimagined change but, in fact, fostered and encouraged it.

Looking back, it is clear that some of Gloria's influence came from her acute understanding of the times in which she lived and was working. Based in her experience as a journalist, as well as an instinct for what was newsworthy and would connect with people, she was able to help the women's movement understand and take advantage of the changing news and the media, especially the new importance of style and its importance to those seeking to spread its message. She was to reform and activism what John F. Kennedy (JFK) was to politics, and while the attention that it focused on her own looks may have been a curse she had to bear for the rest of her life, it also furthered the movement.

Like her friend, jurist Ruth Bader Ginsburg, Gloria Steinem's own distinctive talents and image were equally suited to her times and the change she sought. *The Feminine Mystique* arrived as the civil rights movement was moving into high gear; and in an era inspired by JFK's style, including the way the glamorous Pulitzer Prize–winning statesman made intellectualism fashionable, the chic, stylish Gloria, Seven Sisters degree in hand, seemingly came out of central casting to lead the charge for women. At the same time, while not lacking in ego, she would be the last to say she did it alone. While she did not seek the mantle of the face of the revolution, she was savvy enough about the way the media worked to understand what the movement needed. She was not unwilling to assume the leadership opportunities that came her way while also working to expand the tent and encourage the outreach she knew was needed if true progress and change were to be achieved.

For all her understanding of the importance of image and style, she has often been happiest and even perhaps most effective out of the spotlight and behind the scenes, dealing with the people whose horizons she has sought to broaden and whose opportunities and choices she has sought to expand. Calling herself an entrepreneur of social change, Gloria has steadfastly remained determined to do justice to the women—each and every one—that she has met. While she has long termed herself an organizer, given the nature of the work and the fact that what little documentation there may be consists more in old plane tickets than tangible results, that important part of her work and what will be her legacy is often overlooked. And yet the individual impact has been central to her efforts. Whether it was in the indelible memories that people have taken away from hearing her speak or seeing her sitting on the floor listening as part of a group, she has consistently made both a personal and societal impact. Through efforts that she is proud to note have been part of a travel odyssey that has taken her to all fifty states, she has made an incalculable impact on many levels. But at its core, the lessons that were passed down from mothers to daughters and increasingly to granddaughters, young girls who were now the unknowing beneficiaries of her efforts, were, on a personal level, Gloria's greatest accomplishments.

Ironically, in seeking to figure out why Gloria Steinem matters, one runs head-on into the core of what Gloria Steinem as a person and as an activist, has been all about. Throughout her time as an activist she was committed to the idea that everyone matters: the housewife, the porn star, the single mother, the activist, the victim—everyone. For Gloria, a person's lot in life did not change the fact that every individual had an inherent dignity and deserved respect, regardless of the individual's gender, race, sexuality, or any other artificial distinction that obscures common humanity. There is no denying that over the course of Gloria's long life, she has sometimes stumbled in sharing that message, but there was never any doubt about the depth of her commitment. In fact, given her focus on others, the fact that she should be singled out for a biography and that people should ask why she matters is something she would find preposterous.

In fact, the fruits of Gloria's influence are apparent in countless ways, large and small. As she noted in the updated edition of *Outrageous Acts and Everyday Rebellions,* she has witnessed countless women, as well as some men, engage in outrageous acts and everyday rebellions like leaving a violent husband or lover, proudly proclaiming oneself a feminist, organizing a group to register and vote, leaving home for a week so that a father could learn to be a parent, asking for a long-deserved raise, calling out someone for an inappropriate sexist joke, personally contacting a politician to discuss an issue of particular interest to women, . . . and the list goes on. But in typical fashion, what she fails to mention is that in many of those cases the rebellious or courageous action was inspired by her own words or her own rebellious example. However, regardless of the source, each of those actions reflects an empowerment and an altered consciousness. Those are the foundation of the message that is so central to the continuing efforts. They are all offshoots of the efforts that Gloria began so long ago and has continued ever since.

"Why does Gloria Steinem matter?" To those who came of age in the 1970s and early 1980s, this seems like a trick question. So widely quoted were her feminist views, so ubiquitous were reports of her actions—political and social—and so widely viewed was her face, with its aviator glasses framed by the long, center-parted hair, that she seemed to be the movement. Yet while she long ago made clear that she was "tired of seeing [her] own" face, she never wavered in her commitment to the cause of equality (Cohen 1988, 317). Indeed, to that generation, any suggestion that Gloria was not someone who mattered, someone to be reckoned, someone whose views were not important, was absurd. Yet with the passage of time and the advent of new generations for whom history is yesterday's news, the question is not so much, does she matter? but, who was, and is, Gloria Steinem? The fact that she is no longer in the forefront of the nation's consciousness is, in its own way, a reflection of why she matters. Because, in fact, much of what Gloria fought for is now taken for granted by generations of women who think the country has always been the way it is now. Yet make no mistake, Gloria Steinem mattered—and still does.

For all the identifiable firsts and milestones, for all the specific barriers surmounted by the women's movement, it is the change in the national attitude and the culture that represents its greatest victory. And no one played a bigger role in achieving that change than Gloria did. Indeed, in the end, the best, the most enduring, and probably for Gloria, the most satisfying answer to the question, "Why does Gloria Steinem matter?" can be found in a conversation with any modern, young American woman. Perhaps she cannot answer the question, "Who is Gloria Steinem?" But when asked, "What are you going to be when you grow up?" she can joyfully and confidently reply, "Anything I want!" In that expression of unbounded optimism and limitless ambition, in that unwillingness to admit to any boundaries, she offers the clearest evidence there is of why Gloria Steinem matters.

1

Roots of Rebellion? Young Gloria and Challenges on the Home Front

Gloria Steinem did not set out to change the world, and certainly, by most standards her background and early life made her an unlikely revolutionary. Her paternal grandmother, Pauline Steinem, had been a leader of Ohio's suffragette movement in the latter part of the nineteenth and early part of the twentieth centuries. Pauline also addressed Congress on the issue and was the first woman elected to the Toledo, Ohio, Board of Education (Stern 1997). Yet little in Gloria's early years pointed to her pursuing a similar path of activism. Rather, her childhood and precollege years were focused on the daily challenges of life. But this focus helped Gloria develop a worldview that would impact the rest of her celebrated life. Many of her early experiences, including the challenges she faced, fueled a determination to never be dependent on others or limited in her ambitions. These ideas were central to a feminist movement designed to provide new and unfettered opportunities for the largest part of the American and global population, whose freedom she sought to advance for most of her adult life.

Gloria was born on March 25, 1934, in Toledo, Ohio. Her parents were so excited about their new daughter that the accompanying birth announcement termed her arrival a "world premiere." Gloria was the second of two daughters born to Leo and Ruth Steinem. The Depression-era baby was a response, at least in part, to the insistent entreaties of her nine years older sister, Susanne, who desperately wanted a sister. Not only was

Sue's wish granted, but the older girl was allowed to name the family's new addition, and she happily bestowed the name of her favorite doll, Gloria, on her new baby sister. It was not the last important role Sue would play in Gloria's life (Stern 1997).

Gloria's parents were a distinctive pairing. Her father, Leo, was the youngest of four sons. His father, Joseph Steinem, was a successful businessman, and his mother, Pauline, was actively involved in public affairs at a time when most women stayed home. Leo was a fun-loving, independent entrepreneur and aspiring entertainment impresario, a man who, Gloria once observed, was inordinately proud of the fact that he never wore a hat and never had a boss. Gloria's mother, Ruth, was the daughter of Joseph and Marie Nuneviller. Joseph was a railroad engineer, while Marie had been a teacher before having her children, Ruth and a sister, Janey. Growing up, Ruth was bookish and insecure. She spent her first two years in college at the prestigious Oberlin College. When the family could no longer afford Oberlin, she transferred to the University of Toledo, where she lived at home and worked as a part-time bookkeeper to help the family's finances. Ruth graduated from the university with a degree in math in 1920. She remained at the university for another three years, earning a master's in American literature and also teaching math. Her path crossed Leo's in the fall of 1919. Leo was the editor of a student newspaper that he and a friend had founded. Ruth, having just transferred, gravitated toward the paper, and Leo, as impressed with her looks as her writing talent, made her the paper's literary editor. She quickly climbed the ranks at the paper and was soon editor in chief—and Leo and Ruth became a couple (Stern 1997).

Despite their differing personalities, Leo and Ruth married in the summer of 1921 before a justice of the peace. While such unions were increasingly common in the United States, the pairing of the Jewish Leo and the Christian Ruth came amid a period of heightened anti-Semitism and anti-immigrant sentiment in the United States. Recent incidents, such as the lynching of Atlanta businessman Leo Frank, who was Jewish, and the hotly contested nomination to the Supreme Court of that body's first Jewish member, Louis Brandeis, highlighted the nation's increasing anti-Semitism. The phenomenon also fed the resurgence of the Ku Klux Klan, whose early 1920s attacks were focused on Jews and Catholics. Unfortunately, Leo and Ruth were not exempt from the feelings of this fractious time. Ruth recognized that their union would meet with opposition, so in the hope of breaking down barriers, at first, Ruth and Leo only told family members that they were engaged. Then later that year, the couple had a formal wedding ceremony performed at Ruth's home. But despite the couple's effort to give their families time to adjust, the marriage still met with opposition in some quarters, and a number of family members on both sides boycotted the affair.

As a wedding present, Leo's parents gave the couple a plot of land in Toledo as well as funds sufficient to build a home. Having promised her mother that upon graduation she would try teaching, Ruth taught calculus for a year, but hating the work, she turned to her real love, writing, and got a job with the *Toledo News Bee*, which soon afterward was purchased by the *Toledo Blade*. Over the next few years, while pursuing a rewarding career as a writer, Ruth was as happy as she had ever been. When Susanne was born in 1925, Ruth took a year off from work, but in the fall of 1926, she excitedly returned to the *Blade* as the grandmothers pitched in to care for the family's newest addition. Meanwhile, Leo worked at a range of jobs, including serving as a photographer for ad agencies, while pondering a move into the entertainment field (Marcello 2004).

In the summer of 1926, with financial help from his father, Leo and Ruth Steinem bought thirty acres of land on Clarklake (it is often spelled Clark Lake, but Gloria herself has always written it as one word), in Michigan. There they built a cottage. Ever the entrepreneur, Leo undertook to build a summer resort, which he christened Ocean Beach. They soon built an additional Mediterranean-style house large enough to accommodate visiting family members. In 1928, Leo built a dance pavilion at the end of the pier he named Ocean Beach Pier. Leo's grand enterprise meshed with the beginning of the Big Band era, and in its early years, big names such as Harry James, Guy Lombardo, Duke Ellington, and Count Basie included Ocean Beach Pier on their summer tours. To facilitate the musicians' appearances, Leo built a separate cottage to house the touring entourages (Stern 1997).

Gloria's earliest years were happy, full of activity and adventure. In summer, the family lived at Clarklake, and Gloria reveled in the freedom the resort allowed children. She spent most of her time dressed in a series of red bathing suits that were chosen by her mother to help her pick her daughter out in a crowd. Of course, not even the red bathing suit helped when Gloria ducked under the pier, scavenging for loose change that had fallen into the water the previous evening. She raised a puppy, took piano lessons, and even, at one point, had her own horse. At nine years old, she discovered tap dancing. One of the cigarette girls at the Pier taught the basics to Gloria and her best friend at the time, Jackie, and they later took lessons in Jackson, the closest town. To her family's rueful dismay, Gloria soon was dancing seemingly everywhere she went (Marcello 2004).

While Clarklake represented a stable summer existence for the first ten years of Gloria's life, once the summer season had ended, the family traveled regularly to California and Florida to escape the cold while satisfying Leo's nomadic, entrepreneurial instincts. In fact, to ensure that the less adventurous Ruth could not settle at Clarklake, Leo constructed the various residential domiciles at the resort without adequate heating to survive the Michigan winters. Consequently, the family's winter travels to the warmer climes were a necessity. Pulling a trailer behind their car, the family would usually look for a trailer park where they could take showers and settle in for the night. Once they reached the chosen destination, the trailer became their home. The family alternated between Clearwater Beach, Florida, or Laguna Beach, California. Sue and Gloria generally found the long treks boring, with Gloria dismissively rejecting her mother's admonition to look out the window at the countryside. But Gloria adapted, and while she would later recognize that the lack of consistent, formal schooling left her with some holes in her educational foundation, it also provided the voracious reader with lots of time to pursue her passion. Indeed, she once said that she had initially learned to read from candy wrappers and the Burma Shave billboards that dotted the highway landscape. At the same time, the nomadic nature of her early life made her independent and adaptable, traits that would serve her well in the years to come. And while the experience clearly left gaps in her knowledge, it also fueled her curiosity while giving her real-life experiences that few of her peers could match (Steinem 2015).

Another central element of these years was Leo's traveling antique business, the kind of entrepreneurial enterprise that characterized his life. Given the nature of their travels, the Steinems specialized in small china and glass objects as well as antique jewelry. Years later, Gloria would say that while her father was usually the trader, her mother had a better eye for the antiques, as well as the patience and industry to actually read up on them. But it was clear to all that the traveling operation was a perfect fit in Leo's freewheeling approach to business. Over the years, Gloria would often play a role in her father's work. She could be the smiling helper wrapping items before the sales, but she had more fun playing the young daughter of the struggling father who was forced to sell family heirlooms to support his daughters and wife. While Gloria was enjoying helping her father, not to mention the chance to play act, many buyers went away thinking they had made a one-of-a-kind purchase from the forlorn traveling merchants (Stern 1997).

In the end, being the considerably younger daughter of these ill-fitted parents meant that Gloria's early years were a mix of highs and lows. In early 1944, the couple's marital discord reached its peak when Ruth learned Leo had mortgaged the whole Pier and Clarklake property. Tired of the economic instability that had marked their life together, Ruth determined that they should separate. That decision was followed in 1945 by divorce, itself an interesting phenomenon, given that to her dying day, Ruth held onto the belief that she was not really divorced. She was steadfast in her belief that since she and Leo had been married twice—the secret ceremony and the formal, family-sanctioned one six months later—but had only divorced once, the bond sealed in the second ceremony was never broken (Heilbrun 1995). That belief aside, relations had been deteriorating as their economic fortunes sagged. The situation was only worsened by the wartime restrictions on gas that impacted travel and recreation across the country and made life particularly hard for resorts like Ocean Beach Pier. It was a particularly tough time for young Gloria, especially once Sue departed for college, leaving Gloria with her warring parents.

While Gloria realized fairly early that her life and that of her family was not normal, life in the aftermath of the separation was not either. Ruth and Gloria left Michigan and moved to Amherst, Massachusetts, where Ruth rented a small house less than ten miles from Smith College, where Sue was a junior. Although they stayed for only nine months, the time in Amherst was idyllic and represented a period of unprecedented calm that Gloria would remember fondly. It also represented a distinctive stage in her growing up and in the evolving family dynamic. While she missed her father, she did not miss mediating her parents' arguments. Also, being settled in one place for a whole school year, Gloria was, for the first time, able to attend school on a daily basis. Finally she had the chance to engage in the usual group activities, such as kickball, that marked a normal ten-year-old's world (Stern 1997).

At the same time, Ruth, who over the years had experienced periodic bouts of apparent depression, seemed to benefit greatly from the newfound familial tranquility. For the most part, she was calm and on an even keel in their new surroundings, and she made a concerted effort to give Gloria a more normal and complete life. Ruth tried to make up for lost time, exposing Gloria to things that their nomadic existence had caused her to miss. Foremost among these was having Gloria baptized, a ceremony that was performed at Amherst's Congregational Church. Ruth found the ceremony more meaningful than her daughter did. Indeed, Gloria would later observe that despite, or perhaps because of, her mixed Jewish and Christian heritage, she never had great interest in, nor found any real identification with, either side of the religious divide that marked her formal identification. She has long noted that when she is with people who are touting the virtues of one or the other, she is apt to highlight her own competing roots. In either case, her baptism notwithstanding, her youthful views on religion seemed little different from those she held as an adult (Marcello 2004).

The end of the 1944–1945 school year meant the end of a period that, in retrospect, was an idyllic, if aberrational, calm period in Gloria's young life. Sue planned to spend the summer in New York City working for Georg Jenson, a well-respected silver company, so Ruth and Gloria moved to Scarsdale, New York, where Ruth served as the house sitter for a former college friend. Sue often came out from the city on weekends, but with Ruth unable to afford a car, she and Gloria did little and went nowhere.

Soon life dissolved into a state all too reminiscent of the pre-Amherst days. Ruth reverted to her depressed state and was subject to frequent hallucinations. Lacking any kind of care or adult supervision, she spiraled downward. Meanwhile, Gloria again found refuge in books, which for so long had provided solace, but the carefree social interactions that had characterized her school year in Amherst became little more than a distant series of pleasant memories (Stern 1997).

As the United States emerged from World War II at the end of the summer of 1945, the Steinems dispersed. Leo who had headed to California after the separation returned briefly to help Ruth and Gloria move back to Toledo while Sue returned to Smith for her senior year. With the ending of summer, the cloud of uncertainty that had hung over the year in Amherst disappeared, only to be replaced by an unpleasant certainty when Ruth decided to divorce Leo. While time may have colored her memories, Gloria recalled that it was harder for Sue, who had youthful memories of a more joyful family life, than it had been for her, to whom the divorce represented an end to the fighting that had marked her youth (Heilbrun 1995). However, while one part of Gloria's life came to an end, she was about to embark on a period that would test her in a way nothing else ever had.

The return to Toledo began one of the toughest extended periods of her young life. For most girls her age, these years were a time of excitement as they began the march first through middle, or junior high, school and then high school. It was a time to experience a new sense of adventure as well as a range of social interactions. They often began to enjoy the sometimes mysterious time when a boy began to catch a girl's eye and vice versa. And for some students—such as Gloria's sister Sue (and likely Gloria as well)—attention turned toward college and the future for which such an educational experience would be an important stepping-stone. But the years from 1945 to 1951 held little of such excitement for Gloria. Oh, she would sample bits and pieces of normal, but she was in a very abnormal situation: the centerpiece of her life was the care and support of her mother, a woman whose sense of reality was limited, who regularly suffered hallucinations—which were often terrorizing and led to behavioral aberrations—and whose fears often served to make her a prisoner in her own home. And through this whole period, from the time she was eleven until she was seventeen, Gloria was often the only person—the only thing—that stood between Ruth and potentially dangerous and self-destructive behavior.

In fact, Ruth's year of normality in Amherst soon became just a memory, and her erratic, inconsistent behavior returned with a vengeance, rendering Gloria a virtual prisoner. Beyond the basics, such as going to school and grocery shopping, Gloria seldom ventured far from home. Her mixture of concern for her mother as well as her fear of being embarrassed by Ruth's erratic behavior was the greatest constant in her life. It was not easy.

Ruth's behavior was inconsistent, often inexplicable, such as the time Gloria discovered that her mother had painted the windows black so they would not have to watch the indecent behavior—of which there was none—of the people next door. All of this—and more—left Gloria in a consistent state of anxiety.

The situation could be traced back to a time before Gloria was even born. While the family generally cited the time in 1930 when Ruth had what the family termed a "nervous breakdown" and was sent to a sanitarium, the breakdown, in fact, seemed to have its roots in a series of events in the preceding year.

In the summer of 1929, a teenage boy had fallen off a water ride at Clarklake and had broken his neck. Ruth, who had been on the pier and witnessed the accident, was inconsolable and needed to be given a sedative by a family friend and local doctor, Kenneth Howard. The medication, which came to be called "Dr. Howard's medicine" by the family, was in fact a mixture of chloral hydrate and potassium bromide, a combination that in large quantities was known as knockout drops or a Mickey Finn (Marcello 2004).

While it would prove to be the start of a longtime dependence on the medication, in the short term it did the trick. And yet Ruth remained fearful of repercussions from the accident even when a subsequent lawsuit was dismissed. Given her very real, lingering anxiety and shaken by the stock market crash—which jolted the nation's confidence—as well as by the death in December of Leo's father, followed two months later by the death of her own father, the once vivacious woman Leo had married was suddenly anxious and needy. Sometimes she would physically hold onto her husband in seeming desperation. She sometimes went days without sleep. In desperation, later that spring, Ruth entered a sanitarium (Stern 1997).

She returned home after a few months, but the birth of a stillborn son in January 1932 sent her into depression, and she became all the more dependent on "Dr. Howard's medicine." While Ruth was able to refrain from using the medical concoction while she was pregnant with Gloria, it had nevertheless become a central part of her life and would be a constant companion during the years she and Gloria would live together in Toledo. In later life, Ruth would be formally and officially diagnosed as having anxiety neurosis. But only after Gloria was in college, Ruth was living with Sue, and more advanced and less debilitating medication had become available did "Dr. Howard's medicine" no longer play a major role in controlling and limiting Ruth's life (Steinem 1983).

So it was that in the fall of 1945, in the aftermath of their return to Toledo, and for the next six years, the potentially overwhelming burden of caring for Ruth fell to Gloria. Out of these circumstances emerged a routine and style of life that Gloria would pursue throughout that time period.

While the year in Amherst gave Gloria a taste of what daily school attendance was like, it was, ironically, only when she returned to Toledo and was saddled with the additional burden of caring for her mother that Gloria finally enjoyed a consistent and stable school experience. And despite all the other burdens, it was a school experience she relished. Yet, like many aspects of her life at that time, it was one she compartmentalized as she attended first to her mother and the care of their home, always fearful that Ruth would do something that would either embarrass her or simply increase the burden in some additional way.

Ruth inherited the old family homestead at 747 Woodville Road in East Toledo when her parents died; the former family residence had been remodeled and then housed three apartments. However, when Ruth and Gloria returned to Toledo, all the apartments in the house were occupied. Thus they initially were forced to rent a basement apartment in West Toledo, the upscale side of town. Gloria liked the area but was taken aback by the size of the apartment, which was in fact built in a space behind the utility closet in a local boardinghouse. To get to their one-room bedroom/living room, they had to walk past a huge boiler furnace. Meanwhile, the kitchen and bathroom were even farther back. And if they tried to look outside through the limited windows, all they saw were the tires of the cars parked outside. With space being limited, mother and daughter shared a bunk bed, with the younger and more agile Gloria occupying the top level (Stern 1997).

Once they got settled, Gloria started sixth grade in Monroe Elementary School. Relocating had taken some time, so Gloria got a late start on the school year. However, while she again enjoyed the stability that school provided, the late start, coupled with her erratic early education, left her having to fake her way through some knowledge that was assumed of a sixth grader. But the quick-witted Gloria was able to surmount the gaps. Indeed, despite being both a newcomer and joining a class that had pretty much progressed through school together, she quickly made friends. Conveniently, her soon-to-be best friend lived in the boardinghouse. Sixth grade offered a number of new challenges and experiences. While the boys often seemed intimidating, she vowed to make one her boyfriend. Even more of landmark was getting her first pair of glasses. With her parents and Sue all having glasses, getting her own pair made Gloria feel more grown up. Despite the distinctive dynamic at home, once Gloria settled in at school, she started to feel more normal (Marcello 2004).

The feeling of comparative comfort would be short lived, for as the summer unfolded and seventh grade loomed, Gloria's life was again upended. As sixth grade came to an end, the tenant in the basement apartment in Ruth's building on Woodville Road moved out. Consequently, Ruth and Gloria prepared to move yet again. After a series of discussions, the upstairs occupants, the Barnes family, whose two daughters would soon become Gloria's friends, opted to move to the basement apartment. This left Ruth and Gloria with the smaller, upstairs one. An additional inconvenience arose from the fact that the upstairs apartment's kitchen didn't have a sink—and in all their years there, they never got one. Leo came to town to help with the move, but Gloria made it clear she was not happy about relocating to East Toledo which she, like most of the area's residents, saw as the wrong side of town. To make matters worse, the house was rundown and the neighborhood, dominated by the stench of the long-forgotten factory area it had been, was unappealing. The local male residents were for the most part factory workers, truck drivers, and clerical workers, while the women were most often mothers and housewives. Few were educated, and there was an air of resignation among the many who were struggling to get by. It was an environment that only reinforced the often-dispiriting nature of Gloria's daily existence (Stern 1997).

The challenges surrounding the move to Woodville Road were only increased when Ruth's hallucinations became more pronounced. After an extended struggle, Gloria finally convinced her mother to see a doctor, the only one Ruth trusted, a man who had treated her at the sanitarium back in the early 1930s. After only a short meeting with Ruth, her condition clear, the doctor advised Gloria that her mother needed to be institutionalized and admitted to a state hospital immediately. Despite her youth, Gloria had seen news articles about the often-abusive treatment that patients at such hospitals received, and while caring for her mother was an obvious burden, Gloria refused to even consider such a possibility. In addition, the savvy preteen knew that even if it were a safe option, given their limited income—an almost subsistence-level amount that came from a combination of sources including rent from the other Woodville Road tenants, Gloria's occasional dancing performances, and the lease on Ruth's part of the Clarklake land—the cost of hospitalization would be prohibitive. Instead, Gloria determined to shoulder the responsibility and care for her ailing mother—and herself—as best she could (Marcello 2004).

And care for them both she did. In fact, during the Toledo years, Gloria ran the household. She paid the bills—usually writing out the checks for Ruth to sign. She did the laundry. She shopped for groceries, and she put out the traps to catch the rats that were a constant reminder of their difficulties. She also cared for her mother who was often sick or struggling with the effects of Dr. Howard's medicine, one of which was frequently slurred speech, something that led some of the few neighbors who interacted with Ruth to think she had a drinking problem. In addition, Gloria went to school, but compelled to rush home at the end of the school day to check on her mother, she seldom played outside for fun. Rather, excursions for Gloria, be they to the grocery store or the doctor, were almost always undertaken with a specific purpose (Stern 1997).

Gloria never asked anyone for help with Ruth, though she did receive some assistance and help from family members in the Toledo area. Still, given that some of the relatives lived within walking distance of Gloria and Ruth's first residence, the limited amount of help and the intermittent contact offered by family members was shameful. Gloria's grandmother, Marie, sometimes came by to help clean the house, but her disdain for their slovenly housekeeping style often served to only heighten tensions. Meanwhile, Gloria's Aunt Janey, Ruth's sister, sometimes bought Gloria clothes, though she evinced little sympathy for her sister's illness. In fact, after one argument between the sisters, Ruth threw Janey out of the house. That incident so badly fractured relations that Aunt Janey told Gloria she could call if ever there were an emergency, but otherwise she would not be returning to the house (Stern 1997).

While Sue's work in the jewelry business often involved traveling, she nevertheless kept in frequent touch with her sister and mother and always returned to Toledo for Christmas. After hearing from Janey about the condition of their home, Sue tried to get Ruth to bring Gloria to Washington, DC, where she was now settled and where they could live together, but Ruth stubbornly refused. Meanwhile Leo's brother, Uncle Ed, a skilled handyman was a major help, keeping their aging oil burner operational in the cold of winter. In her typically stoic fashion, while knowing that other family members were undoubtedly aware of their travails as well as her mother's illness, Gloria never appeared to doubt that Ruth's care, as well as the responsibility for their day-to-day lives, rested with her.

Part of that responsibility involved their income, and often during the dark days in Toledo, Gloria would supplement the family's income by dancing at local Elks clubs, earning as much as ten dollars a night for her efforts. Also, while in high school, Gloria auditioned for the *Ted Mack & the Original Amateur Hour*, hoping that her talent might provide a way out of Toledo. And notwithstanding her later disparagement of her looks and their impact on her life and career, she entered at least one local beauty pageant during that same period, again in the hope that success might offer a way out of her difficult life. However, her second-place finish, behind a woman who had gotten a divorce in order to qualify as "Miss Capehart," did little to hasten Gloria's escape from Toledo (Stern 1997).

Things changed a bit when, in the fall of 1948, Gloria, moved on from Raymer Junior High and entered Toledo's Waite High School. There, despite the ongoing challenges with her mother, Gloria seemed to thrive, compiling a strong record through the end of her junior year in the spring of 1951. When Gloria entered Waite High School, she knew only four girls. One was a close friend from the elementary school that Gloria had attended during her first stint in Toledo, while the other three were, like Gloria, new to the school. The group soon started a secret society of their own, choosing the moniker Chi Alpha Tau (CAT). Gloria and her peers initially intended to limit the membership to their core group, all of whom were required to make good grades and be actively involved in other clubs to maintain their membership. However, they subsequently expanded membership in response to developing resentment among the part of the student body that was excluded. The core five also realized that a larger membership could give them greater influence in the school community, a status they sought and relished (Stern 1997).

With school and its attendant extracurricular activities offering a form of escape, Gloria got involved in a range of things beyond CAT. Befitting her love of books, Gloria joined the Periclean Literary Society, although its mother-daughter events always posed a risk. However, regardless of how Ruth presented herself or was perceived, Gloria always treated her mother with respect. In addition, having joined a Girl Scout troop in junior high that was sponsored by a favorite teacher, Gloria had accumulated a sizable collection of merit badges over the course of her involvement (Stern 1997).

Gloria was also active outside of school. Building upon her tap dancing experience, she also took ballet lessons, and by the time she was a junior, she danced in some junior concerts with the Toledo Orchestra. In addition, she joined a group called the Christian Convalescent Entertainment Society, a traveling group that put on shows at supermarket openings, Elks clubs and nursing homes. While Gloria was paid for some of her appearances, in the end the experience was more notable for the real-world lesson it offered when the group's organizer abandoned the troupe, taking its accumulated funds and leaving a bunch of unpaid performers in his wake. Beyond her dancing, Gloria was involved in an impressive array of additional activities. One was an internship, sponsored by another of the city's high schools, that allowed her to work at a school radio studio, where she learned to work off a script as well as cue records. The experience would lead to a paid afterschool job at a local commercial station. She also got a job working at David's, a clothing store in the city's downtown. No one would have confused her life with normal, but while she was still dogged by fears of her mother acting out in some unexpected or embarrassing way, as she approached the end of her junior year, Gloria had managed to craft a high school career that provided experiences that were rewarding while at the same time preparing her for the next stage of her life (Stern 1997).

Yet none of that could erase the insecurities that Gloria faced throughout her tenure as Ruth's caregiver. She was forever fearful that Ruth would do something that would embarrass her and tear the curtain away from the closely guarded domestic image that Gloria had tried to create for her friends. A constant cloud lingered overhead, always with the potential to undo all Gloria tried to do to fit in and be accepted by her peers. It made the Toledo years a roller-coaster ride, a series of nightmares interspersed with memorable events of middle school and high school. In many ways it was the unpredictability that was the worst part, especially the times when Ruth acted out in public, wholly embarrassing her teenage daughter who, like all her peers, just wanted to be like everyone else. All too typical were the times in the middle of the night when Ruth would start banging on the piano, and if Gloria was home—and she tried to stay with friends as often as she reasonably could—she had to settle her mother down with medicine. Then there was the time that Ruth threw a bowling ball down the stairs of the house, and, five minutes after a neighbor downstairs returned it, she threw herself down the stairs. Apparently unhurt, but muttering to herself, she left an indelible and frightening impression on the two girls, Gloria's friends, who lived downstairs (Stern 1997).

Ruth could be paranoid, hallucinatory, timid, angry, stuporous—or normal. Gloria was never sure what she would find when she checked in on her mother after school. Would she, as once happened, return home to find Ruth's clothes strewn all over the front yard, or would she have to bring her back inside after Ruth had run out into the snow dressed only in her nightgown? On quiet days, Ruth would be quietly waiting at home. On quiet, bad days she would be lying on the couch hallucinating, and on bad days she would descend into her own world, replaying in her mind stories about property stolen from Clarklake or expressing fears about the Nazis who were coming after them because of Leo's family. Or she might just rant—about Leo or about the threats she thought she was experiencing. It was a terrifying time (Marcello 2004).

Too often were the occasions when Ruth awoke from an afternoon nap, disoriented and frightened in the early winter darkness, and unable to remember that Gloria was at her afterschool job, she called the police to find her. The scene that followed, when sirens accompanied the police officers who came to her rescue and took her home, left Gloria embarrassed and with little to say to her friends. The effect was devastating, and when a humiliated Gloria angrily rebuked her mother, who forlornly apologized, it made for a tragic human drama that played out in front of the neighbors, an audience that had no real understanding of the family dynamics or background but made judgments just the same (Marcello 2004).

From the start, the neighbors, as well as Gloria's friends, were aware that things in the Steinem household were different. Not only had they seen Leo come, help with the move, and then suddenly leave, but one day during the summer they moved in, Gloria dragged a pair of wooden hobbyhorses on casters out onto the sidewalk. They were a couple of feet high and had been used at Clarklake by adults who had bounced up and down on the springs propelling the horses down the piers in some highly spirited and hotly contested races. As Gloria tried unsuccessfully to teach her friends, the Barnes girls, how to do it, Ruth suddenly appeared. Dismissing

Gloria's effort, she told the girls that if they were going to do it, they needed to do it right. Then, despite being dressed in what one of Gloria's friend recalled as an evening gown, Ruth hitched up her dress, tucked the front part into her waistband while folding the back between her legs, and climbed up on one of the horses. She then proceeded to triumphantly ride down the street as if she were a jockey in the Kentucky Derby. After galloping back, with great aplomb she climbed off, declaring triumphantly, "That's the way it's done." Then, as the amazed Gloria and her friends tried to process what they had just witnessed, Ruth walked back up the stairs (Heilbrun 1995). It was no wonder the Barnes girls would never know what to make of Ruth.

Such incidents, good and bad, made it impossible for Gloria to find comfort or refuge at home. Over the years she had a couple close friends who would sometimes venture to spend the night at Gloria's and as a result were made privy to at least some of the "secrets" that loomed in the Steinem household, from the rats to the unusual division of household responsibilities. But for the most part, Gloria found her safe spots outside her home, engaging in activities and with friends who provided a welcome diversion from her usual unusual life. Her favorite seventh-grade teacher, the one who introduced her to Girl Scouts and led the troop herself, was an important source of adult support during seventh, eighth, and ninth grades (Marcello 2004).

As an underaged homemaker and given their circumstances, a balanced diet was rarely central to Gloria's day. More common was a bologna sandwich and a lunch box pie on a school day that had likely started with coffee and toast. Meanwhile, what housekeeping she could do among the still unpacked boxes and crates that Leo had helped move was haphazard at best. In fact, Gloria's lifelong comfort with sitting on the floor likely had its roots in her Toledo furnishings. Her bedroom furniture was made up of a mattress and box springs on the floor with an old packing crate making do as a closet. The living room featured stacked books and papers that made up an armchair of a sort. The only real pieces of furniture were a rocking chair and a spinet piano that Ruth had brought with her over the course of their many moves. These comforts of home were complemented by the aforementioned rats that often frequented the apartment, especially after Ruth had the collapsed roof of the garage next door torn down, leaving the rats homeless and anxious to migrate to a new place (Marcello 2004).

Once when Gloria was bitten by a rat, Ruth screwed up enough courage to leave the apartment and take Gloria to a local emergency room for treatment. Deeply touched at the time, Gloria would years later recall the episode as showing the kind of motherly support she desperately wanted. And in fact, in an effort to force Ruth to again assume her maternal role, early on Gloria would fake being sick, hoping to prod her mother into action, but her efforts were in vain and only pushed Ruth into a greater depression over her inability to be the mother she wanted to be and knew Gloria deserved. So Gloria soldiered on at home (Stern 1997).

And, of course, even Gloria's best plans and intentions could be knocked askew when Ruth had a bad hallucination. Few episodes were worse than the time in November 1947 when Ruth, convinced that World War II was raging all around them, sought to avoid arrest by the Nazis by trying to escape. Seeking to evade capture, she put her hand through the window, which resulted in a nasty cut that Gloria had to bandage. The young teen then gave her mother Dr. Howard's medicine in the hope that it would soon do what it did best: make Ruth sleep and, in turn, give Gloria some peace and solace on what was, in fact, Thanksgiving weekend. As she calmed her mother, holding her hand to comfort the ailing woman, she also held Charles Dickens's *A Tale of Two Cities* in her other hand as she sought to complete her homework. Engaging in such a balancing act was not unusual while living in the apartment, whose sporadic heating often forced mother and daughter to sleep together for warmth and whose lack of a sink meant that, when all the dishes were dirty, they had to be dumped into the bathtub to be washed (Marcello 2004).

Given such realities, one of the things that made the Toledo years even more challenging was the fact that Ruth did experience occasional periods of normality and calm. These would raise, at least briefly, Gloria's hopes, only to later dash them when another episode occurred. Ultimately, the uncertainty only heightened anxiety, for during the best of times, Gloria could never forget how quickly things could change, nor could she ever be sure of which Ruth she was dealing with. While Ruth would apologize profusely, it would do nothing to assuage Gloria's embarrassment, and the situation was made all the more difficult by Gloria's inability and unwillingness to explain. When pressed by friends or neighbors, she offered little more than a simple avowal that Ruth was sick. And yet the few friends who pierced the veil and saw the places that Gloria and Ruth inhabited got at least an inkling that it was far more than just that (Stern 1997).

The occasional moments in which Ruth escaped her demons and experienced good times only added to the confusion of outsiders. A prime example was the time that Ruth responded to a notice for auditions for an amateur drama group that was putting on Bible-based productions. A production about Noah's Ark saw Gloria getting an onstage role while Ruth made thunder come alive by shaking metal sheets backstage (Marcello 2004). The happy episode represented a brief period of normality as well as a shared mother-daughter experience that defied their everyday life. In addition, when she was at her best, the former English major taught her daughter to appreciate Dorothy Parker's poetry. She also shared often eccentric bits of motherly wisdom that enhanced their bond. One of the more memorable was Ruth's admonition to Gloria to never eat anything with meringue topping, because, Ruth explained, if the baker had sneezed near it, it would absorb the germs. Heeding her mother's advice, Gloria steered clear of meringue for years. Sometimes, too, Gloria was able to get Ruth to write her a small check that the young teen could cash and then spend at the drugstore or for a movie, like any other child her age. But too often Gloria was confronted with the reality, one that cruelly made her youth irrelevant, that Ruth could not function without Gloria's total support. So Gloria maintained her role as the resident adult and plowed ahead, addressing as best she could the rat infestation—a problem she solved by establishing a network of traps and cages around the apartment—a consistent lack of heat, and the wealth of other issues—that dogged their existence.

Though Ruth became the dominant figure in Gloria's life following her parents' separation and ultimate divorce, Leo did not disappear during the Toledo years. He came for regular visits and often sent the girls presents. He would frequently send oranges from his Florida travels. But befitting Ruth's often bizarre behavior, there were instances when Leo came to visit and Ruth would not allow him in the house. Despite these challenges, Gloria maintained a good relationship with her father, one based in her early years when the family had traveled over the course of the fall and spring. Gloria fondly recalled serving as her father's apprentice on their antique-based travels, and while she later said she found the trips boring, she also recognized that it was there in the back of the car that she became the voracious reader who devoured Nancy Drew and the Hardy Boys as well as comic books such as Batman and Wonder Woman (Marcello 2004). On drives to Florida and California, Gloria also discovered her "friend," Louisa May Alcott, all the while developing the foundation for her later work as a writer and journalist. Ultimately, however sporadic and inconsistent her dealings with her father, he was at the center of some of her earliest memories and lessons about independence and sales skills (Stern 1997). And she treasured the way he treated her as a person whose opinion mattered. Despite the challenges of her overburdened childhood, many of which could have been easily laid at his feet, to his dying day, Gloria professed an understanding of her father's actions as well as an abiding love for the man whose quest for autonomy she would one day mirror (Steinem 2015).

The father-daughter connection was cemented in its own way and for all time in the spring of 1951. With Gloria's senior year in high school looming over the horizon, an opportunity arose that would forever change the trajectory of her life. For years Ruth had sought, with no success, to sell the lot behind the Woodville Road house. However, that spring, the church next door offered Ruth eight thousand dollars for both the lot and the house, which it planned to tear down, clearing the space for a new church annex. Faced with this new opportunity, Leo and Sue joined Ruth and Gloria in Toledo, and together they tried to determine a plan for the future.

Meanwhile, unbeknown to their parents, Sue had shared with Gloria an idea she had long harbored and that she hoped would free Gloria of the state of virtual imprisonment that had become her lot (Stern 1997).

The girls arranged a separate breakfast meeting with their father at the Purple Cow, a small restaurant in Toledo. There Sue proposed that Leo assume responsibility for caring for Ruth for the coming year. At the same time, Gloria would move to Washington, live with Sue, and finish high school in the capital, in preparation for heading off to college. Leo's initial reaction was exactly as Gloria had feared. He dismissed the idea out of hand. He not only noted that he and Ruth were divorced but also maintained that he could not make a living while also caring for Ruth. Following an awkward silence, Sue stormed out of the restaurant. In contrast, Gloria simply and resignedly reminded her father that she needed to get to work. Father and daughter drove silently to David's, the small Toledo clothing store where Gloria worked (Stern 1997). But when she opened the door to get out, to her own surprise, not to mention her father's, she began to sob. Overwhelmed at the prospect of another year caring for Ruth, Gloria could not hold back the tears. Stunned, Leo seemed finally to understand just what his little Gloria had been going through. In a startling reversal, he agreed to take Ruth for a year—a definitive time frame marked by the synchronization of their watches—after which Ruth would again become the girls' responsibility (Heilbrun 1995). The turnaround not only gave Gloria a year of comparative freedom but also, in its own way, served as a launching pad for the rest of her life. Following that initial decision, the girls and their parents all agreed that the proceeds of the sale of the house would be put aside to pay for Gloria's college education. And with that, the plans for her move to Washington got underway. The shared family effort was a turning point in the lives of all the Steinem women.

Ironically, in terms of permanence and day-to-day routine, the years of living in Toledo and caring for Ruth represented Gloria's most stable, if often dispiriting, daily existence. Yet she had no qualms about a change. Rather, despite the fact that it represented yet another move, Gloria was excited on many levels to head to Washington. But not surprisingly, the move was not without incident. Sue had to convince her roommates to accept another occupant, and the other working women were leery of an addition, not to mention one who was still in high school. But to smooth the waters and make way for her little sister, Sue agreed to give up her dog, already a source of some discord among the roommates. In return, Gloria was accepted into the fold. Although a decade younger, her beyond-her-years maturity and sense of responsibility helped calm the waters. Also, the fact that Gloria's more mature dating patterns, which included at least one almost thirty-year-old junior naval officer, helped erase concerns that Sue's roommates may have had about babysitting her little sister. In the end, the general spirit and energy with which Gloria pursued her newfound freedom made her an easy roommate. Throwing herself into her final year of high school, she created no problems for the older women and their living arrangements (Stern 1997).

For Gloria, the year in Washington and Georgetown proved liberating in many ways. Freed from having to care for her mother, and living in a rented townhouse in the Georgetown section of the nation's capital with her sister and her two roommates, Gloria was able to be a teenager and a high school student. While clouds loomed—the anxiety about college plans as well as questions about what would happen to Ruth after this clearly defined one-year interlude—Gloria nevertheless dove into her new life as a high school senior. Despite being a new girl at the city's Western High School, a well-respected school whose peak enrollment was about two thousand students and which was located within easy walking distance from Sue's house, Gloria quickly became a central player in the school's daily life. Because Western was Gloria's sixth school, she was adept at making new friends. The transition was also made easier by the fact that the city's rather large and somewhat transient government and political employee-based population meant that she was not the only new member of the senior class. But more importantly, Gloria's transition served as an early showcase of her impressive ability to connect with people while also demonstrating a quiet but charismatic leadership ability. Those skills quickly translated into election as vice president of both the senior class and the student council. In addition, she joined the Archery Club, served as secretary of the French Club, and was chosen as Miss Western in a contest sponsored by the school paper. She dated one of the class's acknowledged most desirable males. It was, to put it mildly, a marked contrast from her experience at Waite, in Toledo. She also did a solid job in the academic arena. Despite the holes in her academic preparation, she was in her own way an early beneficiary of what would become known as "experiential education," and all of that, complemented by her voracious reading, gave her a broader understanding in many areas as well as a distinctive perspective (Marcello 2004).

While she made a smooth transition to her new life, it also represented a major change. Little things that most took for granted were often new to Gloria. Eating regular meals around a table was a new experience. Her first exposure to a consistent routine, it represented a marked contrast to the haphazard, lingering-around-the-refrigerator approach that had marked life in the Steinem household of her youth. Meanwhile, Western was a decidedly upscale school, one whose high academic standards led those outside the school district to pay tuition in order to attend. With a student body that included the children of members of Congress, of members of the diplomatic corps, and of members of the military, it symbolized at least an element of Washington's elite. And, unlike the schools in Toledo, Western, reflecting the typical segregation that was central to Washington at the time, was all white.

Part of the rationale for moving to Washington was to enhance Gloria's chances for college. Her academic record was mixed, and the gaps created by her haphazard educational journey were especially pronounced in her math education. That fact was made clear by her subpar math SAT score. But while she was not one of Western's top academic students, her performance in nonmath areas, her work in school activities, the way she adapted to her new environment, and her strong performance on both the verbal SAT and the English Achievement Test made clear that she had much to offer a college community. In addition, in an admittedly short time she had made an impact in the school community. All of that, coupled with her distinctive story and the strong recommendations she received from both the school guidance counselor and vice principal, were well received by Smith College. In the spring of her senior year, she was accepted for admission as a member of the incoming Class of 1956 (Stern 1997).

Gloria's graduation from Western on June 12, 1952, was the culmination of a family effort, and she was excited to head to Northampton, Massachusetts, to follow in her sister's footsteps as a student at the prestigious Seven Sisters school. With a foundation that represented a distinctive mix of travel, life experiences, and formal education, Gloria prepared to embark on the next stage of what had already been a singular life. Little could she or any of her friends or family have anticipated where it would ultimately lead.

2

An Inquiring Mind

As the train from Washington, DC, hurtled north to Northampton, Massachusetts, carrying Gloria and Sue to Smith College, the nervousness that had been building in the final weeks of the summer slowly faded away. Sue tried to draw upon her own experience to assuage Gloria's concerns, but her younger sister's insecurities—concerns about how Ruth, back from her year with Leo and living with Sue in Washington would fare—made for some end-of-summer anxiety. And of course, missing the first train and then having to go back to the apartment, where they engaged in a second round of emotional goodbyes with their mother, did not help (Stern 1997). But all of that built-up tension faded into the background, replaced by a sense of adventure and opportunity, as the train barreled through the urban landscape of Baltimore, Philadelphia, New York, New Haven, and Hartford. With Springfield, the beauty of the Berkshire Mountains, and western Massachusetts looming, Gloria felt nothing but increasing excitement at the new adventure that awaited her at the end of the journey.

Once they arrived on campus and Sue had moved Gloria into her old dorm, Laura Scales (Scales House), they went out and bought the requisite bedspread and curtains. Sue then headed back to Washington, confident that her little sister was ready to craft her own Smith experience. In fact, it would become an experience that Gloria would relish. From a library whose open stacks invited the kind of joyful browsing that the ever-curious Gloria loved to the luxury of eating three meals a day that had been prepared by someone else, Smith offered a range of opportunities that

Gloria embraced and would subsequently treasure. She loved the natural beauty of New England, and she exulted in the combination of intellectual stimulation and thoughtful reflection that characterized the school's academic life. Though a far cry from Toledo, in its own way, it would be a defining experience.

The Smith College that Gloria Steinem entered in the fall of 1952 represented a very different culture than what she had previously experienced even during her year in Washington. At a time when the nation's most exclusive private colleges were overwhelmingly single-sex, Smith, founded in 1875, was one of the Seven Sisters—the others were Barnard, Bryn Mawr, Mount Holyoke, Radcliffe, Vassar, and Wellesley—an elite group viewed as the female counterparts to the virtually all-male Ivy League. They were well respected as the women's academic equivalent of the Ivy League, institutions that would produce graduates who would put their education to use in society. But they were also expected to be the breeding grounds for models of womanhood—wives and mothers who would be the supportive partners to the Ivy League graduates destined to join the American establishment and to assume positions of leadership in the fields of business, higher education, and government (Stern 1997).

Despite her somewhat disparate educational background, Gloria quickly settled into the academic routine. Her first-year schedule included courses in English, French, geology, government, theater, and gym. She distinguished herself as a talented writer in English, but only in government, where much to her delight she found herself able to read and understand the works of Plato and Aristotle, did she really feel confident. Not surprisingly, the French and geology classes proved the most challenging. However, in exchange for help from a friend who had received private tutoring in French prior to coming to Smith, Gloria offered lessons in how to put on makeup, a deal that benefited both parties (Stern 1997).

Gloria took geology, thinking it was the least scientific of the required options, and while that may have been true, she nonetheless always remembered the course for the valuable lesson it imparted. One day on a field trip, Gloria spied a single large turtle that had crawled up from the riverbank. As she watched its progress, she feared it was about to move into traffic. Jumping to the rescue, Gloria picked it up and then, with some difficulty, took it back down the hill and deposited it, triumphantly, at the edge of the river. Shortly thereafter her teacher approached and explained that the turtle had likely spent a good bit of time crawling up the bank, intent on laying its eggs at the top. But before it had completed its mission, Gloria had intervened, instead putting it back in the water (Stern 1997). Although she was crestfallen, she would later note that the experience provided a valuable lesson about the danger of authoritarian impulses on both sides of the political spectrum (Marcello 2004). The life lesson also reaffirmed the importance of listening to others. "Ask the turtle" would, in its own way, become a sort of personal mantra, and it would emerge as the foundation of her whole approach to changing the world.

In some ways, Gloria's gym class offered her the greatest challenge. Despite her years of dancing, Gloria was not an athlete, and her years in Toledo had afforded her very limited exposure to the kinds of sports, such as tennis and volleyball, that were common among her privileged classmates. Indeed, she once said that if there were an Olympic team for sitting still, she would be a gold medalist. However, the experience had a major practical benefit, for Gloria was able to turn the junior lifesaving certificate she earned in swimming class into a summer job as a lifeguard in Washington. There, for numerous summers, she oversaw an African American pool in the segregated nation's capital (Stern 1997).

For all her concerns and perceived struggles, her first year laid the foundation for much subsequent success as she earned a place on the Dean's List for the rest of her time at the school. Socially things had clicked from the start, and the feared differences that had haunted her summer thoughts—and that were, in fact, real—seemed to pose no obstacles. Rather, out on her own for the first time, Steinem thrived at Smith. Ever able to connect with people at their level, Gloria helped bridge the social divide with her classmates by teaching many to iron. And as she earned their respect in the classroom, she unhesitatingly brought her distinctive perspective to the discussions, formal and informal, that were so central to her college years.

There was no denying that her background meant that Gloria was different from her Smith classmates, but once she got over her initial anxiety, she became more comfortable. Her years of dancing translated to a grace that made her stand out, and her long, painted fingernails were the envy of many of her classmates. In addition, while she was more likely to wear makeup than her peers, she was always happy to teach them how to use it. And while the Seven Sisters uniform featured Bermuda shorts, Gloria was known for her jeans. All in all, she was recognized for an image of elegance and independence that was admired by many (Heilbrun 1995).

Gloria's open and upbeat personality helped her fit easily into campus dorm life. As someone for whom storytelling would be a central part of life, it was natural for her to connect with her Smith peers by sharing tales of adventures in Leo's traveling show. The winter road trips to California and Florida had yielded countless adventures that Gloria, while holding court in her dorm room, would joyfully turned into entertaining anecdotes while also offering portraits of the many American characters whose differing lifestyles proved fascinating to the comparably homogeneous population that was Smith in the mid-1950s. A particular, if perverse, favorite involved the time that Leo's decision to leave had been so sudden that when they returned to Clarklake for the next summer season, they discovered a sink

> **AVIATOR GLASSES**
>
> One aspect of Gloria Steinem's public persona was her distinctive style, and nothing was more representative of that style than her aviator glasses. Indeed, she is sporting them on the August 1971 *Newsweek* cover that introduced her as the media-crowned face of the movement. The glasses themselves were originally designed for American pilots in the 1930s by Bausch and Lomb in an effort to protect the aviator's eyes, thus the name. While they would become a popular brand of sunglasses, for the pilots they became a stylish replacement for flight goggles they wore previously, which were heavier and thicker. The aviators got their initial public relations boost when photos of General Douglas MacArthur wearing them when he landed in the Philippines in World War II were published in newspapers around the world. In the succeeding decades they became a celebrity staple, with entertainers including Elvis Presley, Marlon Brando, Peter Fonda, Steve McQueen, and Paul Newman sporting the stylish eyewear. But it was not until Gloria donned them that they became a part of feminist attire.

full of dishes that had never been cleaned. While the cleaning was no small task for Gloria and Sue, the retelling was one of the many such tales that helped bond Gloria with her rapt listeners (Heilbrun 1995).

At the same time that she was developing what would, despite their different paths, be a lifelong bond with Smith and her classmates, she was also establishing herself as an individual. She never adopted the Seven Sisters uniform of Bermuda shorts and cashmere sweater, preferring her jeans and sweatshirt, a look admired by many of her peers. That, coupled with her ponytail, a style that was not yet the norm, as well as her advanced use of makeup, made her an object of awe among the many who saw her as more sophisticated and possessing a presence they could only envy (Marcello 2004).

She further established her own niche when, in addition to ironing, she taught friends how to knit (Stern 1997). The verbal, quick-witted Gloria was a star in word games, also—she was known for her ability to take one word and develop it into a one-act play—and she was a ready participant in the late-night dorm discussions that marked college life. Gloria also earned a reputation as a good and sympathetic listener (Marcello 2004). As someone who seemed always willing to help solve problems, her dorm room was a center of seeming nonstop activity and talk. Her approach to her studies was also distinctively her own. Both a night owl and a procrastinator, she became known for her furious, last-minute, pushing-the-deadline approach to papers that others had often worked on for weeks. To the amazement of others, high-quality work would emerge as Gloria worked on the floor of her room, books strewn around in every direction. While the process may have left something to be desired, the results were a source of envy as she consistently earned high marks on her papers while impressing her instructors. Ironically, Gloria was a bit taken aback when one professor observed that given how easily and how well she wrote, she should consider a career that would allow her to continue to write. While appreciating the compliment, she could not help but contest the assessment of how "easily" she wrote (Stern 1997). But in the end, her academic talents, her social graces, and her innate way with people combined to make life at Smith a tremendously rewarding experience.

Given the nature of Gloria's previous home life, the Smith practice of having students live in the same dorm for the whole of their time at the college appealed to her. Each dorm house had groups from each class, with a new class coming in as the seniors moved on. This approach created a sense of family and continuity while also injecting new blood into the mix. Gloria's class in Laura Scales, a group that its members named the "Twelve Foolish Virgins," came from a range of backgrounds. Some had gone to elite boarding schools while others had attended middle-class public schools. And then there were a few such as Gloria, who had scraped by. Each type of young woman played a role in the drama that was Gloria's college life. One of Gloria's closest friends was from a religious Baptist family from Rochester, New York, who found Smith intimidating. In contrast, another classmate, a boarding school grad, was the namesake for her father's invention, Janie's Spot Cleaner, a popular product of the time. Spot cleaner aside, Gloria's more vivid memory of her dorm mate involved the time that Janie became frustrated by Gloria's unrelenting cheerfulness, grabbed her by the leg, and dragged her down the hall, asking why she never got angry and then exhorting her to do so (Stern 1997). Such were some of the memories from dorm life in a school that included those who would casually fling their coats on the closest chair, fulling intending them to land in such a way as to reveal their designer label or mink lining. But for Gloria, it was all new and exciting, and she intently watched and learned from her classmates, trying both to fit in and be an individual.

Typical was her approach to the Smith "uniform" of Bermuda shorts, a clothing choice that she consciously chose to forgo, both because she thought her legs looked fat in them and because she simply thought they were ugly (Stern 1997). Nevertheless, her friends chipped in to buy her a pair. Such was the camaraderie at Laura Scales and the college at large. Indeed, so well did Gloria acclimate herself to life at Smith generally and Laura Scales in particular that over her objections, and while she was in Europe for her junior year abroad, she was initially elected president of the house for her senior year.

Her refusal to run for house president stemmed in part from a concern that she would not even be in the dorm, since money was again an issue. She feared that without some additional financial help from the school—help that was initially refused—she would have to instead live in a house where students paid their board bill by doing all their own housework. Consequently, Gloria determined not to run. However, slow mail delivery across the Atlantic meant the election was held with her name still on the ballot, and she won the post. However, amid continuing questions about whether, without aid, she would even return to the college, a state of affairs she angrily decried in an emotion-fraught letter to Ruth, another Laura Scales member was ultimately selected (Marcello 2004). In the end, though, once Gloria's stellar grades, as well as the necessary recommendations, were received, Smith reversed itself and awarded Gloria the needed scholarship, thus allowing her to enjoy the final year of college in the dorm and with the classmates who had been such an important part of her experience (Stern 1997).

From the outset Gloria was determined to get everything she could out of her Smith experience. But in contrast to many of her classmates, finances sometimes imposed limitations on which outside activities—be they spring break excursions or weekend road trips—she could enjoy. However, when Gloria learned that she could study in Europe for the same cost as being on campus, she jumped at the opportunity, happily making arrangements to spend her junior year abroad. Before heading to Europe, she had an eventful summer. The bulk of her time was spent putting her PE training at Smith to good use, working as a lifeguard at a pool in Washington. But the big highlight of the summer was serving as maid of honor for her sister when Sue married Robert Patch, a Washington attorney. Leo came East to give his older daughter away, completing the joyful family celebration (Marcello 2004).

Feeding a passion for travel that would characterize the rest of her life, Gloria left for Europe in the fall of 1954, crossing the Atlantic on the *Queen Elizabeth*. While the students began their year in Paris and spent the bulk of their time in Switzerland, studying at the University of Geneva, they also traveled widely. As one of the students randomly selected to spend the first semester living in the home of a native Swiss family, Gloria had the chance to see what daily life was really like. However, living outside of town and having to ride a streetcar back and forth to the university, she was isolated from her classmates, a loneliness she tried to combat by indulging in Swiss chocolate. Before she knew it, her weight ballooned to an all-time high, leaving her fearful that she was following in the footsteps of Leo, who was weighing in at as much as three hundred pounds. After the usually willowy and disciplined Gloria determinedly ended her indulgent behavior and got her weight down, she vowed to never allow such a weight gain to happen again (Marcello 2004).

During the second semester, Gloria moved back into university housing, where living with her classmates, she pursued a very active social life.

Meanwhile, as a student of government, she studied a range of political theories and left Europe with a very different view of Marx than she had at the start of her studies.

When the program in Geneva finished, Gloria sought to extend her stay. She was accepted into a program at Oxford University in England where she studied twentieth-century politics and literature. She earned a scholarship, which helped with the costs, and Leo also provided some support. Doubtful that she would ever return to Europe, she made every effort to see all the major English sights, and before heading back to the United States, she and a friend joined a cycling tour of Scotland. For the less-than-athletic Gloria, the trip over the country's hilly terrain was a bit of a challenge, but ever anxious to see and experience new things, she found it to be, for the most part, a very positive experience (Stern 1997).

Returning to the United States just before the start of the new school year, she made the arrangements necessary to pursue honors in her government major. That path required a thesis, and she wrote "Humanist and Ideologue," in which she compared the politics of British authors George Orwell and Arthur Koestler. The work was well received and capped an academic career that culminated in her earning Phi Beta Kappa honors. She was also elected class historian by her peers in the Class of 1956. In addition, in an ironic twist, given the anguish she was experiencing that spring, she penned an essay looking at the question of matrimony versus career for the college's *Alumnae Quarterly*. A family contingent of mother, father, and sister were all proudly in attendance as renowned poet Archibald MacLeish urged the graduates to seek change as they received their diplomas in the spring of 1956 (Marcello 2004).

Central to her senior year was a relationship that would, in many ways, haunt Gloria for much of her life. In the fall of 1955, a former Smith friend who had dropped out of school in order to marry invited Gloria to her Westchester County home for a visit. There Gloria met Blair Chotzinoff. The twenty-eight-year-old Blair and Gloria were immediately attracted to each other. Blair's having once worked for the *New York Post* gave the pair a shared interest in writing. If that were not enough, the dark-haired, green-eyed Blair sealed the deal when he flew Gloria back to Smith in a rented airplane, artfully landing it on the college's croquet field (Marcello 2004).

As Gloria saw more of Blair, she learned that his father, Samuel Chotzinoff, was a classical pianist, writer, and critic, then serving as musical director for the National Broadcasting Company (NBC). Blair's uncle was the world-renowned violinist Jascha Heifetz, and his mother, Pauline, had been a Broadway actress. The family moved in rarefied social circles that included such people as Leonard Bernstein, whom Gloria first met through the family. Gloria was very different from the starlets and occasional strippers who had been Blair's usual dates, and yet it was quickly apparent that Blair's parents were less than enamored with Gloria. His family expressed deep concerns about her liberal politics, her mixed religious background—the Chotzinoffs were determined that Blair should wed a 100-percent-Jewish bride—and her having the gall to disagree with Blair's father, the family patriarch. Given her impoverished background, the elder Chotzinoffs feared that she was little more than a social climber, interested less in Blair than in the family's wealth and connections (Marcello 2004).

But despite these objections, as her senior year progressed, Gloria and Blair spent as much time together as they could, and their relationship only deepened. By all appearances, Gloria and Blair seemed to be moving along the inevitable path of societal expectations with marriage as the ultimate destination. But she was by no means convinced that a wedding ring was the key to "happily ever after." And from a practical perspective, it all seemed premature. Gloria was still in school, and her postgraduation prospects were uncertain. Meanwhile, although Blair flew planes for the National Guard, he had no regular job.

While the young couple was more than happy to simply spend time together, occasionally managing a romantic evening, their future prospects were uncertain at best. Yet despite these questions and concerns, when, in the spring of 1956, Blair asked Gloria to marry him, she accepted the proposal—as well as a huge diamond ring (Marcello 2004). But the reality of it all only crystallized Gloria's doubts, and very soon she broke off the engagement. However, when Blair rushed to Northampton, they had an emotional reunion and the engagement was reaffirmed. Plans for a wedding began. However, the internal debate that would dog Gloria for most of the rest of her life only intensified. It was not really about Blair; rather, it was a debate that centered on the very idea of marriage and on her effort to determine whether a life with Blair represented the right next step.

In the United States of the 1950s, popular culture, the media, and even politics celebrated the role of wife, mother, and homemaker as the idealized, combined role for the American woman. The supportive helpmate who tended to things on the home front while her husband climbed the ladder to professional success was a role immortalized in countless television shows and films of the era. Even those women who emerged from college with a Seven Sisters degree still needed a "Mrs." to complement their BA and make their life whole, or so said the "experts." And of course, once this picture was completed with the arrival of children, there was no need or room for a woman to work in anything but a volunteer capacity. The developing consumer culture made the homemaker role increasingly easy, freeing up time for Mom to be an active member of the PTA or some other equally laudable organization. Of course, all of this was more about completing the family's idyllic life portrait than it was about fulfilling the woman's desires and needs, not to mention her path to personal fulfillment (Marcello 2004). In fact, at this point, less than 10 percent of the nation's women over the age of twenty-two had college degrees, and the percentage for married women was even lower. And with homeownership skyrocketing, the impetus for making a home for a family was even greater. Indeed, during the 1950s, less than 25 percent of married women, and only a little over 10 percent of those with children under age six, worked outside the home. Meanwhile, through the course of the decade, those women who did work earned roughly sixty-four cents for every dollar a man made.

All of this Gloria knew, and all of it left her deeply unsettled. Meanwhile, her parents' differing reactions did little to ease her doubts. Ruth, who liked Blair, was very supportive and, in fact, urged Gloria to get married right out of college. She warned her daughter that if she got a taste of the independent life, she would never take the plunge. In contrast, Leo expressed no strong feelings one way or the other. However, having become a gem expert in the years since he and Ruth divorced, he did note that the big diamond that Blair had given Gloria was, in fact, yellow and thus not as valuable as someone might think, a fact that clearly diminished his regard for his possible future son-in-law (Stern 1997).

As Gloria wrestled with this mass of conflicting emotions, she marched into the future. Prior to graduation, Gloria had met with a guidance counselor at Smith, but she had offered little encouragement. The counselor noted that the few women who earned law degrees at that time were struggling to find substantive opportunities. She noted that even the top students (women such as Sandra Day O'Connor and Ruth Bader Ginsburg) usually got little more than positions as legal secretaries, while opportunities to join the big firms and climb the ladder to partner were virtually nonexistent. Gloria then considered writing-based possibilities. Some of her reviews had been published in the Smith paper, *The Sophia*, and so she decided to explore the field of journalism, but that was no more promising. At an interview with *Time* magazine, she learned that the newsweekly only hired women as researchers, not writers. Meanwhile, her applications for copywriter positions with advertising firms were equally unproductive (Stern 1997).

Intent on pursuing a writing career, Gloria returned to Washington, where, living with Sue and Ruth, she spent the summer looking for a job, volunteering in the Adlai Stevenson campaign, and lifeguarding. A shower thrown by Smith classmates only increased her unease with the prospect of marriage. And yet, with limited opportunities in job areas in which she was interested, a future as a wife and mother seemed the likely option, and the engagement remained on course.

But as Gloria continued to wrestle with the marriage issue, an unexpected opportunity arose that would change her life. Smith's International Relations Organization had just that year established the Chester Bowles

Fellowship, which provided an opportunity for a year of study in India. Gloria had heard of the fellowship back in the spring, but given her engagement and wedding plans, she had not pursued it. However, during the summer, after one of the original recipients was unable to go and the opening was announced, Gloria pounced. She contacted the professor involved and expressed her interest. She apparently indicated that the engagement that had prevented her from initially applying was no longer an issue—and in her still-struggling mind, it may not have been. It certainly was not an issue when, not long afterward, her initiative was rewarded and Gloria was awarded one of the newly created Chester Bowles Fellowships to study in India (Stern 1997).

The receipt of the Fellowship and the decision to go to India brought Gloria's ongoing internal debate about marriage to a head. She decided to retain her independence and autonomy and end the relationship with Blair. Not long before she was slated to leave for London, after a final night together, Gloria quietly slipped out of the room they were sharing, leaving an explanatory note and the engagement ring on the nightstand. Blair was devastated, and his efforts to contact Gloria went unanswered (Stern 1997).

Securing a visa to India was a notoriously slow process, both because of the nation's storied inefficiency as well as national concerns that the student visitors would prove incapable of supporting themselves and thus become wards of the state. Consequently, while the year-long fellowship was supposed to begin in September, it got delayed by paperwork and bureaucratic snags. However, at least in part to escape the emotional turmoil she was leaving behind, Gloria headed to London, where she would wait for the appropriate visas to be issued. When the delays continued, and with her funds dwindling, Gloria looked for ways to support herself. Her lack of the necessary working papers limited her options, but she was able to find a job as a server in an espresso shop. The job was certainly not glamorous, but she recalled it as comfortable while also providing the ever-curious aspiring journalist with countless opportunities to meet new people and learn about the area (Marcello 2004).

A few weeks into her stay in London, the visa delays became the least of her problems as Gloria discovered she was pregnant. While she would later expend incalculable amounts of time and energy in the effort to secure and protect a woman's right to reproductive freedom, in 1956 an unplanned pregnancy, especially for an unmarried woman, was nothing less than devastating. Not only did it carry a societal stigma but the variety of ways to address the problem offered a wide range of risks and dangers. From a loveless marriage to the father to being an unprepared parent; to being a single, unwed mother; to seeing one's reputation and dreams impacted forever, an illegitimate child could scar a person for life, while leaving the child no less vulnerable. At the same time, the discovery that a woman had had an abortion carried no less stigma. And in part because of its illegality, the procedure, usually conducted in less than ideal conditions, carried its own shared of health risks (Marcello 2004).

Alone, frightened, confused, and separated from family and friends by thousands of miles, including the Atlantic Ocean—although she had no desire or intention of letting any of them know of her plight anyway—Gloria wrestled with all of these considerations. She racked her brain trying to find a solution to this problem that threatened to upend her life and quash every dream she had ever had.

Ever the student, Gloria researched every available avenue. She investigated methods for self-induced miscarriages—for the onetime horseback rider, reports of that activity as a solution had some initial attraction—all the while knowing that the clock was ticking and she needed to do something. Abortion emerged as the "best" option, but given its illegal nature, people did not simply flip through the yellow pages in search of a doctor who would perform one. And even if it had been that easy, she would have had reservations about the procedure. Before going down that path, Gloria went to see a doctor, John E. Sharpe. She lied about her situation, telling the elderly physician that the man who had gotten her pregnant refused to marry her (Marcello 2004).

While sympathetic to her plight, the doctor said there was little he could do, although he did give her some medicine that might bring on her period. With the clock ticking, she tried the medicine, but it had no effect. Gloria would later say that it was the only time in her life that she ever considered suicide. She considered heading to France for an abortion before she learned that abortions could be obtained in London if the pregnant woman got two doctors to sign off on the need for the procedure. With time running short, Gloria rushed back to the kindly old physician who agreed to both sign off and refer her to a doctor who would perform the procedure. Years later, after his death, Gloria would dedicate her 2015 book *My Life on the Road* to the kindly doctor who had helped save her life by sending her to the female gynecologist with the words, "You must promise me that you will never tell anyone and you will lead your own life." With those words of encouragement, Gloria headed to the second doctor (Steinem 2015). There, she had to endure a verbal dressing-down from the female doctor, who chastised her for getting into the situation in the first place and then waiting until it was almost too late to be addressed. Then the doctor completed the procedure, and Gloria went home to rest.

She stayed in bed for the first few days after the procedure, telling her friends that she was experiencing back pain. When after a few days, and as promised, the bleeding stopped, she felt an overwhelming sense of relief. Later she would recognize that beyond that relief, the episode had, however unintentionally, given her a sense of empowerment, because she had been forced to take control of her life and the ultimate decision had been hers and hers alone.

When Gloria's visa finally came through from India on January 27, 1957, she was ready to turn the page on her traumatic London experience. But before embarking for India, the inveterate traveler took a quick trip to the southern part of Europe, stopping in Geneva to visit a friend and then going to Greece, where she visited the Acropolis. Yet all of these travels paled in comparison to what she discovered upon her arrival in Bombay on February 24. India was a revelation for the native of Toledo, Ohio, allowing her, for the first time, to look at the world through other than a Western-centered lens. From the outset, she was deeply moved by the abject poverty in which much of the nation's people were mired. At the same time, despite the stark and obvious differences between the United States and India, Gloria felt a strong sense of home, of belonging, of liberation, and she was anxious to explore the expansive nation (Marcello 2004).

Gloria spent her first few days with the family of a Trans World Airlines (TWA) employee before heading to New Delhi, the nation's capital. There she met a young woman, Jean Joyce, an American who had accompanied Chester Bowles to India and then served as his assistant when he was the ambassador. However, she had lost her job when Bowles had left his post with the election of Eisenhower. Loving India, Joyce had been able to remain when she got a job with the Ford Foundation, and she was delighted to have Gloria stay with her until she got settled (Stern 1997).

Gloria was determined to experience the Indian culture as fully as possible. From the start, she made every effort to adapt to the local culture. Anxious both to fit in and experience Indian life, Gloria happily adapted the sari as her preferred attire. The sari itself consisted of unstitched yards of cloth that was wrapped around one's body to form a skirt while the free end was draped over the shoulder. The outfit was completed by a blouse that ended just below the bust as well as a petticoat under the sari. Wearing the sari did not just allow Gloria to show her respect for her local hosts; it also provided her with an opportunity to recast herself as more like a native, thus making her better able to fully experience the culture. And the sari was in many ways more comfortable for her than the Seven Sisters–endorsed Bermuda shorts she had brought with her (Marcello 2004).

At the same time, many of the less palatable aspects of Indian life were clear from the beginning. One of the most obvious realities was the status of women. She and Kayla Achter, the other Bowles Fellowship recipient, lived in Miranda House in New Delhi, where they discovered that they had an 8:00 p.m. curfew—which was actually later than that imposed at most of India's other dorms. In addition, they could only leave campus in groups, but here, too, they were allowed to travel in groups smaller than the usually required four. As Americans in a dorm overwhelmingly occupied by

Indian students, the Bowles Fellows were sources of great curiosity and interest, and their curiosity was reciprocated. Consequently, considerable information was shared across the cultural divide. Questions about American music, religion, and dating abounded, as did concerns about America's political views toward the newly independent India (Stern 1997).

The American women addressed the political questions as best they could, although they were more comfortable singing American songs and demonstrating American dances, efforts to which their Indian peers responded in kind. Their status as singular Americans led to numerous invitations and opportunities to see and experience the Indian way of life. From learning how to eat with her hands to seeing how, in contrast with the United States, a bared midriff was acceptable but bared legs were not, Gloria took it all in, fascinated by all she saw. Similarly, traditions regarding shoes and feet were a revelation. Gloria quickly learned not to wear shoes into another person's house and that shoes or feet must not ever touch another person. At the same time, there were no comparable boundaries when it came to staring at a person or inquiring about some of what Americans thought of as personal information. And of course, the American idea that moving one's head from side to side meant "no" clashed directly with the Indian version, by which the same action meant "yes" (Marcello 2004).

At the end of her first semester, Gloria set off on her own to see more of India. She and Kayla had not hit it off, so they decided to pursue separate paths over the break. Gloria was intent upon visiting Madras, the home of theosophy. A spiritual philosophy strongly influenced by Hinduism, Gloria's mother, Ruth, and her mother, Marie, were both devoted followers of the theosophic ideal, one that encouraged the pursuit of a moral life but in a less authoritarian or self-righteous way than many of the more formal Western religions. It focused on individuals doing their job in their life, doing the best they could in that effort, and not trying to dictate the path of others (Marcello 2004).

Believers in theosophy were strong individuals who were responsible for their own actions, and in seeking to do good, they were to do no harm. While Gloria was never an overtly religious person—she often fended off outside efforts to identify her with a religious label by noting that her parents had given her a mix to choose from and there were pros and cons to both—theosophy could certainly be seen as an influence on much of her life. Beyond the trek to the home of theosophy, the trip also revealed another side of Indian culture. While Gloria was very comfortable traveling alone, in purchasing her third-class railway pass, she learned that in order to avoid unwanted attention from men, women were given a separate car. In fact, men were not allowed to touch women in public; not even a handshake was acceptable. Meanwhile, married women were not just considered possessions of their husbands; this status made them liable for beatings or other punishments if they did not show proper respect or obedience. While Gloria was deeply distressed by such behaviors and customs, she did learn much from the Indian women. Like her dormitory discussions, the train rides served as female-only classrooms, exposing Gloria to the thoughts and ideas of the Indian people, while also giving her a sense of what the Indians knew and wanted to know about Americans (Marcello 2004).

Seeking to take in as much of India as she could, Gloria traveled all the way to the southern tip of India, stopping in Kerala. A communist government had recently taken control of the region, and the former government major interviewed ten plantation owners in an effort to determine the government's effectiveness. In addition, Gloria traveled to an ashram, a religious community that was run by a Gandhi disciple who had pioneered the Bhoodan, or land gift, movement, an effort to get property owners to contribute part of their land to the poor. At the ashram, Gloria met a missionary who convinced her to join his group (Steinem 2015). He made her realize that she was no different from any of the many others traveling in a country whose diversity was evident in the more than a dozen languages fully in use. He was also interested in having a female member, because his overwhelmingly male group could not connect with Hindu women. Unable to go into male quarters, Hindu women could not be brought into discussions that took place there. The minister thought Gloria could serve as a bridge, a point of connection for that effort. For her, it represented a chance to help the Indian women improve their status. From the start of her visit, Gloria had been struck by the cultural inequality in India, so the opportunity to help address some of that was something she welcomed. Seeing a chance to perhaps improve their status in the world or at the very least to raise their awareness of the wider world in which they lived, Gloria happily agreed to join them (Marcello 2004).

In reality, her work with the group consisted primarily of listening to the complaints of the local people they encountered on their journey. She did serve as an effective bridge to the female community, but it would be years before its members became a part of any national discussions on larger issues. Meanwhile, in seeing the group work to try to address the many land-based problems they encountered, she learned valuable lessons in group problem solving and mediation. In typical fashion, over the course of their daily walks, Gloria demonstrated her easy familiarity with the culture, often bathing in streams encountered along the way, wading in fully clothed to cool herself with the sari and then drying as she continued along. At night the group would stop in villages where local residents would feed them rice cakes and sweet milky tea. They would also share their sleeping mats.

Despite her enthusiasm and determination to be one of the group, Gloria's feet soon suffered under the burden of the long daily walks. They became badly blistered and then infected, and she was forced to get rides on the oxcart that accompanied them or take the bus back to the ashram, thus reducing her time with the Bhoodan marchers. After her feet finally healed, she traveled to Bombay. There, staying at the local YWCA, she determined to squeeze some additional time out of her stay, having exhausted the funds provided by the fellowship (Heilbrun 1995).

Before leaving India, Gloria undertook some final excursions that included visits to Rangoon, Burma, and Calcutta, as well as Tokyo and Kyoto in Japan. In typical fashion, that final foray included an even more interesting series of encounters. Indeed, waiting in the Rangoon airport, she struck up a conversation with a woman who turned out to be a fellow Seven Sisters alum, having gone to Vassar. Her husband, Y. H. Kwong, was on his way to Hong Kong, and they spent the whole flight in conversation, during which Gloria learned that the businessman's ventures had included the construction of the Burma Road. Upon their arrival in Hong Kong, he graciously invited her to stay at the family apartment. However, ever determined to experience the local culture, she opted to stay at the local YWCA.

After a couple of days and many bedbugs, she got back in touch with Mr. Kwong, who not only welcomed her into his home but brought her along on a number of meetings with visiting Burmese officials with whom he was working in an effort to secure war reparations from the Japanese. A flight to Tokyo on a cargo plane piloted by a U.S. flyer who had decided to remain in the region after his World War II service as a member of the Flying Tigers offered one final adventure. To her great delight, he allowed Gloria into the cockpit and encouraged her to talk with the ground crew on his radio—to the surprise of all. Finally, in July 1958 she set sail for the United States. While she was officially in steerage class on the *President Cleveland*, the always charming Gloria endeared herself to the crew, who would sneak her to a higher deck, where the now-experienced world traveler would easily mingle with the wealthy passengers (Stern 1997).

Money was a consistent challenge over the course of her time in India, for the Bowles Fellowship did not begin to cover the full cost of the experience. But being her father's daughter, Gloria found a way. She did a variety of writing projects, ranging from a promotional brochure for TWA to an article on the Ajanta and Ellora Caves as seen from the tourist perspective. In addition, she wrote a work titled "The Thousand Indias." A series of essays originally intended as a book, they ended up being published as individual essays by the tourist bureau of the Indian government. Additional writing projects included a brochure for a documentary film company and some travel pamphlets and newspaper supplements. Beyond her writing, Gloria further supplemented her income by helping a local Indian man design sandals for export—and then writing the advertising material to help launch the product—and she also did some modeling, helping sell saris, toothpaste, shampoo, and cold cream (Marcello 2004).

Ironically, Gloria the aspiring writer had difficulty producing the fellowship reports that were required of the recipients. While the reports were supposed to depict the "mysterious East" for the Western audience back home, Steinem did not find India particularly mysterious. In fact, so comfortable did she feel that she made it a point to try to avoid the more tourist-oriented areas, preferring to explore the non-Western part of the country, an approach to her travels that meant that she often went days without seeing another Westerner. For Gloria, part of the attraction of India and much of what made the experience so rewarding were her determination to try to experience their culture. While she could not deny she was a student from the United States, she had no desire to be seen as an American tourist. Rather, she sought to live as the Indians did. Living on the food that the villagers ate, sleeping on mats in the women's quarters, washing in the stream alongside the natives, and not only wearing the traditional sari but having it dry on her after bathing in the local stream, gave her a different and distinctive experience from the typical American tourist (Heilbrun 1995).

Years later Steinem would look back on her Indian trip as a life-altering experience. She termed it one of those events that divides one's life into before and after periods, and she added that there were lessons she learned in India that remained central to the rest of her life. Foremost among them was the idea that if you hope to help people change how they live their lives, you must first understand how they live them. Similarly, for a woman who was already respected for her listening skills, she took away the sense that if you want people to see your point, you need to sit down with them and let them first see you. Her time in India left her with a sense that nothing could be more rewarding than pursuing one's passion and that if a person did that, other things would take care of themselves. Coming home with that idea etched in her psyche, Gloria looked forward to pursuing a career in journalism in New York City.

Returning to the United States in the late summer, Leo met Gloria at the boat, and the cash-strapped father and daughter plotted their respective next steps. Leo's initial effort to get Gloria to help him sell aerosol cans held no attraction for an aspiring journalist just home from world travel. Also, she was anxious to head to New York, where she hoped to build upon her Indian experience. But she did succumb to his entreaties to try Las Vegas, where Leo's "lucky" little girl won enough to allow them to continue east. On the next leg of the journey, in a scheme that hearkened back to some of Gloria's childhood travels with the family, the struggling father was forced to sell his daughter's rings, as she reluctantly, mournfully, slipped the presumed family heirlooms off her fingers in exchange for immediate cash. The seemingly forsaken pair enticed many buyers, who believed that they were getting a great bargain from the traveling fire sale that financed the Steinems' cross-country trip. For Leo, it was another chapter in an entrepreneurial story, while Gloria saw it as a great adventure as she reacclimated herself to the United States (Steinem 2015).

Gloria came back from India determined to do something about the poverty she had seen. The experience had spoken to her fundamental humanity and was something of a spark for her subsequent career as an activist. At the same time, she got an early lesson in the fact that activists must make connections with others to achieve change. Years later, after a life of travel, she ruefully recalled that the many cabdrivers whose ears she bent must have hated her as a fare (Heilbrun 1995). Yet the experience in India was invaluable, and once she found her audience, she would employ many of the lessons she had learned in India in her feminist organizing efforts.

In the meantime, she turned to journalism as a way to change the world. But the young girl journalist found it a tough beat. As she looked for a job in New York, she stayed with some women whose lack of apparent jobs, coupled with long nights out, initially left her wondering about how they supported themselves, before realizing that they were at least "semi-hookers" (Stern 1997). It was a realization that reaffirmed how hard it was for a single woman to make it in New York. Fortunately for Gloria, a contact from her India days helped her find something, and while it forced her to put her journalistic aspirations on at least a short-term hold, it would prove to be another valuable experience.

While in India, she had met Clive Gray, a onetime vice president of the National Student Association (NSA). He remembered being impressed with her knowledge of India. He was looking for young people to staff a youth festival in Vienna that he was preparing to launch, and he thought of her. The 1959 festival was the latest in a series that had started in the mid-1940s. The early ones had been officially organized by a collection of international youth groups who were known to have communist ties. In addition, the earlier festivals had been held in communist countries. All of this had led to a skepticism within American youth group circles as well as a reluctance on the part of the United States to encourage American participation. But with the 1959 festival scheduled for Vienna, the U.S. State Department pulled back on some of the policies that had previously made it difficult for students to attend the earlier communist country–based festivals. In fact, it now urged the NSA, which because of communist affiliations had essentially kept itself at arm's length from the groups that had organized the earlier efforts, to send Americans. As Gloria was to learn later, the CIA was also supportive of American participation, seeing it as a way to gain a better understanding of youth culture in some of the communist and communist satellite countries (Stern 1997).

Given her interest in government and all things international, Gloria was aware of the program and had, in fact, been interested in attending the

1957 festival held in Moscow, but Indian travel restrictions had made that impossible. But two years later, with her Indian experience in hand, Gloria was very receptive when Gray approached her about working for the 1959 effort. A series of interviews with others involved with the festival, many of whom were former NSA officers, went well, and Paul Sigmund, a Harvard graduate student who was slated to run the festival, ultimately offered Gloria the job of executive codirector of the Independent Service for Information (ISI) at the Vienna Youth Festival. Her responsibilities included helping recruit students for the festival—the intelligence community and the State Department were looking for articulate and thoughtful students who could hold their own in the head-to-head exchanges with their Soviet-sponsored counterparts. However, she was primarily involved with public relations—getting press coverage for the festival as well as working with the media and writing various festival sponsored publications. While the work seemed interesting and Gloria needed a job, given some of the organization's history and the ongoing controversy over communists in government, she had some initial reservations (Stern 1997).

Senator Joe McCarthy had recently been censured by the Senate for his anticommunist activities, but the American fear of communist associations was still real. Gloria was concerned about the possible taint on her efforts and its possible impact on future prospects. But, in the end, she took the job and relocated to a basement apartment in Cambridge, Massachusetts, an aspect of the position that was perhaps its least attractive feature. For despite her Seven Sisters pedigree, the apartment brought back memories of Toledo, and she felt like an outsider in the Harvard-dominated intellectual circles in which the organization operated. In addition, while she found the work interesting, if not wholly satisfying, her social life was limited to her fellow workers. And while she was getting a chance to write, it was not the type of writing she had hoped for. But in typical Gloria fashion, she threw herself into her work, and the results were impressive (Marcello 2004).

In fact, over the course of the next year, she engaged in a wide range of activities involving a list of impressive people. Among her major accomplishments was convincing CBS television to make a documentary about the festival. When, barely three weeks before the festival was to start, the network reneged on its original promise to make an hour-long documentary, asserting that it was not sufficiently newsworthy, Gloria went to New York to meet with C. D. Jackson, a former Eisenhower aide and a powerful figure in the media. Jackson was publisher of *Fortune* magazine as well as a former president of the Free Europe Committee, the parent body of both Radio Free Europe and Radio Liberty, networks that directly broadcast information to countries behind the Iron Curtain as part of the American effort to spread democracy.

Jackson had not only significant clout but also a deep interest in such programs as the festival, which sought to spread the message of American democracy. Gloria had worked with him earlier in the project and in fact, had gotten him to help secure financing for four delegates, including rising scholar Zbigniew Brzezinski and socialist leader Michael Harrington, whose already high profiles made their traveling with the delegation problematic. This time she knew that his broad experience and countless media connections could make him a formidable advocate on behalf of the festival. After meeting with Gloria, Jackson agreed to write Frank Stanton, the president of CBS as well as a member of the board of Radio Free Europe, and explain the importance of ISI's work to the Cold War effort. Stanton responded by meeting with Gloria, and while he refused to commit to an hour-long program, he agreed to producing a half-hour program. Gloria headed to Vienna with the promise of both a CBS cameraman, who would record the action, and a top correspondent (Stern 1997).

After months of preparation and planning, the festival got underway during the last week in July. The participants and their attitudes offered a telling window into the forces at work in the Cold War. The American delegates combined an upbeat idealism with a sense of adventure as well as a desire to party and enjoy life in that distinctive city. In contrast, their Soviet bloc counterparts were all business, no doubt in part because they were far more tightly monitored by their adult supervisors. In the end, however, participants on both sides were able to complement their discussions and workshop sessions with trips to the ballet and the opera, and all enjoyed the fireworks that added to the spirit of the event.

Gloria wrote press releases and selected delegates who could then share their views with the waiting media. She served as the head of both the Independent Information Center, which effectively communicated with the festival participants, as well as the International News Bureau, which published a daily newspaper in five languages for festival attendees. While the communists mounted a major campaign to prevent the distribution of such news and views, the general consensus was that the communist youths were exposed to a considerable amount of Western information—to what end remained unknown. Gloria's work in all of this was well received and she was showered with praise.

In the end, the work with ISI not only offered Gloria countless opportunities to hone her skills but also gave her contact with the numerous other young, ambitious recent college graduates involved with the project, beginning a network that would eventually stretch from coast to coast and into foreign outposts as well. For instance, the man who had hired her, Paul Sigmund, would go on to head the Princeton political science department and marry Barbara Boggs, the daughter of Democratic House leader Hale Boggs and the sister of newscaster Cokie Roberts. In addition to the contacts and positive impression she made among her peers, Gloria returned to the United States having left positive impressions with an impressive array of national power brokers ranging from Frank Stanton, C. D. Jackson, and Zbigniew Brzezinski to future journalist Walter Pincus and the *New York Times*'s Abe Rosenthal (Stern 1997).

Making those contacts would be one of the enduring hallmarks of the experience and a foundational part of her wide-ranging influence. In fact, over the course of her professional life, the contacts she accumulated and the relationships she developed—the way she networked before the concept had truly been developed—allowed her to both transcend and break down the "old boys network" that had been so critical to limiting female opportunity while maintaining dominance in seats of power and influence. It was a world she was intent on redefining, and it had its start in the earliest days of her own career. Indeed, whether the product of a personal, social, romantic, or work relationship, Gloria never failed to make the kind of impression that would allow her to go back to and seek assistance from a given individual in any of countless ways when she later needed to do so. The range of her contacts was mind boggling.

Gloria's experiences in India and with ISI were the final chapters in her formal education, further broadening her global perspective while giving her additional experience dealing with the media. They also gave her invaluable contacts that would be helpful later in her life. The time had come to put all of that to use. So after the close of the festival, Gloria returned to New York, intent on becoming a journalist whose efforts could impact the world.

3

Journalist, Activist, and Feminist

When she returned to New York in the fall of 1960, Gloria was determined to make her mark. However, she was quickly reminded of why she had accepted the ISI position: New York City teemed with well-educated, ambitious men and women looking to jump-start their careers. But Gloria was undaunted. She was also connected. In fact, shortly before she left Cambridge, while she and Paul Sigmund were working on their final report of the festival, she had a visit from Walter Friedenberg. Steinem and Friedenberg had had an intense relationship while she was in India, but as was typical for Gloria, they had parted as friends. The reunion led to an introduction to his friend Harold Hayes, an editor at *Esquire* magazine, and Harold's wife, Susan. Through Hayes, Gloria met, and would soon become a couple with, Robert Benton, *Esquire*'s art director, who would go on to cowrite *Bonnie and Clyde* and direct *Kramer vs. Kramer*. Susan Hayes helped Gloria get a job as an assistant to Harvey Kurtzman, the creator of *MAD* magazine. Kurtzman was preparing to launch a humor magazine *Help! For Tired Minds*. Taking on a part-time job that became a full-time commitment, Gloria soon found herself writing captions, setting up photo shoots, and persuading comic stars such as Milton Berle and Dick Van Dyke to appear on the cover. While she tended to omit the job from later reflections on her early, more serious, career stops, she nevertheless did it well. Terry Gilliam, who replaced her when she left and would go on to direct some of the Monty Python films, praised her efforts (Marcello 2004).

In her off-hours, Gloria spent time around the *Esquire* offices, and in her quest to build her career and get better established, her ties at *Esquire* proved helpful. Soon she was writing captions for fashion spreads and recipes for bachelors as well as authoring a growing number of small but uncredited items. Her first byline came in the July 1961 issue with a piece titled "Sophisticated Fun & Games" (Marcello 2004).

At the same time, given the lack of consistency that a freelance career entailed, when ISI (which had changed its name to the Independent Research Service [IRS]) called to ask about her assuming her former position in advance of the 1961, Helsinki-based festival, Gloria was willing to listen. Unwilling to box herself in and be forced to bypass freelance opportunities, Gloria agreed to help on a limited basis. She agreed to volunteer as time allowed while also promising to work with the press during the actual festival.

She quickly proved an asset, helping find the group a new headquarters in New York, a two-room office in a Thirty-Seventh Street townhouse. In addition, she helped the new director, former NSA president Dennis Shaul, in numerous ways as they prepared for the festival. She was particularly involved in recruiting people to work on a set of festival newspapers such as the ones they had produced in Vienna. The list of people she recruited included some future media heavyweights, including future *Washington Post* managing editor Robert Kaiser. She also recruited volunteers from *Esquire*, including Clay Felker, who left Helsinki tremendously impressed with the range of Gloria's talents, a recognition that would help make him an important mentor and facilitator of her career. Meanwhile in Helsinki, while again serving as the point person for press relations, she dealt with press luminaries such as Daniel Schorr and Marvin Kalb. In addition, she was able to do an article about the festival with her "Dateline: Helsinki, the Last Red Festival," appearing in the October 1962 issue of *Show* (Stern 1997).

Leo died in the spring of 1961, a result of complications of a car accident. Sue and Gloria only learned of the accident after he had been in the hospital for several weeks. Sue had four young children to care for, so it was Gloria who traveled west to see their father. However, on April 21, 1961, as he was being moved to a convalescent hospital, Leo suddenly hemorrhaged and died, just four days before his sixty-fourth birthday. Gloria was en route to California, and Sue had her paged in Chicago, where she was changing planes. It was a horrible way to receive the news, but it somehow seemed an apt end for a relationship that had become increasingly distant. After hearing from Sue, Gloria continued on her journey, flying to California to claim the body and make arrangements (Steinem 2015). The body was cremated and brought back to Washington for a painful memorial service for the girls and their mother. The loneliness and aloneness that surrounded Leo's death were something they would not allow to be repeated with Ruth.

The sudden death represented a singularly unsatisfying end to the often-complicated but nevertheless close relationship that Gloria had with her father, a man who had left her with a raft of memories and lessons. But like the revealing revelation that was her essay "Ruth's Song," it wasn't until the publication of *My Life on the Road*, with its chapter "My Father's Footsteps," that Gloria publicly came to terms with the important role that Leo had played in her life. Whether while directly a part of it or as a ghost who hovered over every one of the thousands of miles she traveled, he was helping her exercise the freedom, autonomy, and joy of living that were central to his own life and to hers. That was the core part of Leo Steinem's bequest to his younger daughter.

If you had seen them standing side by side, you would have been hard-pressed to see the resemblance between the lithe, sometimes almost stick-thin, Gloria and her obese father, whose shadow would engulf her. Yet if you compared their travel logs, you would see that they were joined at the hip in pursuing their respective dreams and in their unwillingness to stay still, always believing that the next big score, in Leo's case, or the next receptive individual or audience, in Gloria's, was ready to be found.

Leo was an erratic presence, but he was also a model, however unintentional, for what she would become and how she would approach much of what she would do. The freelance life suited her fine and continued the family tradition of never having a boss. And while she may have worked for Clay Felker at *New York*, as a part of the founding team as well as a columnist, she wasn't exactly punching a time clock. But in picking her subjects, in traveling and crusading, she was living the life of a social entrepreneur before the phrase was invented, and her father would have been proud. She developed a lack of concern about insecurity after years of watching Leo's never-ending travels end well; it left her with a confidence that things would always work out. It was an experience that offered a vivid, if skewed, example of a singular approach to life. At the same time, it fit well with her unbounded optimism.

It was certainly not the norm in the 1940s, but the Steinem family's itinerant, nomadic, lifestyle saved the ever-curious Gloria from the rote and formulaic version of American education that characterized the postwar world and produced the vanilla 1950s lifestyle that the rest of her life directly rebuked. Not surprisingly, Gloria came to see how her father had helped make her into who she would become. But it wasn't just the lifestyle; it was the personal style. Ever the individual, he treated her and all others the same way—with dignity and respect. In valuing her opinion, in making clear that he enjoyed her company, in treating her better, as she recalled, than he treated himself, he offered a view of interpersonal relations that would impact the rest of her life. Indeed, the lessons in organizing that she learned in India—lessons about understanding the experience of the people with whom you are working, about sitting down and listening, about dealing with people face to face in person, she had, in fact, already seen through life with Leo. Theirs was a distinctive relationship, and while it was not always smooth and had its share of gaps and disconnections, it had been profound. From the countless little lessons he had imparted to taking Ruth for that all-important senior year in Gloria's high school life, in the end, Leo had done more than either of them could have realized to help make her the Gloria Steinem the world would come to know (Steinem 2015).

With the festival behind her, Gloria returned to New York intent upon jump-starting her career—and her life. The New York Gloria sought to conquer was a vibrant mix of excitement, adventure, and opportunity. Seeking to maximize their experiences while minimizing their costs, Gloria and her friends would regularly go "second-acting," where they would sneak into a Broadway theater at intermission and catch the second act. A long time tradition among young, impoverished theater buffs and aspiring actors, it required little more than a confident air and was often only the first part of an evening that might later include a postperformance get-together with the actors, who were still on an adrenaline high, followed by an automat breakfast for all (Leland 2016).

At the same time, her new career focus got a boost from her old friend Clay Felker, then an *Esquire* editor. Gloria would look back at the assignment by Felker of an article on the newly developed contraceptive pill as her first big break. While she had written a number of short, unsigned pieces for the magazine, this piece represented her first major assignment. Working diligently and amassing mounds of information, and aided by a patient Felker, Gloria produced an article, "The Moral Disarmament of Betty Coed" that appeared in the September 1962 issue of *Esquire* (Marcello 2004). That breakthrough was followed by what was undoubtedly the best remembered work of Gloria's freelance career, "A Bunny's Tale," an investigative piece that appeared in consecutive issues of *Show* in May and June 1963.

The *Playboy* exposé came about when Gloria was also working for *Help!* magazine, which led to work with *Show*. It was there that the idea for the *Playboy* article emerged out of a typical brainstorming session at which ideas for possible articles were randomly tossed around. Gloria jokingly suggested that they should hire someone to infiltrate the Playboy Club, a part of the increasingly popular Playboy empire and a phenomenon that was becoming a signature part of the urban landscape. Playboy Clubs, nightclubs owned and operated by Playboy Enterprises, drew upon the mystique of the popular men's magazine *Playboy*. The magazine offered a mix of nudity, high-quality writing, and interviews with newsmakers and was a symbol of the nation's increasingly liberal, if sexist, views on sex. The clubs, which first opened in 1960 and featured scantily attired "Bunnies," played upon that attraction. The idea among the *Show* staff that someone should pose as a signature Playboy Bunny resonated with the group; one meeting participant said that they did not need to go outside the magazine, suggesting that it would be an ideal assignment for Gloria. Having put the idea out there, she suddenly found herself the one asked to make it a reality (Stern 1997).

Apprehensive about the prospect but comforted by the fact that the ad for the Bunny position called for women between the ages of twenty-one and twenty-four, the almost thirty-year-old Gloria headed off to the interview, figuring that that experience alone would provide sufficient material for an article. But when she arrived at the initial screening using her grandmother's name, Marie Catherine Ochs—by this time she had published enough that her byline might blow her cover—her assertion that she was indeed twenty-four was accepted, and she was told to return the following week to meet the Bunny Mother.

A week later the increasingly hesitant Gloria also convinced the Bunny Mother of her necessary youth before she was passed on to the costumers, who gave her the iconic costume, showed her how to enhance her bosom, and presented her with both her bunny ears and the renowned cottontail. Offered the job without a background check or an additional interview, she accepted. Now welcomed into the hutch, the Bunny-to-be was ushered back to the Bunny Mother, who had her complete a four-page application. Gloria made up most of the answers while leaving the Social Security number question blank. Although she was told to bring in her card the next day, she never did, and it apparently never mattered. The Bunny Mother also presented her with the Bunny Bible—officially the Playboy Club Bunny Manual. A physical with the Playboy physician as well as training sessions were scheduled. Gloria Steinem was a Playboy Bunny.

Gloria remained for only a month, but that was more than enough time to allow her to present an illuminating look at the life of a Playboy Bunny. From the training sessions to the lessons in walking and serving, from insight into the way a Bunny's responsibilities impacted the tips she might be able to earn to the way she treated her customers—or allowed them to treat her—Gloria offered her readers an eye-opening view of the Bunny experience, which turned out to be far from glamorous.

The focus of "A Bunny's Tale" was originally intended to be on the working conditions the Bunnies experienced, with a particular focus on their low pay and poor working conditions. However, over time the feminist issues that it also exposed became more clearly recognized. For in a very straightforward way, Gloria's article illuminated the many basic indignities the Bunnies suffered on a regular basis. From being pinched by the purposely too tight uniform that often left the Bunnies experiencing leg numbness to being monitored by private investigators making sure they were adhering to the dress code and behavioral guidelines, their experience offered painful lessons in female powerlessness.

Inflated and unfulfilled promises of two hundred dollars to three hundred dollars in weekly pay were common, as were directives to react appropriately to the entertainers who worked at the clubs: Bunnies were expected to laugh when the comics performed. Knowing she was only in it short term, Gloria could go home at night and regale friend with stories. She talked about being stiffed for a tip at the coat check station by Radio Corporation of America (RCA) chairman Robert Sarnoff and recounted how, dressed in full costume as she descended the spiral staircase that connected the club's two floors, she realized that she was fully visible to the males gawking on the street below. As if that were not enough, one of the room directors told her to go back up and do it again, urging her to give the boys "a treat." While desperate to avoid the degradation, she also remembered that disobedience of a direct order was an automatic fifteen demerits. Such was life in the Playboy Bunny hutch. Indeed, in the month she was there, Gloria lost ten pounds, nearly ruined her feet, and weathered all sorts of propositions. By the end of her stint, she could only marvel at the different unsuccessful ways a man could try to ask for a Bunny's phone number.

At the same time, she was fully aware that most of her fellow Bunnies did not have the freedom to leave that she did. Consequently, being deeply empathetic to the challenges they faced, Gloria worked hard to understand and depict their plight in a meaningful way. Furiously, but surreptitiously, taking notes, talking with other Bunnies in an effort to broaden the perspective beyond her own experiences, Gloria portrayed an inhumane and sexist work experience. The Playboy Club News asserted that the "Playboy Club world is filled with good entertainment, beautiful girls, fun-loving playboys ... like a continuous house party. Cheerful Bunnies feel as though they are among the invited guests," but Gloria depicted a daily existence devoid of basic respect for the women, who were seen and treated as little more than objects to be exploited to the benefit and profit of their bosses. Her fellow Bunnies had a wide range of backgrounds. There was the young mother looking to pick up extra money and some college students looking for part-time work, but the bulk of the girls seemed to be aspiring models. They hoped that the Bunny experience, not to mention the cheesecake photo sets that each Bunny was subjected to and that were reportedly sent to Playboy headquarters in Chicago, might result in the ultimate goal—selection as one of the magazine's monthly centerfolds, itself a stepping-stone to a career in the entertainment business.

The group also included young women who chose to work as Bunnies because they had insufficient skills to do much of anything else. In fact, they expressed surprise that, given the secretarial skills Gloria professed to have, she was bothering to be a Bunny. Indeed, after resorting to seeking physical protection by wearing shoes three sizes too big and wrapping her ribs in gauze to protect against the pinching of the uniform, Gloria wondered the same thing.

While a bond quickly developed among the Bunnies, their relationship with the busboys was more complicated. A good, efficient busboy could ease the physical load and allow a Bunny to serve more customers and thus make more money. But for some, that efficiency meant clearing the table of the Bunny's tips as well, while "speculating" that the customer must have stiffed the poor girl. This curious dynamic meant that in addition to customer relations, the Bunnies had to make nice with busboys to whom, outside the club, they would seldom have given the time of day. Gloria's extended description of the glamorous life of a Bunny was comprehensive and enlightening. She included a list of the items that were the most effective bosom stuffers—who would have guessed that the unathletic Gloria would have found a use for gym socks as well as silk scarves, Kleenex, and perhaps cathartically, cutup Bunny tails, among other items. Meanwhile, she also recounted her explanations to new Bunnies about how to serve roast beef while convincing the customers that their piece was rare, medium, or well done when in reality they were all the same. And of course, some of that presentation was based in the distinctive, wiggly Bunny walk designed to keep the Playboy customers satisfied. It was a devastating piece of journalism, and the two-part saga conveyed the experience in a compelling way (Steinem 1983).

"A Bunny's Tale" appeared in consecutive issues of *Show*, May and June 1963, and was a seminal event in Steinem's career. And yet for all the attention it garnered as well as the positive feedback she received, for a very long time, she said that it had been a mistake and a hindrance to her career. Despite the intended focus on working conditions, the bulk of the attention was instead, but not really surprisingly, on sex, or more properly on that aspect as it applied to the Bunnies and also to Gloria herself. Unfortunately, since much of the response was based on her looks and on her ability to pass herself off as a twenty-four-year-old, aspiring Bunny, it did little to enhance her credibility as a journalist. It opened the door to editors seeking to offer similar ventures (Heilbrun 1995), but for Gloria, the idea of going undercover as a prostitute had no allure, especially since she had started to get assignments more in line with the political and social issues she was most interested in writing about. And in fact, in the aftermath of "A Bunny's Tale," *Show* withdrew an assignment to do an exposé on the conservative bias of the U.S. Information Agency and instead offered a series of more frivolous subjects for her to pursue. After years of trying to make her mark, she was seemingly trapped by her new higher profile.

Frustrated by this new roadblock, when one editor noted that "A Bunny's Tale" had put her on the map, the ever-willing traveler countered that it was the wrong map (Stern 1997).

No less a double-edged sword was her first book, a work that came out just a few months after "A Bunny's Tale." *The Beach Book* was an indirect product of Gloria's romantic relationship with Robert Benton. Published by Viking in 1963, it had begun as a joint project with Benton and was tentatively titled *The Pleasure Book*. An anthology, Steinem and Benton planned to combine some already published writing with some original works and illustrations. While working at *Esquire*, the duo had already created a number of clever, if somewhat sophomoric, pieces, and Gloria had also produced a couple similarly themed pieces for *Show*. One example was titled "The Student Prince, How to Seize Power Though an Undergraduate." In an era increasingly focused on image, the article, which appeared in the September 1962 issue of *Esquire*, offered advice on how students could fake their way to an interesting persona. Tips included renting a painting to grace the wall of their apartment and explaining its subsequent disappearance at the end of the rental by noting that the artist was having a show. Also, students working their way through college were urged to take interesting jobs such as selling blood or driving a beer truck. These were preferred over the more conventional, if more lucrative, standard options such as waiting tables, a job that was especially unattractive if it was on campus, in a fraternity or sorority (Stern 1997).

When Gloria Steinem and Robert Benton broke up, he urged her to complete the project, suggesting that she work with Sam Antupit. Viking approved the change, and in 1963 the twenty-nine-year-old Gloria published her first book. When it was almost done, she, Antupit, and the publisher realized that most of the material was about the beach, so the title was changed to *The Beach Book*. As planned, the final version included a mix of previously published items as well as a number of original although unsigned chapters by Gloria, all complemented by a range of artwork and photographs. It was a collection notable for its variety, with chapters ranging from "White Skin as a Status Symbol" to "Noah and the Flood," taken from the Bible. Photographs included shots from D-Day as well as the famous photo of swim trunks-clad JFK surrounded by admiring women. Meanwhile selections and quotations from authors such as Joseph Conrad, T.S. Eliot, and Cornelius Ryan, as well as a piece by Amy Vanderbilt on swimming pool etiquette, were all a part of the eclectic mix. One section that Gloria put together, titled "Things to Read While Lying on Your Stomach," included a seven-day supply of reading material, with the length of the material aligned with the amount of exposure a sun worshipper could enjoy. To top it off, the book's jacket was foil lined, so it could serve as a reflector, a touch that did not sit well with the American Cancer Society, which wrote Viking a letter of protest. To add a wholly unexpected element to the project, the always well-connected Gloria got John Kenneth Galbraith to write the introduction. The book was a pleasant diversion for the upper-class beach crowd that was its intended audience, but had its author not gone on to bigger things, it would likely have never been heard from again (Steinem 1963).

Those bigger and better things were still in the future, however. In fact, while her star as a writer and journalist was slowly rising, neither the publication of "A Bunny's Tale" nor *The Beach Book* had any substantial impact on the career of the still-struggling freelance writer. "A Bunny's Tale" is an enduring part of her early legacy, one that was magnified and introduced to a new generation in 1985, when after years of resistance, Gloria finally allowed it to be made into a television movie. But at the time, it represented little more than the high point of a still-developing career.

Gloria continued to find herself getting mostly women's issues assignments; between "A Bunny's Tale" and her 1968 move to *New York* magazine, the bulk of her bylined work was pieces published in *Glamour*. Even the occasional plum assignments in the *New York Times* and similar publications came in the form of pieces such as "Nylons in the Newsroom," which appeared on November 7, 1965. Similarly, even more extensive pieces, such as her profile of New York City first lady Mary Lindsay, "She Will Not Vegetate in Gracie Mansion," which appeared in the *New York Times* magazine on January 9, 1966, just after her husband took office, focused on the female and social sides of their partnership. At the same time, while his work on behalf of Eugene McCarthy's insurgent presidential campaign had reaffirmed Paul Newman's standing as one of the leading social activists in the film community, Gloria's profile of the award-winning actor, a piece that appeared in the May 25, 1968, issue of *Women's Own*, was titled "Paul Newman: The Trouble with Being Too Good-Looking." It highlighted not only the limits that preconceived notions had on his activist efforts but also, in its own way, the impact of such views on her efforts to become a reporter of hard, political news (Steinem 1983).

Part of what made Gloria distinctive and effective in almost everything she did was the way she so often and so effectively defied established guidelines and boundary lines, and this period was no exception. Indeed, nowhere was this singular ability more evident than in the way that in her journalism career she both advanced and reported on the city and the nation's changing social and political agenda. Understandably she initially took almost any assignment she could find to pay the bills, but none of the work stirred her imagination. In fact, it often left her frustrated. Gloria wanted to be a political reporter, and she wanted to address the issues of the day. Perhaps to compensate for her career, Gloria was becoming increasingly involved in politics and social activism. As a political science major at Smith, she had studied the process, and the academic experience had been complemented by a stint as a summer volunteer in the 1956 Adlai Stevenson presidential campaign. But it went beyond practical politics for Steinem: public policy and international affairs had long been of interest to her, and her experience in India, coupled with her work with the ISI, had expanded her perspective and given her a more experience-based, global view of politics. All of this meshed well with the times, for the civil rights movement had morphed into the antiwar movement, and a women's movement had begun, so Steinem could find many issues that she could investigate as both a journalist and a citizen. Often forgotten amid much of the hype was the fact that "A Bunny's Tale" was undertaken as an investigation of working conditions and was not a meant as a feminist tract—even if over time it was seen as one (Stern 1997).

Similarly, while reformers' major focus was on the growers on the West Coast, a developing issue in the 1960s was the plight of the farmworkers. An unorganized group earning, at best, five dollars a day, their efforts, exploited by the agricultural combines, were the centerpiece of the nation's agricultural production. Early on, Gloria, despite having some deep-seated concerns about Cesar Chavez's misogynistic attitude toward women, became a strong supporter of his effort to gain union recognition for the farmworkers. While she had misgivings, she could not deny what Chavez had accomplished. Working with Dolores Huerta, he cofounded the National Farm Workers Association (NFWA), which evolved into the United Farm Workers (UFW) union. Adopting a Gandhi-inspired, nonviolent approach to their protests, with high-profile hunger strikes, garnered the movement considerable media coverage. It also led to resentment about the attention Chavez was receiving, but by the mid- to late 1970s, the growers in California and Florida had come to recognize the UFW as the bargaining agent for fifty thousand field workers in those states. All of this was in the future, though, when Gloria, in her typical fashion, responded to a request from an old friend, Marion Moses, who was a close ally of Chavez (Marcello 2004).

In the spring of 1968, Moses was in New York trying to raise awareness of the farmworkers' plight, but it was slow going until she called Gloria, who immediately arranged a lunch and asked Moses what she needed. What she needed and what Gloria offered was a lifeline. Not only did Gloria allow Moses to stay at her apartment but she quickly introduced her to members of the media while offering ideas on fundraising. Gloria opened doors to a later appearance by Chavez on *Today*, and she got reporters from *Life* and *Time* to meet with Chavez, with *Time* ultimately putting him on the cover of its July 4, 1969, issue. In addition, Gloria did her own interview with him for an article in *Look*. And earlier that spring, when

Chavez had arrived in New York, Gloria had met with him and helped plan a fundraiser for the Farm Workers at Carnegie Hall. The fundraiser, while a financial success, also represented a public relations triumph. With attendees and donors including Jacqueline Onassis, Paul Newman and his wife, Joanne Woodward, Woody Allen, and numerous other members of the celebrity elite, the event served to raise the movement's visibility to an unprecedented level (Stern 1997).

When Chavez later dispatched aide Dolores Huerta to New York in an effort to follow up on these efforts, Gloria not only provided her with a place to stay but also helped raise money and gave her an entrée into the city's liberal inner circle. Gloria was particularly happy to help Huerta, whose equal efforts as cofounder of the NFWA were usually getting second billing at best. Indeed, the only woman on the board of what ultimately became the UFW, she first came to prominence when she helped organize the Delano grape strike in 1965. Then she solidified her position within the movement when she served as the organization's negotiator in winning the workers' contract following the strike. Over the course of her decades as an activist, she would be the recipient of numerous awards, including the Presidential Medal of Freedom. However, in these early stages, Dolores and the farmworkers to whom she was so deeply dedicated needed all the help Gloria could offer. So while Gloria continued to use her column to publicize the group's efforts, she also continued to share her seemingly endless list of contacts to put Dolores in touch with people whose sympathies could be turned into financial support for the Farm Workers (Stern 1997).

Gloria's involvement with the farmworkers reflected the ongoing, if sometimes sporadic, activism that marked her early years in New York. While she was sympathetic to the civil rights cause, to her later regret, she never got on the buses and joined those who were going south to actively participate in the marches and voter registration efforts that were being staffed largely by northern students and recent graduates. However, she did go to Washington in 1967 to demonstrate against the war in Vietnam, as part of the Women's Strike for Peace. The march was one of the annual events that had originated in 1961, when over fifty thousand women across the United States had marched in opposition to the aboveground nuclear testing in which the government was engaged. By the time Gloria joined the 1967 effort the Women Strike for Peace had changed its focus to the Vietnam War, where it became a centerpiece of the antiwar activities and marches that were directed at the Johnson and Nixon administrations. And it was there that she first met Bella Abzug, a longtime antiwar activist and a figure who would loom large in her future political endeavors. In addition, Gloria also helped organize antiwar demonstrations in New York. In 1968 she joined a group of writers and editors who made a commitment to withhold the part of their taxes that they saw as going to fund the war (Heilbrun 1995). Gloria's involvement with social causes was in part a product of the uncertainties of being a freelance journalist and a woman, a status that made life in New York a constant challenge. Indeed, while not yet a feminist, Gloria nevertheless was reminded regularly of her second-class citizenship in the journalistic community. Typical was a particular cab ride in 1964: when squished between New Journalism icon Guy Talese and prize-winning author Saul Bellow, whom Steinem had recently interviewed for a profile that would appear in *Glamour* the following summer, she was made to feel all but invisible as Talese, whose wife Nan would go on to be one of the publishing world's most powerful figures in the latter part of the twentieth century, leaned over Gloria and said to Bellow, "You know how every year there's a pretty girl who comes to New York and pretends to be a writer? Well, Gloria is this year's pretty girl." Although an older, mellower Gloria would later look back and claim that Talese had intended it as a compliment, at the time, Gloria was mortified and could only wonder what Bellow thought of his recent interviewer (Steinem 2015).

No less typical of the ongoing challenges as well as the rewards of being a freelance journalist, especially one with an unshakable activist streak, was Gloria's piece "Ho Chi Minh in New York," which appeared in *New York* magazine's inaugural issue in April 1968 (Steinem 1968b).

It was not only a trailblazing article but also, in its own way, a telling illustration of the way the ever-inquisitive Gloria worked. She was already caught up in the antiwar movement when an offhand conversation with a

---

NEW YORK

Besides its critical importance in both Gloria Steinem's career as a journalist and the launching of *Ms.*, *New York* magazine played an important role in advancing the women's movement. With its roots as a Sunday supplement to the *New York Herald Tribune*, a redesigned version was launched as an independent magazine in the spring of 1968. A pioneer in 1960s journalism, *New York* established a bold, brassy template for local magazine coverage, one that was envied and copied but never successfully matched, in major cities all over the country. The magazine's editor and founder, Clay Felker, was a major proponent of the New Journalism, and the work of some of its most famous practitioners, such as Tom Wolfe, appeared in the magazine, which added to its influence. The magazine also featured the work of such New York journalistic icons as Jimmy Breslin and film critic Judith Crist. Felker's mentoring of Gloria Steinem, first at *Esquire* and then at *New York*, where she wrote the "City Politics" column, was of undisputed importance to Steinem's career. In addition, *New York*'s pages were where some of her most important work, including her award-winning article "After Black Power, Women's Liberation," first appeared.

middle-aged man and a group of young veterans in a local diner in rural Virginia led her to follow up on the older man's comments about Ho Chi Minh and the long-term history of U.S.-Vietnamese relations. The man's initial comment that we were on the wrong side of the war piqued Gloria's interest. The World War II vet described the Ho Chi Minh he had come to know while fighting in Asia. There Ho Chi Minh had been not only an ally against Japan but also an admirer of FDR and his postwar intention to end the colonialism that was central to the prewar world. Steinem was fascinated when she learned that he and some fellow vets had gone to the State Department to issue a reminder that Ho had been an ally and assert that he could be again, but to no avail. It was an eye-opening experience and when, in the course of their conversation, he learned that she was a journalist, he urged her to write about the North Vietnamese leader who, he said, had once lived in New York City (Steinem 2015).

Returning to New York, Steinem was determined to learn more, and sure enough, there was more to be had. She began to investigate, and the efforts, building upon what she had learned from the veteran whom she later called the "Prophet in the Diner," opened up a whole new world. She discovered that Ho had, at one time, been a cabin boy on a French freighter and had lived in New York—Manhattan and Brooklyn—working as a pastry chef and maybe a photographer. He may have also traveled to Boston. Her research led to a greater understanding of the roots of the war as well as Ho's longtime advocacy of Vietnamese independence.

She also wrote of his efforts to persuade Woodrow Wilson to include the nation's cause in the Treaty of Versailles and how it all led to the Vietnam War that she and her fellow Americans were experiencing. Gloria's efforts produced a piece that offered a very different view of a man long vilified in the American press. However, much to her distress, production issues meant that the piece that was ultimately published was shortened by almost two-thirds, but not before she had sent a telegram to the revolutionary leader, seeking to confirm some facts. While she received no response, she was pretty sure the telegram probably ended up as part of her FBI file. In the end, Gloria was able to produce a piece unlike anything else that had appeared in the American press, as she offered a very different side of the feared communist leader at a time when U.S. efforts in Vietnam had reached a crisis point (Steinem 2015).

The Ho Chi Minh piece created a decisive turn in Gloria's career. In the midst of the 1968 presidential campaign, while the country seemed to be imploding, she played a major role in helping Clay Felker launch *New York* magazine. The venture would propel her career in many positive ways. Felker had long been a mentor and a big help to Gloria at *Esquire*. Meanwhile, unknown to Felker at the time, she had returned the favor when she had convinced Tom Guinzburg to hire him at Viking after he had left

Esquire. That stint helped tide him over until a year later, when he was hired to edit the *New York Herald Tribune*'s magazine, *New York*. He soon turned it into a vibrant publication, one that competed with *Esquire* for readers and writers. When the *Herald Tribune* folded in 1967, Felker, Steinem, and others decided to start an independent version of the former newspaper supplement (Stern 1997).

After almost a year of organizing and fundraising efforts, in much of which Gloria played a part, the magazine's first issue, dated April 8, 1968, was produced. For Gloria, it represented an extraordinary opportunity. She got an unparalleled education in the publishing business, being exposed to all aspects of the fledgling enterprise. Reflective of the nature of the start-up, and given the already extensive network that she enjoyed, Gloria demonstrated an impressive willingness to think outside the box when, recalling his obsession with British-style crossword puzzles, Gloria asked her friend, Stephen Sondheim, to create puzzles for the new magazine. The much-decorated composer and lyricist willingly undertook the assignment for a year before having to turn his full attention to the musical *Company*, for which he won both Tony and Grammy Awards. As much fun as such creative forays may have been, the greatest reward for her efforts as a founding editor was the column, "The City Politic." Becoming a political journalist just as the presidential election was moving into high gear, she was able to gain entrée into a number of campaign venues, where her work sometimes blurred the line between journalist and activist (Heilbrun 1995).

Actually, before *New York* hit the newsstands, Gloria had already been actively involved in campaigning. At the same time that she had been seeking to establish herself as a journalist, she was staying active in the political arena. She continued the volunteer efforts that she had begun on behalf of Adlai Stevenson, when she was still a student. In 1960 she had undertaken mundane tasks such as getting Chinese food for Kennedy volunteers, and in 1964 she helped run a disco as a fundraiser in support of President Lyndon Johnson's campaign. But through it all, her primary focus at that time was trying to establish herself as a political reporter. In 1964, she got her first look at Robert Kennedy, who had left the Johnson administration following the passage of the Civil Rights Act to run for the U.S. Senate from New York. Steinem felt an immediate kinship for a man who seemed as uncomfortable talking to a crowd as she did. At the same time, four years later she would be disappointed when Kennedy initially refused to challenge Lyndon Johnson and his Vietnam policies. Instead, she volunteered on behalf of Minnesota senator Eugene McCarthy when he was willing to enter the primaries and challenge the president over the war in Vietnam. The experience was eye-opening and would prove to be the basis of an insightful article.

In fact, her early work for McCarthy as well as her subsequent writing about him reflected Steinem's distinctive view of politics. She was, she reflected later, one of a group of writers and editors united by one thing—desperation—but that was enough to get them to troop over to the McCarthy headquarters in New York after work and do the things volunteers did—especially volunteers for a candidate who himself said he had no chance to win. Looking back—and in fact, the idea was made clear in her article, "Trying to Love Eugene"—at base the anti-war Democrats did not really like him and were not really for him. But as she showed, they had no alternative: McCarthy was willing to run. In contrast, while Steinem's friend John Kenneth Galbraith had been the first to speak out against the war, the Canadian-born Galbraith could not run for president. Similarly, George McGovern, if no more charismatic than McCarthy, had in fact, been ahead of him on the war, but he had a difficult Senate reelection campaign that forced him to the sidelines. And then, of course, there was Bobby Kennedy, who could not only rally the antiwar forces but could also connect with the other parts of the Democratic coalition, especially minorities, in a way that no other candidate could. But ultimately none of them was running. And so they clung to Gene, trying to convince themselves he was the right choice (Stern 1997).

Steinem's personal recollection of McCarthy painted the picture of a man who for all his failings was nevertheless an intellectual, a man who wrote books and had once supported Adlai Stevenson. She admitted she and her colleagues turned a blind eye to his fervid pursuit of the 1964 vice presidential nomination that ultimately went to his fellow Minnesotan, Senator Hubert Humphrey, whom he would subsequently battle for the 1968 nomination.

McCarthy was a journalist's nightmare. Unresponsive and dismissive, he treated them all as intellectual inferiors and second-class citizens. Yet for an activist journalist such as Steinem, the campaign was one she could only dream of. Indeed, while the candidate was hard to love and sometimes even to stomach—and some of her colleagues credited her with being one of the first to highlight the unfortunate reality that McCarthy seemed to be his own greatest fan—the Children's Crusade that he inspired not only made for great copy but was an inspiring movement to be part of.

But before long, as McCarthy became too hard to love and Kennedy's entry into the race seemed like little more than an exercise in opportunism, after McCarthy had wounded President Johnson in New Hampshire, the situation became chaotic. The divide between the antiwar sides, the Kennedy and McCarthy forces, groups that needed to join together to achieve their shared goals, instead got enmeshed in internecine warfare. Meanwhile the body counts in Vietnam and in the riot-torn cities at home grew. Amid all of this, an increasingly confused and disillusioned Gloria

Steinem pulled back. She withdrew from the campaign trail and instead sought refuge in neutral ground, redoubling her efforts on behalf of Cesar Chavez's farmworkers, using her newfound journalistic platform on their behalf.

In looking back and with the benefit of additional campaign experience and a more hardened view toward politics, Gloria recognized that in 1968 she had begun to develop a more personalized political view, one that went beyond politics and focused on the personal. But fearing how that approach would be seen by her peers, she was unwilling to abandon McCarthy despite the fact that she would later write the aforementioned, devastatingly insightful piece about the candidate. In the end, she would regret the fact that fear kept her from supporting Kennedy, for by the end of the primaries but before his death, she had come to believe he was the only candidate who had the ability to bridge the divide and create a new Democratic coalition of Latinx people, Blacks, antiwar activists, and blue-collar workers who were suffering the ravages of war fueled inflation.

All of this made for a meshing of the personal, political, and professional: at the same time that the country was reeling, Gloria achieved her ambition to become a political reporter, all the while experiencing the same fears and doubts that other Americans had. In the immediate aftermath of Martin Luther King Jr.'s assassination, Gloria, goaded by Felker, who reminded her that she was a reporter, headed to Harlem, where she followed Mayor John Lindsay. She later chronicled his efforts as he personally walked through the city's largest Black area in an ultimately successful effort to prevent New York from erupting into violence as so many other cities across the country were doing (Stern 1997).

The chaos of 1968 led to a meshing of her personal and professional interests, and as a result, the 1968 campaign was the first time that she really straddled the line between political reporter and political activist. On the journalism side, she wrote incisive pieces on Pat Nixon and McCarthy that added to the electorate's understanding of the candidates and their efforts. Gloria's profile of the aspiring first lady revealed both her own journalistic tenacity as well as an ability to connect on a personal level. Indeed, after speaking almost as from a script about the wonders of the many campaigns she had undertaken with her husband, the frustration that had built up came pouring out, and Pat Nixon began to open up. Recalling the countless indignities she had suffered, all perhaps embodied in the "good Republican cloth coat" of her husband's 1952 Checkers speech, Pat showed Gloria a previously unseen side. She deflected Gloria's questions about her hopes and dreams and instead lashed out about those who, like Gloria, had it easy, never for a moment recognizing that, glamorous though she may have appeared, Gloria's Toledo years excluded her from Pat's deeply resented, class-based antagonists. The portrait Gloria sketched offered new insight into the relationship of a man and a woman who had spent much of their life on the campaign trail, with Pat, at least, having clearly paid a price for the experience (Steinem 1983).

Meanwhile, Gloria's portrait of McCarthy got to the heart of the ambivalence that many felt about him. Gloria won praise from many of her fellow journalists for the way she combined journalistic legwork with access to the candidate, all colored by an emotion-based hope that McCarthy could be the difference-maker his supporters sought. In her piece she painted a picture that identified earlier, and explained better than most, the way in which the admiration and enthusiasm that had been so apparent when he had begun his challenge to the president had been undermined by his own self-regard, diffidence, and indifference, traits that left many of his once devoted followers deeply disillusioned (Steinem 1968e). And her subsequent labeling of Senator George McGovern as the "real Eugene McCarthy" was equally insightful, if no less devastating, reflecting her own disappointment at McCarthy's lack of commitment to the cause he had helped ignite.

Then, while she was still reporting, she got involved with McGovern's late-starting, convention-based campaign, an effort that further demonstrated to her that there were other ways she could have an influence. For instance, while she bridled at the attention it received, the chic Gloria did much to spruce up the often-dowdy midwestern lawmaker, adding a touch of style to his uninspired wardrobe. More importantly, however, she was able to use her contacts to get him access to the New York media, including interview sessions with editors from *Time* and the *New York Times*. Ironically, these efforts offered her a disconcerting reminder of the still-existing gender gap. Often, she was one of at most two women present, and it was clear that the editors, who made countless lady jokes while apologizing for swearing, were ill at ease. She emerged from the experience recognizing that she was not cut out to be a press secretary. But perhaps most importantly, her work with McGovern revealed one of her singular talents, one that would be a central, if often unheralded, part of her influence for years to come—she was an exceptional fundraiser. When she had first approached McGovern and asked how she could help, he had almost laughingly told her she could bring money. However, no one was laughing when soon afterward, she appeared with a check for ten thousand dollars, the first of many contributions she would secure on behalf of his candidacies (Stern 1997).

Having helped nudge McGovern into the race, Steinem attended the Chicago convention as part of McGovern's group. The Chicago convention itself was an education but not one she absorbed passively. In fact, while she was passing out literature in support of the farmworkers and welfare rights on the convention floor, she was pushed around by Mayor Daley's security force and even had her glasses broken. The whole experience further expanded her network of contacts, and she later wrote about it for *New York*.

In the aftermath of the convention, she helped McGovern, who was up for reelection in South Dakota and feared that his presidential gambit might hurt his reelection prospects. Gloria made a tangible contribution to the effort, raising substantive amounts of money while also making appearances on local TV and radio. Also, reflective of her political acumen and bowing to the realities of a midwestern campaign, when Gloria campaigned for the senator in South Dakota, her wardrobe featured two long skirts and proper sweaters. McGovern ultimately won with the largest margin of his career. In return for her help, he spoke at a fundraiser for Chavez and the farmworkers (Stern 1997).

One of the things that made Gloria's political reporting so distinctive was the way she was able to present the personal side of the equation. Her work was not caught up in deep-seated political analysis but rather focused on the human side: not the gossipy aspects one might see on the style pages but, rather, who the people were, whether candidates themselves or those who surrounded the candidates and would ultimately share power if victory was achieved. She offered portraits of people based on how they reacted to the crowds they were at once seeking to impress, seduce, and inspire. In Gloria's hands, readers were treated to portraits that went beyond the position papers and the sound bites and instead allowed them to see what kind of person would be sitting in the Oval Office and how the person's character might impact his—because there were no female candidates that year—performance there.

Her work demonstrated an impressive ability to get at the humanity or lack thereof that characterized the range of people she covered. Her journalistic efforts in that singular election year of 1968 were not always carried out within the long-established lines of journalistic objectivity, and, certainly, her status as a columnist gave her some flexibility in her coverage. But in the end, despite the often-personal nature of her writing and the humanity that had long been central to her very being, it was her own intellectual honesty that allowed her to write pieces and report in ways that did not jeopardize the credibility of her work, no matter her personal views. Nowhere was that more evident than in her treatment of Eugene McCarthy.

Gloria capped her coverage of the 1968 campaign with an impressive piece on Richard Nixon that garnered the cover of *New York* magazine less than two weeks before the election. In a mix of the personal and the professional, Gloria offered a profile of Nixon that, without saying as much, clearly sought to change the minds of the many who, like her, had left the Chicago Democratic Convention resigned to not participating in the general election. While they had taken to sporting blank white buttons that more clearly than anything else illustrated their sentiments and despair, her portrait of Nixon reminded them of what was at stake. Indeed, while the dispirited Democrats sulked, the Republicans had been happily sitting back, proudly proclaiming to anyone who would listen that their candidate, the red-baiting former senator, onetime vice president, narrowly defeated presidential nominee, and vanquished candidate for governor of California was the "New Nixon" and worthy of a second, or third, look.

Bereft of hope, but still possessing the reporter's curiosity, Gloria decided to see if "Tricky Dick" really had changed. The result was a fascinating, prescient, and underappreciated examination of Richard Nixon. For all the campaign's efforts to convince the American people that in 1968 there was a "New Nixon," Gloria consistently found herself coming back to Nixon's own comment that those who speak of a new Nixon don't really know the old one very well. She offered a portrait of a tightly controlled campaign that would, in fact, be translated into the tightly controlled administration from which Watergate would spring. That portrait of control also served as an interesting complement to Joe McGinnis's classic *The Selling of the President* and all it had to offer. Appearing on the newsstands in the campaign's waning days, Gloria's telling portrait of a man whose heavily scripted campaign left no room for error—or humanity—served as a final preview for voters who had not made up their mind. Gloria's effort to find a man who had changed had come up empty, but in the process, she had offered voters a cautionary tale (Steinem 1969b).

The result of the election left Gloria unhappy, and while her professional fortunes were clearly on the rise, personally she was adrift, exhausted, and disillusioned by the events of 1968. But while she initially seemed to some friends like a lost soul, uncertain of a direction and lacking real purpose, the ever-resilient Gloria, in fact, remained committed to making a difference, and she approached 1969 with a renewed sense of purpose. Ultimately, she would "find" feminism, making a discovery that would change not only her life but also the nation's political and social landscape. But first, Gloria got involved in a more quixotic effort: the 1969 New York mayoral campaign of Norman Mailer, whose running mate as the candidate for City Council president was her fellow journalist Jimmy Breslin. They had, in fact, initially sought to have Gloria join the ticket as the candidate for comptroller, but beyond her woeful lack of any of the qualifications needed to serve as the city's top financial officer, the woman who years later, after literally decades of speaking before countless crowds from coast to coast, still said the prospect of speaking in public frightened her, quickly dismissed the idea of running. It would not, however, be the last time that anyone envisioned the possibility.

Gloria's willingness to work for the duo, especially the famously misogynist Mailer, was a puzzle to many. Breslin and Mailer certainly represented a different type of politics from what Gloria had covered in 1968, but that may have been what she needed. In 1969 Jimmy Breslin was on his way to crafting a career as a journalist and author that would make him a legend in New York. Already recognized as the guardian of the city's working class, he had been a colleague of Gloria's at *New York* before moving to the *New York Daily News*, where his columns would be a barometer of life in the city for decades to come. A New York native whose father deserted the family when Breslin was only six, he understood the challenges of the working people who were the backbone of the city, and no matter how big he became, he remained committed to being sure that the city's power elite did not forget them. It was that mindset as much as anything that led the forty-one-year-old, future Pulitzer Prize winner to run for City Council president. Meanwhile, his running mate, Norman Mailer, was one of the nation's most outstanding and most controversial novelists. His 1968 work *The Armies of the Night* won him his first Pulitzer Prize as well as the National Book Award. To many, the New York native was a man whose talent was rivaled only by his ego. And yet that talent, first displayed when Mailer rocketed to fame with his 1948 novel *The Naked and the Dead*, would allow him to tower over the American literary scene for decades. At the same time, he was as well known for his personal life (he ultimately had six wives) and his outspokenness on virtually any subject, including feminism—which he treated with disdain—marked by a highly publicized debate with Australian feminist Germaine Greer. Never averse to the limelight, Mailer's mayoral candidacy was little more than another ego-driven escapade, and Gloria's support of the effort remained forever a mystery to her many friends (Stern 1997).

Her involvement with the campaign continued to baffle both observers and friends even when she later explained that she did it in hopes of shaking up the city's political status quo. To that end she helped raise money and featured the effort in a number of her columns, including "The Making (and Unmaking) of a Comptroller," where her own resistance to Mailer and Breslin's entreaties, a resistance that saved everyone from one of the greatest candidate/office mismatches in memory, was revealed. In the end, the effort, one that featured Mailer's promise to make New York City the nation's fifty-first state while also calling for the construction of a monorail around Manhattan, was a sexist disaster. The unlikely candidates won only 5 percent in the Democratic primary. However, it did reveal once again Gloria's preference for making her substantive impact and contribution through working behind the scenes while primarily dealing with small groups. While observers all agreed that the Mailer-Breslin effort was quixotic in the extreme—their slogan "Vote the Rascals In" said much about the candidates' approach—her involvement reflected yet again Gloria's longtime preference and tendency to work for causes far more than candidates. While Gloria would later say that the overriding motive for her involvement was her longtime association with and high regard for Jimmy Breslin, that explanation also reaffirmed her lack of any doctrinaire leanings. Indeed, Mailer's longtime role as a thorn in the side of the feminist movement made this even clearer, since her support of his 1969 effort did not make her immune from future attacks by the irascible and overly macho writer (Steinem 1969b).

Ironically, for all her subsequent prominence, Gloria was, by her own account, a latecomer to the feminist movement. More than a few commentators have noted the irony that 1963 saw the publication of both *The Feminine Mystique*, by Betty Friedan, Smith Class of 1942, and *The Beach Book*, by Gloria Steinem, Smith Class of 1956. And yet while Gloria has never been anything but clear about the fact that she came to the movement late, she has also noted that she was not oblivious to the women's movement. She acknowledges, too, that she found herself increasingly sympathetic to its goals. At the same time, as *New York*'s political writer, not to mention the only female writer on staff, her male colleagues, with whom she was very close, were adamant in urging her not to get involved with "those crazy women." And while she had made clear her willingness to cross the journalism/activism line, she was nevertheless reluctant to become actively involved in this effort. In fact, on a number of occasions she had rebuffed direct invitations to join National Organization for Women (NOW) (Stern 1997).

But for all her reluctance, those evolving views began to resonate in a wholly different way after she went to a meeting in late March 1969. The gathering, an abortion rights speak-out held at Judson Memorial Church, in Greenwich Village, was sponsored by the radical feminist group the Red Stockings. And while Gloria may have attended the event believing it could provide fodder for her *New York* column, she later cited it as a career turning point, one from which she would develop a concept of feminism and women's rights that she would pursue the rest of her life. Arriving as a journalist, she left as a budding feminist, her life unalterably changed (Stern 1997).

Sitting on a windowsill, the proverbial fly on the wall at the standing-room-only gathering, she heard women of all kinds, from all backgrounds, as they shared their stories of dealing with unwanted pregnancies. Learning that one in three American women had needed an abortion at some point in their lives and then hearing the testimony from those who had had them—from women who had risked their health, not to mention flouted the law—she suddenly felt a deep and shared kinship. She also had a newly heightened awareness of women who, like her over a decade before, had experienced the fear, the pain, the loneliness, and the anguish that were so central to the experience of having an abortion. These public confessions created a new level of understanding and appreciation, one that went beyond the intellectual approach to which she had previously consigned her treatment of the issue. Suddenly it became clear that as women they needed to talk about this experience, to ask why it was illegal, and to consider the other aspects of their lives that had long gone unexamined. Hearing these women represented an awakening, one that led to a reassessment of her years in New York, with its sudden recognition and resulting resentment of all the little humiliations that had made her efforts all the more difficult. Suddenly Gloria began to read every bit of feminist writing she could find (Steinem 1983).

With her *New York* column offering a ready-made platform, she quickly launched herself into the fray. While the meeting may have marked her arrival as a feminist, her April 7 "City Politic" column, "After Black Power, Women's Liberation" (Steinem 1969a) served as the official announcement while also being one of the first mainstream media reports on the women's movement. The piece, which gained immediate attention and subsequently earned Gloria the Penney-Missouri Journalism Award for its early explanation of feminism, made clear her belief in the subject's importance. Interestingly, while Gloria's feminist awakening may have been based in a meeting devoted to abortion, her April 7 call to arms barely mentions that particular subject, a practice that was, at that time, illegal in forty-nine states. Nor does the article offer much of a real sense of Gloria's personal thoughts on the issue. Rather, it is a piece of reporting that offers one of the first discussions of the developing women's liberation movement. Applying a longer lens and putting it all in a broader context, Gloria offered a short but informative look back. She made some important connections with the civil rights movement, while also noting its own role in the ongoing revolution that however inexorably, was opening up new opportunities for the long-oppressed majority of the nation's population.

At the same time, she painted an optimistic picture of the movement's development and direction, while noting that, like most reform efforts, it was not one like-minded monolith but, rather, had its different branches. She then illustrated that reality through a number of telling examples, ones that helped illustrate the commonality of aspects of discrimination, the ones that know no racial or socioeconomic lines, while also noting that there are others rooted solely and firmly in gender. Also, in a twist that would soon carry no small amount of irony, Gloria's quick historical tour paid homage to the role of Betty Friedan and her pioneering work *The Feminine Mystique*. At the same time, while acknowledging the importance of Friedan's main constituency, the middle-class, educated woman, Steinem noted that no group was immune from the discrimination that met women at every turn. While recognizing that this effort had been met with no small amount of opposition, she saw it as one that could transcend the class lines along which it had tended to be viewed.

The article concluded with an interesting, if not novel, thought but one that over the years would become a central tenet of Steinem's view. She argued that the movement was not just about women but was an important part of the drive for human equality and freedom: "The idea is in the long run," she wrote, "that women's liberation will be men's liberation, too" (Steinem 1969a, "After Black Power").

Ultimately, of course, Gloria's personal epiphany was destined to have an impact of far greater magnitude than just her own life. Gloria's psychological and intellectual embrace of feminism came at the right time, as her past experiences and skill set were perfectly aligned with the needs of the movement. In fact, she quickly became a force in an effort that was rapidly gaining public notice. That heightened awareness matched a desire from the mainstream media for a figure who could represent the feminist cause. With her personality, skills, experiences, and beauty, Gloria fit the bill.

In fact, the column and the announcement it represented—that Gloria Steinem, girl reporter, was a feminist—suddenly changed her life. Many who knew her saw nothing new, observing that if you looked at her life and work, it was clear that she was a feminist, even if she had not recognized it. But with it now plain for all to see, her developing public profile, coupled with her strong statement and her Hollywood looks, made her a perfect spokesperson for the developing cause. Except for one thing: few things were more terrifying to Gloria than speaking in public—even for a cause to which she was deeply devoted. Consequently, in the immediate aftermath of the article, she took refuge in the whimsical Mailer and Breslin campaigns.

The campaign could only hold off the inevitable for so long. At the same time that Gloria used her column to tout the dynamic duo's effort, invitations for her to speak, to hit the road for the feminist cause, poured in. Finally, on June 17, the Democratic voters of New York ended the sideshow as Mailer finished fourth in the five-candidate race, with his 5 percent barely edging out Congressman James Scheuer, then in the third term of a career in the House of Representatives that would ultimately span almost thirty years. With the campaign's end, Gloria could no longer avoid her fate, and yet the idea of going on the road, even for the cause of women's rights, was absolutely terrifying.

She was happy to have her voice jump off the page, but offering those same thoughts in front of a live audience was something very different. Yet she did not just recognize that there was a receptive audience out there just waiting to hear and be heard; she knew, too, that so much of what she had done before—in India, with the youth festivals, in the 1968 campaign, and as a reporter—had prepared her for just this kind of effort. And so it was that Gloria Steinem agreed to begin to travel and speak, a decision that would kick off a half-century odyssey that would help reshape the national consciousness.

She began by working out a plan whereby she and Black activist Dorothy Pitman Hughes would offer a multiperspective presentation. It was an approach that not only took some of the pressure off Gloria but also helped bring home the broader ideas about the women's movement: that it was not only related to the civil rights movement but also, at its core, an important part of a humanity movement. That message was a central part of Gloria's approach from the beginning. Now she would have the chance to share it (Steinem 1987).

4

To the Barricades

The publication in 1963 of Betty Friedan's *The Feminine Mystique* is often seen as the start of the second wave of feminism. Friedan's work was a product in part of the frustration she, an accomplished Smith graduate, had experienced in trying to make a satisfying life that went beyond the societally sanctioned framework of wife and mother. After Smith, Friedan had originally begun graduate studies, but under pressure from her then boyfriend she turned down a PhD fellowship. Instead, she turned to writing, initially working for a number of newspapers and periodicals and then doing primarily freelance work after she married and began raising three children. In 1957, she did a survey for her Smith reunion and, after the results yielded a vague but real sense of dissatisfaction and a lack of fulfillment, Friedan began to write articles about what she termed "the problem that has no name." Readers responded to her work with heartfelt expressions of gratitude at learning that they were not alone. From all of this, she decided to expand her work into a book, and when the final product was released in 1963, *The Feminine Mystique* hit a chord with the nation's middle class. Talking to a national audience about women having the right to grow, talking about their experiences in a way that made them realize that they were not alone, the book became a best seller and Friedan became a celebrity. More importantly, the seeds were planted for a reexamination of American society and the role women played in it (Cohen 1988).

The Feminine Mystique was a phenomenon. Yet for all its success and influence, the roots of a major change were, in fact, already in evidence as the nation entered the 1960s. In 1960 the government began to consider a response to a report from the President's Commission on National Goals. The all-male commission, whose eleven members included former Harvard president James B. Conant, DuPont president Crawford H. Greenwalt, federal appeals court judge Learned Hand, University of California president Clark Kerr, and General Alfred M. Gruenthe, who had served as Supreme Allied Commander in Europe from 1953 to 1956, issued its report just after the election of John F. Kennedy. In retrospect, it could have been a blueprint for President Lyndon Johnson's Great Society.

Included in the commission's report was the assertion, "Every man and woman must have equal rights before the law." It added, "Vestiges of Religious prejudice, handicaps to women, and most importantly, discrimination on the basis of race must be recognized as morally wrong, economically wasteful, and in many respects dangerous" ("Text of the Report" 1960). It was a noble pronouncement, but despite the high-flung rhetoric, it was unrelated to the later inclusion of women in the Civil Rights Act of 1964, which was, depending upon one's source, either a fortuitous accident or a tactical error rooted in the belief that proposed equality for women was so outrageous, it would sink the whole bill. Either way, the groundbreaking legislation barred discrimination based on gender and provided a legal basis on which a movement dedicated to expanding the rights of the long-suffering majority of the nation's population could build.

While the inclusion of gender in the Civil Rights Act may have been a happy accident, there was nothing accidental about the developing organizational efforts among women that began to emerge in the mid-1960s. Foremost among these was the NOW. It was born out of frustration when, in 1966, a group of women attending the Third Annual Conference of Commissions on the Status of Women decided to take action. They were disturbed by the government's failure to put into action the newly created means to end discrimination, especially the Equal Employment Opportunity Commission (EEOC) as well as the provisions of the Civil Rights Act of 1964. Being particularly incensed at an EEOC ruling that separate, gender-based job advertising did not constitute sex discrimination, a small group decided to act.

With Betty Friedan offering her hotel room as a gathering place, a meeting took place that included Pauli Murray, Inka O'Hanrahan, Rosalind Loring, Catherine Conroy, Mary Eastwood, Dorothy Haener, Shirley Chisholm, and Kay Clarenbach. The women determined to create an organization to advocate for their goals. While the acronym "NOW" came from a sketch Friedan had made on a napkin, the organization would develop into something that provided a focus for the nation's developing wave of feminism, turning it into a force that would change American society forever. Before the conference was over, the group met again; Catherine Conroy reportedly placed a five-dollar bill in the middle of the table, challenging each of her colleagues to match it and then to sign on as a founding member of NOW. Thus, the NOW was founded (Cohen 1988).

In the wake of Friedan's book and the newly enacted legislation, the nation appeared ready for a new campaign for women's rights, one powered by a new generation of feminist activists. NOW hit the ground running, and when it held its first formal conference in October, the organization not only elected Friedan president, while naming Clarenbach chair of their board, but also issued a formal Statement of Purpose. It declared that NOW was an organization intended to pursue actions that would help make women full and equal participants in American society, on the same level as the nation's men. They added that they sought to make an impact in an array of policy areas, including employment, political and legal rights, and education, as well as four other areas covered by the task forces they established (Cohen 1988).

It was a powerful kickoff, one that quickly caught the attention of the media. And in one of their first formal actions, NOW mounted a legal challenge to the EEOC's earlier decision on the segregated advertising, the ruling that had been so central to the group's founding. In August 1968, the EEOC reversed its decision, and a 1973 Supreme Court decision upheld the ban. It was the beginning of a new age. But the movement entered that new age lacking a leader or a face with which it could be identified. It also was hampered by the disparate and competing ideas and ideology that marked the quest for female equality. Devotees of Simone de Beauvoir's more academic approach clashed with the white, middle-class suburbanites who had seen themselves in Friedan's *Feminine Mystique.* Meanwhile, Black women, who had been consigned to second-class status in their own civil rights movement, fared no better when the battles were waged along gender lines. But the era was one in which the media increasingly latched onto an individual, so one person was needed who could be the singular representative or leader, no matter how complicated or multifaceted the reality. Consequently, as it approached the 1970s, the movement found itself in need of a singular force who could lead the pursuit of the still-developing feminist agenda.

Into this void stepped Gloria Steinem. From the very beginning, Gloria had sought to cast a wide net, asserting that if something was not good for all women, then it was not good for any living thing. She saw the women's movement as part of a larger human rights movement, one in which all benefited as each formerly oppressed group was brought under the tent of equality. Gloria's background led her to the belief that inequality could bedevil any group or be based in any classification; age, gender, race, ethnicity: they could all be targets of inequality. But she sought to bring them all under the net of human and civil rights, a concept that transcended labels and even geographical lines, a stance that, in contrast with some of her American allies, had her seeing feminism as a global cause.

From the outset Gloria brought political experience and a fine-tuned political antenna to the movement. It was not much of a leap from political reporter to political activist and now to feminist activist, and in fact, she had straddled the line for years. In addition, in walking with others in India, she had quickly demonstrated an uncanny ability to connect with others, a talent that was furthered by her ability and willingness to listen, especially around the talking circles that provided one of the most enduring and impactful lessons she took away from being there.

And finally, to the chagrin of many, and no one more than herself, Gloria brought a glamour and a physical presence that in a highly charged media age could assuage the media's desire to personalize and simplify the movement. In the same way that the civil rights movement was, in fact, far more than Martin Luther King Jr., so, too, was feminism more than Gloria Steinem—she certainly knew that—but to media starved for a point person, the beautiful, glib, media-savvy Gloria was a godsend.

Meanwhile, within the movement she was a potent symbol. On the one hand, her attractiveness—and the fact it was always a part of perceptions of her—reinforced the longtime idea of judging women by their looks. At the same time, she was also a rebuttal to those who saw feminists as little more than unattractive—if not plain ugly—unhappy, unfulfilled, women who were dissatisfied with their lot in life because of those attributes. In a word, they saw a feminist as the embodiment of what was known as an "old maid." In contrast, there was Gloria. Beautiful and accomplished, vibrant and upbeat, single by choice, an independent achiever, she was everything naysayers said a feminist could not be but was instead something very different. Indeed, rather than being an old maid, the new face of feminism seemed almost to be a female version of the swinging bachelor—in control of her own life and enjoying what it had to offer.

For all her beauty, it was not wholly because of her looks that Gloria was anointed a feminist leader by the media over the other individuals vying for the honor. No less important were her presence and style. The same skills that had made her a star at the countless word games she had played at Smith made her a star at producing the pithy lines that journalists loved to quote. She represented a marked contrast to feminist peers such as Betty Friedan, who tended to pontificate in a seemingly endless manner. While Gloria Steinem would get more philosophical the longer she stayed involved, she never lost the ability to provide the one-liners, such as her famous "This is what forty looks like," that so aptly and effectively made her case while also endearing her to the media. And beyond the words and the basic beauty was a presence that added to her stature. From early dance performances to the personal, but no less real, roles she had played during the Toledo years, Gloria had developed the ability to present. Whether it was at a press conference, in a talking circle, or at a meeting with a prospective advertiser, Gloria presented herself in an authentic, appropriate, and usually very effective way (Cohen 1988).

Not surprisingly, as the movement grew, it also fractured, or more accurately the existing divisions became too much even for the media to ignore. It was easier for the media to portray it as a big monolith of shared purposes headed by a single leader, but that was not the reality. Split over issues of abortion, lesbianism, and its relationship to the Black civil rights movement, among others, clashes took place across class lines as well as marital ones. In fact, the movement Gloria joined in the spring of 1969 was one whose energy exceeded its organization and cohesiveness. For many, Gloria's arrival helped address that, but to others she became a lightning rod for the personal, ego-driven tensions that would characterize the movement of the 1970s.

Gloria's emergence did not represent a threat to all the early leaders. One person who was not threatened by Gloria was Bella Abzug. A boisterous, outspoken, self-proclaimed radical attorney and activist, Abzug's early career was marked by her work in the civil rights movement as well as on behalf of victims of the McCarthy-era "red scare." She was also an early opponent of the war in Vietnam and a leader of the antiwar movement that developed in the 1960s. Critics charged that she was a communist, but in fact she had refused to join the party at a time when many friends had done so. She charged that the party was too ideologically rigid and that she was committed to the freedom guaranteed by the Constitution, freedom she sought to protect through her legal efforts. In 1970, Abzug won election to the House of Representatives, vowing to shake things up in Washington. While she would only serve three terms in the House before losing a bid for the Senate, Abzug was a leader in the House and her central role in the National Women's Political Caucus (NWPC), a bipartisan organization aimed at increasing women's participation in politics, reflected her determination to increase the role of women in the political process. For Abzug, Steinem was a resource, a means to connect with groups that were not part of her existing circle. Indeed, one savvy observer of New York politics, seeing how Abzug took Gloria under her wing, opined that Bella, who had been involved in many of the political causes that Gloria had admiringly observed, taught Gloria about aspects of politics that, despite her previous experience, were totally new to her. At the same time, for the bellicose, office-seeking Bella, being with Gloria meant being at the center of attention, for Gloria was a magnet for the media. In a singularly and awkwardly sexist characterization, one observer referred to Gloria as Bella's arm candy, but there could be little doubt that Gloria's charm and attractiveness added to Bella's power and appeal (Zarnow 2019).

Once Gloria took the plunge, her personal life and the women's movement became virtually interchangeable. At the same time, to a media ever intent on identifying a singular face of a movement, a cause, or an organization, her admittedly late arrival on the scene was no deterrent to their effort to make her the face, if not the leader, of the developing movement. Thus the articulate, photogenic, media-savvy Gloria was quickly christened the face of feminism. It was not an illogical decision. In fact, utilizing the skills and contacts that she had been developing as far back as her days at Smith, she would focus on changing the nation's balance of power as it related to the menu of opportunities available to all Americans. Once engaged, Gloria became a nonstop advocate for women's rights, with strategy sessions, fundraising efforts, and public events all blurring together.

A simple glance at the number of activities and organizations with which Gloria has been involved can leave an observer exhausted, and while you cannot help but be impressed, at the same time, you may also wonder whether she has perhaps overextended herself and sometimes traded quality for quantity. And yet the distinctive background she brought to the movement undoubtedly impacted her efforts. For instance, despite the fact that she joined the movement in 1969, the immediate embrace by the media, coupled with her longtime political involvement, made her an obvious asset when elected officeholders Bella Abzug and Shirley Chisholm, along with other female political leaders, looked for additional figures to help found (as discussed in greater detail below) the NWPC (Stern 1997).

Similarly, her travel abroad as a Smith student, and even more importantly, her almost two-year sojourn to England and then India, had given her a global perspective that made her more intent on pursuing a more worldwide effort than many of her American allies. This added a dimension to her activism while also creating another source of tension in a movement that, while often portrayed by the media as a focused monolith, in fact, had numerous splinter sectors based on personality and/or ideology, all of which reflected the diverse nature of the national and global female populations. Ironically, these conflicts presented challenges for which Gloria was an ideal mediator.

With credibility and identity created and then certified by the media, Gloria quickly became a much-sought-after public spokesperson for the feminist cause. One of her earliest appearances came on May 6, 1970, when she testified before the U.S. Senate on behalf of the Equal Rights Amendment (ERA). The amendment, a proposed addition to the Constitution that was first introduced in 1923, was passed by Congress in the spring of 1972. Gloria's testimony was just one of the many public appearances that marked her emergence as a feminist leader (Stern 1997).

In 1971, Gloria sought to return to her journalistic roots, not to mention her comfort zone. She believed that while the movement needed to develop a cohesive voice, it also needed to provide a voice for the women of the nation who had long gone unheard and unheeded. Determined to use her skills in that way, she embarked on an effort to provide that national platform. *Ms.* magazine, a pioneering publication that would become the centerpiece of both her efforts and her feminist legacy, was Gloria's response to this need. (See below for background on the run-up to and impetus for *Ms.*) The first magazine to be created and operated entirely by women, it first hit newsstands as part of a year-end issue of *New York*, and the reception was remarkable, exceeding the expectations of observers and staff alike. But when its first solo issue hit newsstands in the spring of 1972 and sold out in a just over a week, it became a cultural phenomenon and a centerpiece of Gloria's feminist legacy (Thom 1997).

At the same time that she was immersed in the development of *Ms.*, Gloria was being pulled in other directions. Reflective of her multifaceted involvement in the women's movement, in July 1971, she joined feminist author and fellow Smith alum Betty Friedan, political luminaries that included Congresswomen Bella Abzug and Shirley Chisholm, Republican leader Jill Ruckelshaus, Native American activist LaDonna Harris, and Lyndon Johnson confidant Liz Carpenter, along with veterans of the civil rights movement and organized labor, to help cofound the NWPC. The bipartisan group's goal was to increase the number of women actively involved in politics. Motivated in part by the continuing failure of Congress to pass the ERA and with an eye to the upcoming presidential election, the group sought greater female representation at the national party conventions while also encouraging more women to run for office (Stern 1997).

While garnering impressive media coverage, highlighted by a *New York Times* article topped by a picture featuring Abzug, Chisholm, Friedan, and Steinem, the launching of the NWPC showcased the developing tensions within the growing movement. It also offered an example of both Gloria's singular style as well as her evolving place in the movement. Perhaps because of the impressive list of political heavyweights involved with the creation of the NWPC, clashes over strategies for, the structure of, and the approach to governing the organization were rife, with Friedan and the newly elected Congresswoman Abzug heading competing forces as they vied to be recognized as the group's leader and spokesperson.

Steinem backed Abzug, whose political skills she admired, but in some respects the question of who was to speak for the movement was taken out of the organization's hands. Indeed, while Gloria played a role of mediator in the NWPC, the media focused their attention on her, and her public profile was raised to new heights when *Newsweek* featured her on the cover of its August 16 issue, under a banner that proclaimed "The New Woman." And yet, more typical of her equally important impact, not to mention her preferred role, was the group's mission statement, which was adopted with few even knowing she had written it. The few who did know—or later discovered it—were impressed as much by her ability to articulate the group's mission as by her selfless approach to serving the cause (Stern 1997).

As Gloria became more and more active in the feminist movement, her relationship with the media became complicated. As a working member of the fourth estate, and fully aware, if defiantly dismissive of, her looks and their power, it could not have been a surprise when she and neither Betty nor writer-activist Andrea Dworkin nor anyone else was chosen to grace the *Newsweek* cover. On the other hand, the Seven Sisters, Phi Beta Kappa graduate deeply resented the idea that her looks were the reason for her prominence and influence. And yet her willingness to work behind the scenes, to make countless unheralded trips to the boonies to encourage and help organize a band of enthusiastic women who wanted change, was a far better reflection of her commitment and her priorities. In fact, on more than a few occasions she had to be dragged to an event by those who resented, but nonetheless needed, Gloria to be in the picture—often more literally than figuratively.

In the aftermath of her feminist epiphany, the focus of her writing changed as well. With a newfound feminist sensibility coupled with a regular column, she was less willing to accept some of the more fluff-like freelance pieces she had previously done. Instead, with her *New York* column, "The City Politic," offering an opportunity for commentary on a range of city-based subjects, her outside freelance work, including a *Glamour* profile of radical Irish leader Bernadette Devlin and a *Look* magazine piece titled "Why We Need a Woman President in 1976," seemed to reflect her newfound feminist perspective (Stern 1997).

Befitting her background as a political reporter, Gloria knew that politics could play an important role in advancing the feminist agenda. She was also well aware of the limitations of the political process. While the feminist cause became the centerpiece of her life, her earlier study of international relations, her time in India, and her journalism experiences led her to embrace and advocate for a broadening of the feminist ideal. She worked hard to help people understand how the women's movement was intimately and inextricably related to the ongoing Black civil rights movement as well as the antiwar movement, and that all were a part of a human-rights-centered vision that transcended the nuts-and-bolts aspects of politics.

And yet despite her broader vision, from the beginning, a central factor in Gloria's influence was her involvement with the political process. In fact, her relationship with South Dakota senator George McGovern was in some ways typical of the vast interlocking web of her contacts and causes. The network not only fueled her efforts but reflected her broad-based humanistic and inclusive approach to both politics and personal relations.

Steinem had first met McGovern in 1965 at Boston's Logan Airport, when both were en route to the Vermont home of John Kenneth Galbraith.

Although a backbench senator in the 1960s, McGovern gained prominence as an early opponent of the Vietnam War. A decorated fighter pilot in World War II, McGovern came to politics from a different direction than that of most of his colleagues. He earned a PhD in history from Northwestern University and initially planned to pursue a career as a history professor. But he got involved with the South Dakota Democratic Party and eventually served two terms in the House. In 1960 he mounted an unsuccessful bid for the Senate, and following that defeat, he served in the Kennedy administration as director of the Food for Peace Program. In 1962 he again sought election to the Senate and that time was successful, winning a narrow victory and becoming only the third Democratic senator in state history. In the Senate, he soon became a vocal opponent of the war as well as a staunch advocate on behalf of agricultural interests. Steinem, whose own introduction to Galbraith had come only a few years before at the home of mutual friends, shared a three-hour ride with the senator, and it left her deeply impressed. Finding him unpretentious, kind, humorous, and frank, she was pleasantly surprised that despite her being a journalist, he was open about his politics and especially his opposition to the Vietnam War. Meanwhile, by the end of the weekend, after seeing Steinem easily mix with the Galbraiths and guests such as Kennedy administration luminary Arthur Schlesinger Jr., McGovern was no less impressed by Gloria. Things reached a new level in 1968 when Steinem, in a radio

---

Ella Grasso

Ella Grasso was the first woman to be elected governor of an American state, Connecticut, who was neither the spouse nor widow of a former governor. Grasso's election represented the culmination of a career that over the course of two decades took her from the state legislature to the office of state secretary of state, two terms in Congress, and then the 1974 gubernatorial race. As governor, she had to address the challenges brought by the Arab oil embargo of the mid-1970s as well as the broader, "stagflation"-based economic downturn, but she remained popular, winning reelection in 1978. She resigned at the end of 1980 and died from ovarian cancer barely a month later. Although frequently mentioned as a candidate for a cabinet post, Grasso remained loyal to Connecticut and showed herself to be a strong chief executive and an inspiration for the many women who would subsequently go on to seek the governor's office in states across the country. In a touch of irony that connected Steinem to Grasso, throughout Grasso's tenure in the Governor's Mansion, Connecticut's senior senator was Abe Ribicoff, the organizer of the McGovern campaign meeting to which Steinem was denied entrance when Ribicoff declared, "No broads allowed."

interview intended to promote her *New York* cover article "Trying to Love Eugene," castigated McCarthy and the way he treated the campaign and especially his idealistic and youthful supporters, and then observed that George McGovern was probably the real Eugene McCarthy. Steinem quickly found herself in the middle of an effort, largely of former Bobby Kennedy supporters, to find a candidate who could stop Humphrey. Her comments helped fueled an effort to make McGovern that man. When he jumped into the race, Steinem was there with him, doing pretty much anything she could to help him and his cause (Steinem 1983).

Given those roots, in July 1969, when McGovern began to consider a run for the 1972 nomination, he invited Steinem to an organizational meeting. However, the meeting's organizer, Connecticut senator Abraham Ribicoff, made clear that despite McGovern's explanation of the various roles that Steinem had played in his previous efforts, *no* women were welcome at the gathering. It was a slap in the face for Steinem, one she never forgot, still citing it decades later as an early part of her feminist awakening. She fully recognized that if he had said, "No Blacks" or "No Jews," there would have been political hell to pay but somehow "No broads" (see the "Ella Grasso" sidebar) was acceptable. But in typical fashion, rather than stew about it, Gloria took it as a useful and motivating reality check about the status of women in the politics of the time, clear evidence of why the NWPC was so necessary. At the same time, it proved highly ironic, given that one of the few positive legacies of the McGovern campaign, as well as the party reform overseen by McGovern, was the major increase in the involvement, profile, and influence of women in the post-Vietnam-era Democratic Party.

Despite McGovern's early rebuff, when the 1972 campaign actually got underway Gloria, albeit somewhat awkwardly, became actively involved—in multiple campaigns. While she would later somewhat ruefully observe that she would have been more comfortable attending the Democratic convention as a member of the press, between the war and the emergence of a female candidate, Gloria was unable to stay on the sidelines. But she had ties to both Shirley Chisholm and George McGovern, and her efforts to balance them were awkward at best. In fact, it was a complicated matter, a mix of the personal and the political. Gloria was thrilled that her NWPC ally Chisholm was running, and she showed her support by running, albeit unsuccessfully, as a Chisholm delegate. She had long admired Chisholm, the first African American woman elected to Congress, winning a seat representing Brooklyn in 1968. A tough, outspoken former state legislator and teacher, her slogan "Unbought and Unbossed" summed up her independent approach to politics. Not satisfied with the large field of candidates seeking the Democratic presidential nomination in 1972, Chisholm joined the race in the early spring, and her candidacy became a rallying point for both women and Blacks. Even though in the end it was unsuccessful, it nevertheless represented an important historical milestone. It was all that and more to Gloria, who continues to count her authorship of the speech that Chisholm delivered before a national television audience at the convention to be one of her proudest political achievements. And yet, given her strong opposition to the war, she did not see it as illogical to urge voters to support the antiwar candidate, Senator McGovern, in the primary states where Chisholm, who had entered the race later, was not on the ballot. But ultimately, her efforts not only proved frustrating to both sides but also left her open to much criticism. She was accused of being both indecisive and wanting to have it both ways by politicians and the media alike. Yet to those who had long followed her politics, the awkwardness aside, her efforts seemed an accurate reflection of her tendency to care more about issues and causes than individual candidates (Chisholm 1970).

In this case, Steinem admired Chisholm, a woman who had long said she had experienced more discrimination as a woman than as an African American, and she was also strongly supportive of the idea of a female candidate. In addition, Steinem's continuing efforts to better mesh the civil rights and women's rights movements made Chisholm all the more attractive as a candidate. At the same time, Gloria did not just strongly oppose the war in Vietnam; she also thought that McGovern was a far more credible candidate.

Despite all of this division, Gloria did attend the Democratic National Convention, and in addition to writing Chisholm's speech, she delivered a well-received address in support of Texan "Sissy" Farenthold for the Democratic vice presidential nomination. But in the end, the convention was, in many ways, a major disappointment. In addition to the fallout from her own awkward effort to support both Chisholm and McGovern, she also felt betrayed by a strategic decision of the McGovern campaign's high command, one that purposely torpedoed a challenge mounted by the NWPC against the makeup of the South Carolina delegation. The McGovernites said it was a necessary move in advance of the significantly higher-stakes battle over the delegate-rich California delegation. But to the feminist forces, it was a betrayal, one that was magnified when the McGovernites also retreated on the abortion rights issue. The campaign's explanation that it was necessary so as to be better positioned for the upcoming fall general election campaign offered little solace. For Gloria and company, it was a bitter lesson in practical politics in a system still overwhelmingly controlled by men. While women had been allowed at the convention, their voices were not yet being heard (Steinem 1983).

And yet despite those disappointments, her commitment to McGovern had deep roots, and with the war in Vietnam still raging and Richard Nixon the alternative, Gloria could not abandon the beleaguered senator. Rather, she traveled widely, at one point being part of a group called the Grasshopper Special. Organized by NWPC colleague Liz Carpenter and including Schlesinger, McGovern's daughter Terry, and civil rights leaders Myrlie Evers and Aaron Henry, as well as journalist Hodding Carter III, the group campaigned actively for the South Dakota Democrat (Stern 1997).

Gloria refused to abandon McGovern, and she understood the reality of pragmatic politics. At the same time, the fact that the campaign culminated in McGovern's landslide defeat did nothing to assuage the hurt or the sense of betrayal. In the end, Gloria could do little but reflect upon the overall 1972 election effort as a difficult, but valuable, learning experience. In retrospect, 1972 also represented the last time she was ever so deeply involved in an individual campaign, at least at the presidential level. While she would continue to campaign well into her eighties, she would increasingly turn her attention and energies to broader-based movement efforts while also traveling all over the country to help develop the grassroots organizations so critical to raising awareness and fostering female empowerment. Her formal political efforts have represented individual choices and not support for any particular organization or party. Following 1972, Gloria's active support would go to those candidates who sought to further her feminist/humanist agenda.

In the aftermath of her feminist awakening—and as the 1970s approached—Gloria the journalist initially had sought to use her column to support the women's movement. She recognized that there was a receptive audience spread across the country, anxious and open to hearing about feminism, and she needed to respond to that group. And yet doing so would force Gloria to face her single greatest fear: public speaking. Confronting that fear, she undertook to go on tour, and it quickly became a direct, distinctive, and powerful way for her to contribute to the cause. In fact, over the course of many years, paired first with Dorothy Pitman Hughes, a New York childcare activist whose work Gloria had profiled in a *New York* column, then Margaret Sloan, a Black activist from Chicago, and finally Florynce (Flo) Kennedy, a charismatic, larger-than-life African American attorney, Gloria made countless inspirational appearances all over the United States. These efforts not only did much to raise the national consciousness but also helped make Gloria a more human and accessible figure to the thousands of women who heard her speak, and even more importantly, saw her listen. The efforts added a human dimension that made real the figure they had only seen on television or the cover of a magazine (Steinem 1983).

The partnerships had initially stemmed from Gloria's fear of public speaking. However, beginning shortly after her April 1969 *New York* column, "After Black Power, Women's Liberation," the pairings not only served to raise awareness of the feminist movement but also helped foster a connection, which was of deep importance to Gloria, between the civil rights and women's liberation efforts. They also helped mitigate the concerns of those who saw the movement as one that only addressed the concerns of upper-class suburban whites. And they added credence to Gloria's long-expressed view that the women's movement was just one part of a larger movement for human equality. As these partnerships were, in the early 1970s, arriving on the back of the civil rights movement of the 1960s, they were establishing a logical and important connection. No matter the locale or the audience, they would sweep into town, make their presentations, and then allow the members of the audience to tell their stories, providing them with the opportunity to share with their fellow citizens and help them understand that they were not alone. After Hughes had her baby, but before she decided to limit her travels, she and Steinem would appear, baby in tow, with Steinem holding the child while Hughes talked and then Hughes often nursing the baby during Steinem's presentation. It was a different approach, one that in its own way illustrated some of the challenges all women faced (Steinem 2015).

In the early days, when the movement was continually trying to counter a perception of lesbian domination, Gloria recalled that she was sure that, despite their distinctive stories, not to mention Gloria's jet-set image, many in their audiences believed the baby was Hughes and Steinem's child. Yet such perceptions and reactions did nothing to dampen their enthusiasm or determination to spread knowledge of the feminist cause while helping empower women, no matter their stage in life.

Gloria and her speaking partners appeared before a wide range of audiences. They spoke to student groups, welfare mothers, political activists, and others—but their fundamental message was unchanging as they sought to help people understand that the movement was about providing opportunities. They encouraged their audiences to break out of the artificial and societally imposed constraints that had often characterized their lives. They spoke of the new jobs and careers that were slowly being opened to women. They acknowledged challenges but made clear that if their audience members made the effort, change could be achieved. The movement, they said, was about helping individuals fulfill their potential while at the same time allowing for individual choices. They appeared before the audience two women at a time, each with a distinctive story that reflected their differing background and experiences. They encouraged their listeners to join the effort to strike down the barriers that limited all of their opportunities. Opponents' charges to the contrary, they didn't dictate one path through life, nor did they belittle those who wanted to be stay-at-home mothers. But they did make clear that they sought a society in which the range of choices was the same for both men and women (Steinem 2015).

These appearances were at once a contrast with and a complement to the countless other things Gloria did to advance the feminist cause. For every high-profile, publicity-generating effort of hers, there were innumerable low-key, personal endeavors in which she was engaged. She did local fundraisers that jump-started political careers, provided mentoring, took on short-term housemates, and "adopted" assistants, who learned about organization, feminism, and commitment at her knee. Traveling all over the country, she became a one-woman consciousness-raising machine who also made real the goal of the NWPC to elect greater numbers of women to public office.

Gloria's wide-ranging travel and her countless presentations have reflected her determination to push the feminist agenda through the creation and development of organizations that supported the movement at the grassroots level in a consistent, collaborative manner. Many eventually would come to see Gloria's efforts to develop organizations that would support and further the movement as primarily a reaction to the conservative 1980s. In fact, however, they not only predated the conservative ascendancy but were a central a part of her organizational and leadership approach from the beginning. Indeed, they were often products of or at least nurtured by the traveling presentations she and her partners had offered in the farthest reaches of the country. One of the earliest was the Women's Action Alliance that Gloria helped found in 1971. The group, which pioneered the dissemination of information addressing nonsexist, multiracial children's education was an important contributor to the movement until the alliance's dissolution in 1997 (Stern 1997).

The presentations tour was also noteworthy for the way it served as a workshop for her distinctive leadership approach. While some of the presentations were to large audiences in huge auditoriums or gymnasiums, whenever possible, Gloria sought as small and intimate a gathering place as possible. She sought to create venues in which she could draw upon the lessons she had learned in India, utilizing the talking circles she had seen there. In that way, she could begin to listen and learn from the women. And in sharing their stories, they could learn from each other. Such efforts established bonds and connections that would fuel the still young movement (Steinem 2015).

It quickly became apparent to Gloria that central to the women's movement was the need to give women a voice, to get their words out, to hear their stories, and to share them with others. At the same time, her feminist awakening brought a reduction in her own writing. While she continued to do her column for *New York*, it appeared less often, and her outside writing also became less frequent. But as much as she wanted to return to her writing, she put it aside, instead encouraging the words of others. All the while, though, and however unconsciously, she was looking for a way to get the stories out, to provide a voice for that half of the population that had for so long gone unheard, and if she could not write it, she would do all she could to see that it was written by others. It was out of this desire, coupled with an ever-greater understanding of the American people, all shaped and informed by her wide-ranging travels, that *Ms.* magazine emerged.

Ironically, in looking back on Gloria's career as an activist, she probably spent more of her time on her seemingly endless, often-unnoticed jaunts to some of the most obscure corners of the United States than anywhere else. And yet, for Gloria and her companions, anywhere that there were women for whom equality was a quest and not a reality—a gymnasium, theater, community center, union hall, sports stadium, or even someone's living room—was a place worth visiting. It also offered a story worth hearing from a life worth respecting. Those ideas represented the central tenets of her efforts. Looking back years later, Gloria would say that these efforts were based on the lessons she had learned about reform in India, coupled with the long-ago lesson from her Smith geology class about the need to "ask the turtle." She wanted and needed to learn their stories—from there she could act and organize.

Her wide-ranging travel did much to combat the disillusionment and disappointment that politics often brought on. Gloria's earlier political and organizing work gave her a broader perspective and helped achieve a broader diversity in the women's movement than might otherwise have been achieved, and the many gatherings, large and small, that she addressed only reinforced those broadening efforts. Indeed, in looking at her role—real and perceived—there is an irony to the fact that while in many ways she became the public face of the movement, her greatest contributions and influence were arguably behind the scenes as an organizer and fundraiser. When the initial creation of the NWPC threatened to come apart amid a battle between Friedan and Abzug, it was Gloria who mediated the dispute. It was through her efforts that compromise was achieved on some key issues, and she then followed that up by traveling the country to help organize and fund local chapters.

In addition, and reflective of her big-picture view of feminism, Gloria often credited the Black feminists who preceded her and who played important roles in the civil rights movement with teaching her about feminism. She was also quick to highlight Shirley Chisholm's often-reported declaration that she had endured greater discrimination because of her gender than because of her race. In addition, Gloria had consistently spoken about the important role of Blacks in the movement, a fact that partly explained her support for Chisholm in 1972 despite her longer and earlier association with George McGovern.

In the aftermath of Nixon's resounding victory, feminists turned their attention to the ERA. While the amendment, which had first been introduced in Congress in 1923, had been passed overwhelmingly by Congress in the spring of 1972, after initial early success it ran into substantive opposition (Steinem 2015). A group that billed itself Stop ERA (Stop Taking Our Privileges), headed by Phyllis Schlafly, began an active campaign designed to prevent ratification by the required thirty-eight states. Phyllis Schlafly was a longtime conservative, Republican activist who played a particularly influential role as the leader of the effort to stop the ratification of the ERA. She earned her bachelor's degree and later a law degree from Washington University, in St. Louis, and she also earned a master's in government from Radcliffe. She worked for a time as a teacher before turning to the law. A longtime Republican activist, she ran for Congress unsuccessfully in 1952 and also was defeated for the presidency of the National Federation of Republican Women in 1967. She wrote a widely circulated book, *A Choice Not an Echo*, attacking New York governor Nelson Rockefeller during the 1964 campaign, when she was a strong supporter of Arizona senator Barry Goldwater. But it was in the early 1970s, when she led the effort to prevent the ratification of the ERA, that she rose to national prominence. As the organizer of the Stop ERA campaign, she changed the very nature of the debate. While proponents talked about equality, Schlafly and her group argued that if the ERA became law, it would end gender-specific privileges such as alimony and the "dependent wife" benefits under Social Security. She raised the specter of coed bathrooms and women being drafted into the army. It was a stunningly successful effort (Critchlow 2005). The early success of the ratification campaign led observers to initially think that ultimate ratification was a foregone conclusion. Indeed, following its congressional passage in the spring of 1972, twenty-two states had ratified the amendment by the end of the year, and another eight approved the provision in 1973. However, while the amendment had received overwhelming bipartisan support in Congress, as the organized opposition led by Stop ERA appeared, what had been a flood of support dropped to a trickle. Only three states added their names to the rolls in 1974, and one each came on board in 1975 and 1977.

Ironically, the bicentennial year of the nation founded on the belief that "all men are created equal," saw no states express their support for female equality. The ratification movement stalled, and only a last-ditch effort to extend the ratification process another three years kept the effort alive. Further complicating the process was the fact that in addition to trying to secure support in the remaining states, the proratification forces had to fend off efforts by additional states to rescind their initial ratifications. In addition, the defeat of efforts to implement state ERAs—including resounding popular vote referendum rejections in both New York and New Jersey—emphasized the strength of the opposition.

Going back to her testimony before a congressional committee, Gloria had been an active proponent of the amendment, and she made it a regular part of the presentations she was making across the country. As the original March 22, 1979, deadline to achieve ratification approached, feminist leaders pulled out all the stops to achieve victory or at least secure an extension on the deadline. Publisher Katharine Graham had Gloria come speak to the *Washington Post*'s editorial board, which opposed the extension. Gloria recalled the meeting as one of the most anxiety-ridden of her life, and the fact that she was unable to persuade them to support the extension only magnified the painful memory (Stern 1997). While a three-year extension was approved by Congress, it was not enough to make ratification a reality, and when time expired on June 30, 1982, proratification advocates remained three states short of success.

5

The Activist Life

In 1975, in the midst of increasing media reports of growing divisions within the women's movement, the Red Stockings targeted Gloria. A radical feminist group begun in February 1969 and centered in New York, in their early days they were particularly active in achieving reform of abortion laws. But the group had long been critical of groups such as NOW, which they saw as simply seeking institutional change while ignoring the interactions between males and females that are at the heart of female oppression. Consequently, apparently seeking to undermine her increasing prominence as a public face of the movement's establishment, they released a report alleging that Gloria was a former CIA operative.

The timing was clearly no accident. With Congress in the midst of a series of hearings and investigations aimed at determining the full and exact extent of the agency's activities, new bombshells about everything from Watergate to the overthrow of governments in South and Central America were hitting the front pages of the nation's newspapers on an almost daily basis. Consequently, tying an adversary to the beleaguered intelligence agency, the nation's leading spymaster, was a surefire way to tarnish a reputation, even if it was a case of guilt by association (Stern 1997).

Gloria originally ignored the Red Stockings attack. She had long ago acknowledged her work in the later 1950s and early 1960s with the CIA-backed Independent Research Institute. In interviews with both the *New York Times* and the *Washington Post* in 1967, following disclosures by *Ramparts* magazine of the CIA ties, she had explained that the work was aboveboard and provided an opportunity for American students to gain a better understanding of their counterparts in the Soviet Union while offering similar opportunities for the Soviet-sponsored participants. Thus in 1975, she did not believe it warranted further comment. However, after months of silence, feeling betrayed and hurt, especially at charges that implied that her "commitment" to feminism was little more than a political gambit, she issued a six-page letter. While released to the public, the document was really directed to a number of small feminist publications that had been most dogged in their demands for the full story. While the explanation mollified some, for others it only added fuel to the fire, especially since, forever protective of her image, the explanation, rather than fully clearing the air, only added to the confusion. That, in turn, provided an opportunity for Betty Friedan among others to attack Gloria on other grounds (Stern 1997).

Gloria's insecurity seemed to make her fearful of how people would react if she simply acknowledged things and moved on. In the end, while nothing new emerged, the whole episode was put to rest only after Gloria threatened to go court to prevent the publication of a Red Stockings book, *Feminist Revolution*, which contained the allegation. In response, an acceptable revision in the book was made. There were lessons to be learned from the episode, but as Gloria moved on, it was not clear that the biggest one—that she would be best served by accepting her past for what it was and moving on, an approach that would have minimized the damage here—had truly been understood (Marcello 2004).

Gloria's approach to this subject is similar to some of the other small, but not insignificant, aspects of her life that are not easily explained away or are in conflict with some other, more central aspects of her life or career. Such cases defy easy explanation but often find Gloria putting the blame or responsibility on someone else. For instance, given her longtime rhetorical support of civil rights and her record of activism, she has always been defensive about her failure to actively engage. She bemoaned the fact that she had not joined the many others of her age and generation who traveled south, rode the buses, and worked in the voter registration efforts that were so central to that period. Her explanation for that lapse has always centered on Robert Benton's reluctance and fear that her solo engagement in the effort might hurt their relationship. However, that explanation is undermined by the fact that their relationship came to an end well before the 1964 Freedom Summer campaign. She was also asked about her longtime practice of fudging her actual age: it was only as she got older and had famously and proudly declared, "This is what 40 looks like," a comment she has updated with each passing decade, that she has she been upfront about her age. But even when admitting the longtime lie, she still clung to the equally longtime explanation that only on the advice of

Tom Guinzburg as well as her sister, Sue, had she acceded to society's preference for youthful female self-presentation (Stern 1997). Similarly, after the publication of her article "Women and Power," an exploration of how women used sex to attain power and an issue some observers saw hitting close to home, Gloria made it clear that it had been Clay Felker's idea. She made it equally clear that it did not reflect her experience. In its own way, Gloria's insecurity left her vulnerable to further criticism, which, as it had with the Red Stockings and CIA, only made matters worse.

More politically volatile, but no less important, was Gloria's work with reproductive rights. Given her awakening at the Red Stockings abortion speak-out, it is fair to say that it has been an issue at the forefront of her feminist efforts. However, the issue sometimes arose in unexpected ways, leaving Gloria, the reluctant, media-crowned face of feminism, caught in the middle of the developing culture wars. Yet her unwanted status made her a touchpoint for opponents, to whom she was the embodiment of all their grievances. Nowhere was this clearer than in the way her image became embroiled in a song that highlighted the cultural divide that *Roe v. Wade* had exposed in the nation.

The early response to *Roe v. Wade* was comparatively muted. In fact, it was not even the lead story in the news on January 22, 1973, for not only was the decision handed down in the shadow of Richard Nixon's second inauguration only days before but Lyndon Johnson's death that same day relegated the Supreme Court's ruling to secondary status, behind the recaps and tributes that accompanied the passing of the architect of the Great Society and the force behind the legislative side of the civil rights revolution. And yet in no time, the abortion decision became a symbol of a seemingly intractable cultural divide. Rooted for so many in moral absolutes of freedom and life, it was an issue ill-suited to be addressed by a political system based in compromise. Instead, it became a veritable litmus test for political candidates and judicial nominees in a way that only furthered and hardened the divide.

Typical of the issue was the way the 1974 song, "Having My Baby," by Paul Anka, became an early, if comparatively low-key battleground in the developing culture wars. Anka's song, one that would go to number one on the charts, was controversial on many levels, but it was adopted by pro-life forces as a tribute to the idea of having a baby and all the reasons why a woman should not abort a pregnancy. It arrived on the scene early enough in the ultimately violent political and cultural wars that there was little organized opposition. However, that did not prevent some defenders from dragging pro-choice feminism in general, and Gloria in particular, into the fray. One reviewer, assessing the lyrics, glibly commented that a line referencing the mother's refusal to choose an abortion had to have represented a lyrical embodiment of Gloria Steinem's worst nightmare. And as if his disdain for her views were not clear enough, he added that he couldn't believe that the support voiced by Anka's female vocal partner, Odia Coates, could have resulted in anything less than a hand-delivered telegram from an indignant Gloria.

Four years later, in 1978, Gloria headed to Minnesota, invited by Father Harvey Egan of St. Joan of Arc Catholic Church of Minneapolis to join him and to give the sermon to his congregation. Egan, whose church had long welcomed gays and lesbians while also supporting peace efforts across the Americas, saw all this as reflecting what Jesus's teachings are all about. As part of this openness, he had a long tradition of inviting laypeople, usually social activists, to join him and to share their thoughts in this way.

Steinem was well aware that Egan was not a favorite of the Catholic hierarchy, and despite concerns about getting him in trouble, she accepted his invitation, only to arrive to an organized protest focusing on Gloria's pro-choice position on abortion. Although taken aback by the rowdy crowd, she was comforted by Egan's assurances that the positive response had been exceptional and that, despite his having scheduled another mass to accommodate the greater demands to hear Gloria, there was still a waiting list (Heilbrun 1995).

While her anxiety only grew as she waited and the Mass began, her nervousness was assuaged when Father Egan's call for "Glory Be to God for Gloria" was met with laughter. And her talk about ancient original cultures and the time when religion was untainted by the patriarchy and was a special bond between individuals and their god, an approach that does not limit who is or who could be a god, was well received. Afterward, Gloria and Father Egan were greeted by a long line of congregants who shook hands and offered thanks despite the howling protesters who crowded the sidewalk outside the church.

Reflective of Gloria's place in the cultural landscape of that era, the story did not end upon her return to New York. Rather, she would soon learn that Archbishop John Roach, Egan's superior in the church hierarchy, had not only reprimanded him but publicly apologized for him, an action that made national news. Gloria next saw Egan a couple of days later when he, in Minneapolis, and she, in Washington, were interviewed on the *CBS Morning News* about the incident. The interview, she noted later, was not focused on anything she said in her homily but simply on the fact that she had been invited. While Gloria expressed her concern that she had hurt Egan and his place within the church, he was his usual jaunty self, noting that under the new guidelines he had been given requiring him to use outsiders only from a preapproved list, he was still able to draw upon the wisdom of Mickey Mouse, Peter Rabbit, and Lawrence Welk. In fact, a couple of weeks later, Gloria discovered that the church had dropped the hammer when she saw a *New York Times* front page headline declaring, "Pope

Forbids Homilies by Laypeople." Being addressed by the pope was not, she said later, something she ever expected. And yet, years later, long after Egan had died, she was reminded of the way change does come, even if it takes time (Steinem 2015).

Almost forty years after the incident, while visiting Minneapolis, Gloria ran into a young boy, who, recognizing her, worked up the courage to tell her that he knew about the incident and that he knew she was the most protested speaker St. Joan of Arc had ever had. She was shocked that he knew all this and was even more surprised to learn that he had gotten it all from the church website. Her admiration for him was cemented when she learned that the young teen—the son of Vietnamese refugees—sought to help Indigenous tribes in the Latin American rain forest. It was, she thought as she watched him walk away through the snow, another reminder that change was always possible and that the efforts to achieve it were never wasted (Steinem 2015).

Beyond these incidents, Gloria's deep commitment in the area of reproductive rights was manifested in her work with a number of organizations and would continue for the rest of her activist career. In 1978, Gloria worked with her friend, Koryne Horbal, on the Minnesota Democratic Labor Party's Project 13, an effort aimed at electing more pro-choice legislators. A group of party-affiliated women decided they would visit every precinct in the state offering workshops and training on the abortion issue. Agreeing to help, Gloria traveled all over Minnesota on a tiny plane. In the aftermath of the effort, and seeing the national success of the right-to-life efforts, Gloria and Koryne decided something more needed to be done, and from there Voters for Choice was born. As a cofounder, Gloria served as president of the organization, which began operations in 1979. The nation's largest independent, nonpartisan political action committee, with a bipartisan board made up of women and men, including former Republican senator Edward Brooke, it was committed to guaranteeing that safe, legal, and accessible abortions were available to all women regardless of where they live, their age, or their socioeconomic status. Gloria continued as head after the group merged with the Planned Parenthood Action Fund for the 2004 elections. Indeed, her work for reproductive rights has never ended, and as the threat has increased, so have her efforts. She was a cofounder in 1992 and continues to serve on the board of Choice USA (which in 2014 changed its name to URGE: Unite for Reproductive & Gender Equity), a national organization that supports young pro-choice leadership while working to ensure that comprehensive sex education remains a part of the school curriculum (Stern 1997).

As she has moved through her life, often basking in praise while at the same time reflecting on her activities, Gloria has heard herself referred to by many titles in wide-ranging efforts to describe who she is and what she has done. While "organizer" is her preferred label, the term "activist" has often been favored by those looking to cast a wide net. And much to the eternal discomfort of the determined collaborator that she has been, she was often hailed as the leader of the women's movement. Interestingly, the one term that has not been heard as much as one might expect, or at least as much as Gloria would once have wanted, is "writer." Few would deny that Betty Friedan's *The Feminine Mystique* was the intellectual spark of the second wave of feminism and that numerous other authors, including Susan Brownmiller, Germaine Greer, Kate Millett, Robin Morgan, and Andrea Dworkin, to name just a few, wrote important works that built upon and furthered Freidan's efforts. But Gloria Steinem, the onetime freelance journalist, also made some important contributions to the literature of the movement.

Befitting her journalism roots, most of Gloria's work was short articles that, especially in the early going, covered a wide range of subjects and reflected a reality of the lives of freelance journalists: they write articles about the things they are paid to write about. Of course, as she climbed the ladder and her work got more exposure, greater opportunities and more choices appeared, but as she was always quick to note, even the success of "A Bunny's Tale," while raising her profile and name recognition in New York, also resulted in a seemingly narrow set of opportunities, including numerous offers for similarly themed stories. Only with the advent of *New York*—which provided both a substantive platform and a column—did Gloria begin to produce on a consistent basis the kinds of articles that could be gathered into a book of collected essays or that simply would pique the interest of a serious publisher, who might then want a book-length treatment of a particular subject. *The Beach Book* had been fun, but Gloria, the writer, longed to write a serious book. While she did not lack confidence in her writing, she nevertheless harbored a feeling that has dogged many writers over the years: books were what real writers, that is, real authors, produced.

In 1978, Gloria made an effort to return to the writing life. While she remained devoted to the feminist cause, she needed a break and wanted desperately to return to her long-neglected craft. Awarded a Woodrow Wilson Fellowship, which included a generous stipend to cover living expenses while she pursued her research and writing during a year at the Washington, DC–based Woodrow Wilson Center, Steinem intended to address the impact of feminism on political theory. She was hopeful that it would be an opportunity to fulfill her dream of writing a book. At the same time, she hoped it would also provide a respite from the grind of being continually on the road, beating the drum for the feminist cause while also wrestling with problems that were besetting *Ms.* All of it had left Gloria exhausted and her friends deeply concerned about her welfare.

Unfortunately, as attractive as the opportunity appeared, the expectations of the Wilson Center did not mesh with a lifestyle—both personal and professional—that had by then become her norm and was characterized by continued travel and activity. It was a merry-go-round that could not stop no matter how much Gloria wanted it to. Ongoing crises at *Ms.* only added to the challenge.

It quickly became apparent that Gloria's plans to spend Thursdays and Fridays in New York attending to *Ms.* and other movement-related activities stretched the limits of the Wilson Center's expectations. The regular luncheons and seminars that fellows attended and participated in were a core part of the scholarly experience that the Center sought to foster. Making things worse was the fact that, reflective of the times and the battles Gloria was fighting, she was one of only a handful of women in the program, so not only was her presence all the more desired but her absences were all the more noticeable. And Gloria's request for a cot in her office, a reflection of her recognition that she did her best writing later at night, did not enhance her stature with the Center leadership.

Things came to a head in March 1978, when she received a letter from the Center's director that took her to task for both her behavior as well as her inconsistent involvement with the program. Gloria responded respectfully but directly. She said she saw the luncheons as a burden, exercises that put her in the position of always having to offer the woman's point of view, and she said she had never seen her role at the Center as including the teaching of a class in feminism. She said she was also tired of being the unending object of forced inquiries by lascivious men who made up excuses to talk with an attractive woman. Finally, she noted that she was deeply involved in the important battle to ratify the ERA, and while she regretted the fact that it had perhaps taken away from her work at the Center, it was not something she felt she needed to apologize for. She closed by saying that she had entered the program in the belief that she would be able to write in an uninterrupted fashion, and she was sorry and a bit disappointed that the program had not met her expectations. Things did not get better, and in October, she again heard from the director, who alleged that someone had used her ID and key to work in her office at night. He also noted that he had seen news reports of her wide-ranging outside activities and hoped she was not taking too much time away from the center. In response, Gloria thanked him and the Center for the opportunity they had given her but also informed him that she was preparing to accept a contract to write a different kind of book and, as a result, did not intend to complete the fellowship project. In bringing to an end what was, in hindsight, a mismatched project, Gloria offered to repay part of the stipend (Marcello 2004).

While the media loved to refer to the women's movement and feminism as though they were one big congenial and well-organized effort, the reality was something very different. A mix of various local and national movements and organizations, social, political, and cultural, racial, ethnic and religious, it was in its own way a reflection of the people—American women—whose diverse interests it sought to advance. While the media may have wanted to find or identify a singular leader of the women's movement, there was, in fact, no such thing, even though more than a few people thought they deserved the crown. All of this only added a level of internal tension to an effort that was already causing reverberations across the American political and cultural landscape. For numerous reasons and to her great dismay, from almost the moment that she announced her new embrace of feminism, Gloria was thrust into the middle of the drama.

Of course, further complicating the whole situation, as it had from the start, were the issues of Gloria's physical appearance and her lifestyle. Attractive, sexy, with a series of high-profile lovers, to many Steinem embodied the freedom and the choices the movement sought to achieve. But to others, the attention paid to her appearance not only threatened to overshadow her message but also represented a step backward at a time when the movement sought to change the focus from a woman's appearance to her ability and performance. Meanwhile, another group saw her living and operating in a stratosphere of glamour and style that made her seem more like a fantasy than a friend: that Gloria was not someone with whom other women could relate and thus the feminism she preached was not a lifestyle to which they could relate.

In some ways, she seemed to be two people. To those who encountered her in the course of her continuing travels, she was transformed before their eyes. In countless gatherings from coast to coast, when she turned the dialogue around and asked her listeners to share their stories, she morphed from the celebrated cover girl and author to the empathetic listener, and in doing so changed the dynamic and bridged the previous divide. But in the early days, when she was seen more as a newcomer than a force, these aspects of what she brought to the table were often seen as a problem.

Given all this, Gloria's early efforts left her vulnerable to criticism. With her feminist credentials not yet fully established, but with her public profile high, Gloria was a prime target for the kind of article that appeared in the October 1971 issue of *Esquire*. In the piece, subtitled "The Awesome Power of Gloria Steinem," journalist Leonard Levitt portrayed Gloria as a girl who shed causes and men as suited her needs (Levitt 1971). She was, he wrote, able to adapt herself to the romantic needs and desires of her current man, able to use each of them to advance herself and her interests while at the same time leaving no fingerprints or hard feelings. As to her activism, he acknowledged her involvement but questioned her commitment. Levitt was also skeptical of her motivations and dismissive of her talents. He accused her of manipulating and using the rich and famous while quoting those who knew her and called her an opportunist who likely saw herself as an idealist for whom any using of others—boyfriends or otherwise—was unconscious and only part of her desire to advance her cause. But he discounted her commitment to any of the causes anyway (Stern 1997).

In many ways, the article just seemed mean, as Levitt quoted one of her writing contemporaries as saying that most writers get involved with politics for the fun of it, but that for Gloria there was an obvious interest in the exercise of power. Quoting that same writer who observed that social mobility, not writing, was Gloria's real talent, Levitt noted that many editors who had worked with her thought she had an overinflated sense of her writing abilities. Gloria would later say that she was both angered and hurt by the Levitt piece. She was also fearful that it would undermine her credibility and effectiveness in a movement which, for all Levitt's skepticism, had clearly become central to her life.

At the same time, Levitt's questions surrounding her sincerity were not helped by the fact that Gloria, who had already revealed a clear concern about protecting her image, had also begun to show a bit of a tendency to reinvent herself. And in doing so, she often revised or rewrote some of her own history. Such efforts did not help negate the charge of insincerity. In the end, despite increased sniping from some feminist quarters, Gloria and her allies were able to fend off much of Levitt's work as a sexist attack on a woman who was threatening to upset the comfortable world he and his male colleagues enjoyed (Stern 1997).

From this incident also emerged the beginnings of a group of supporters whose loyalty to Gloria, a sentiment that she returned in kind, would be central to her life for decades to come. In the end, the little bit of female sniping aside, Gloria's power as an advocate for the movement was widely recognized and tremendously appreciated by the many who closed ranks and came together to support her against unprovoked, unprecedented attacks based in sexism. It was a tough time for Gloria but it also was an introduction to life in the spotlight. While she had been involved with this world for over a decade now, the tables had turned. She was now a high-profile figure in an increasingly contentious movement. New lessons about celebrity and power lay ahead.

While Levitt's full-frontal attack was extreme, Gloria was regularly the victim of low-level barbs and jibes, but she was not alone, as egos and ambition clashed amid the effort to shape the direction of the movement. But during the movement's heyday in the 1970s, no internal battle got more attention than the clash, real or imagined, between Betty Friedan and Gloria. While there were some ideological differences between the women, the clash seemed based more in personal jealousy and animosity than anything else. As a result, other than providing fodder for a hungry press, it seemed to do little to hamper the movement's efforts.

And yet given that it was part of an era when perception often trumped reality, and given too, the dynamism of the women's movement, it is not surprising that the Friedan-Steinem clash made enough of an impact that it was immortalized as recently as 2017 in an off-Broadway play, *The Fight*, by Jonathan Leaf. The drama, while purporting to be fiction, is clearly modeled on the historical characters so as to leave no doubt of its origins, and it offers an interesting take on the rivalry. Whether in fact or fiction, the clash clearly had its roots in Betty Friedan's deep resentment of Gloria's emergence as the face of the movement that Betty believed was "hers." From the foundational impact of *The Feminine Mystique* to her being elected the first president of NOW, the formidable Friedan, who did not count diplomacy among her talents, was never anything but jealous of the way Gloria burst upon the scene. While she was not oblivious to the value and star power Gloria brought to the movement, Betty never forgave the younger woman's failure to know and assume her place. Betty also never accepted that it was others who had anointed Gloria, who, as was made evident in the movement's great event, the Houston Conference, was happy to work behind the scenes, visiting small and often-forgotten hamlets, and listening, always listening, as opposed to being the voice. Indeed, for all of their shared commitment to the cause, at the heart of their difference was the fact that Gloria sought to give others a voice while Betty demanded that she be the voice of a movement. In the end, despite assertions to the contrary, the Smith alums had different views on the fundamental nature of feminism as well as the roles they should play in the movement (Stern 1997).

Betty's antipathy toward Gloria took many forms, big and small. Despite having no knowledge of the precarious financial straits of *Ms.* and with no knowledge of the financial sacrifices that Gloria, publisher Pat Carbine, and other major figures were making, she accused them of profiting from the movement (Cohen 1988). On a more personal level, one that still hurt many years later, Betty had refused to shake Ruth's hand when a local labor leader had tried to make an introduction (Steinem 2015). Years later, looking back on those times, Gloria realized that her efforts to not respond, to not feed the stereotype that women could not get along, only emboldened Betty, but it was reflective of who she was and how she approached most conflicts, often to her detriment.

The fact that Betty had been crowned the "Mother Superior to Women's Lib" by the *New York Times*, proved to be a designation that did nothing to dissuade Betty from believing that it was her movement (Cohen 1988). She seemed unable to understand the impact that she often had, and when she was rebuffed, her responses only reinforced her problems. Typical was the time that after being denied reelection to an NWPC post, she threated a lawsuit, going so far as to dispatch an attorney to check the ballots. He found no irregularities. It was against this backdrop that Gloria was pursuing her own path. Despite her expressed desire to not hold public positions, she could not hold the media at bay, and the attention for which she was a magnet only further enraged Betty. The issue would never be resolved but instead provided a subtext for much of the movement throughout the seventies.

Perhaps the clash was inevitable, so different were their personalities (Stern 1997). But part of it was simply based in clashes over the seemingly smallest things. For instance, Betty was deeply hurt when Smith students selected Gloria as the speaker for their 1971 graduation ceremony, an honor never accorded her (Marcello 2004). Also, Betty seemed to ramp up her criticism in the aftermath of Gloria's appearances on the covers of *Newsweek*, *McCall's*, and *New Woman* magazines, appearances that all served to heighten the profile of the movement as well.

In fairness to all concerned, the clashes were not just examples of petty jealousies and overactive egos. In a movement as large as the women's movement that rolled through the 1970s, there was a range of competing ideas, approaches, and strategies. Ironically, while those differences were real, they were often obscured by some of the big personalities involved.

In fact, while Friedan's *Feminine Mystique* had begun the discussion and awakened people's consciousness about the role of women in society, Gloria's arrival on the scene shifted the debate. Rightly or wrongly, she was seen as offering a more hard-line approach, this despite the fact that her vision had feminism as a part of a broader humanitarian movement. Friedan's middle-class women were soon overshadowed by a more strident group. Second-wave feminism quickly morphed into the women's liberation movement, with Gloria offering—or so it was said by some commentators—a more strident message. Gloria made clear from the beginning that not only was she a latecomer to the effort but that she was about choices in a movement that was part of an even broader humanism effort. However, the media found her quips—for example, "a woman needs a man like a fish needs a bicycle"—far more newsworthy than her extended discussions on the importance of a broadly inclusive effort. That reality, coupled with a media presence and style that were the envy of every public relations flack in the country, meant that inevitably the battle lines—or at least the parameters for a newsworthy conflict—were drawn (Stern 1997).

While on the one hand, Gloria's personal life was central to her appeal, giving lie to those who claimed that the only people who were feminists were the ugly losers who could not get a man, aspects of her personal life were seen by some as intimidating. Many applauded the way, as one woman expressed it, Gloria was someone who could play the game, could win the game, and then could say the hell with the game. And yet how Gloria seemed to play the game was sometimes overbearing to many. Her big-tent approach, one that included lesbians, single mothers, and those who opted not to marry, was an ideological basis for some of her differences with Betty Friedan and the more middle-class approach that was at the root of *The Feminine Mystique*. But Gloria's personal declaration that she would never marry and did not want children left many young feminists conflicted, unsure of the appropriateness of their own choices or desires. Over the years, many young acolytes were fearful that they were letting Gloria and the movement down if they took a step back and decided to have children and raise a family. While Gloria's rhetoric said it was all right, for many, the power of her example said something else. It certainly was not her fault, but it represented an occasional lack of understanding of just how much influence she really had.

For the most part, Betty's issues with Gloria were personal (Cohen 1988). At the same time, again, reflecting the middle-class roots of her arguments in *The Feminine Mystique*, Betty was also outspoken in her concerns that Gloria, Bella, and others were hurting the movement by their efforts to add issues of abortion and lesbian rights to the feminist agenda. All of this was exacerbated by the fact that Betty preferred to air her grievances in public forums, calling press conferences to makes charges that garnered headlines, raised her profile, and divided the movement (Stern 1997).

Through it all, whatever the motivations, Gloria tried to remain above the fray. At the same time, she was always protective of her image and also determined to have others get it right. She bridled at charges that she swept in and grabbed the spotlight from the early pioneers such as Betty. She noted how terrified she was of public speaking, recalling the time she initially turned down an invitation to address the 1971 *Harvard Law Review* banquet out of fear, only changing her mind when friend and attorney Brenda Feigen Fasteau convinced her of the impact such an appearance could have in the effort to achieve equality (Steinem 2015).

Similarly, Gloria recalled how, despite making clear her desire not to be the liaison with the press of the newly created NWPC, she was still selected in absentia. While she knew the selection forever irritated Friedan, Gloria reluctantly filled the role. And in the midst of an early squabble over the leadership of the NWPC, one focused primarily on a battle between Betty and Bella, Gloria reasserted her long-held view that they needed to get away from centralized leadership, declaring in frustration while pointing at Bella and Betty, "I am tired of seeing your face, and yours, and I'm tired of seeing my own" (Cohen 1988).

For all her struggles and deep desire to be more than her image, Gloria's distinctive place within the movement, at least in the early days, was captured in an article in the March 8, 1970, *New York Times Book Review*, in which Marylin Bender surveyed the literature focusing on the liberation of women. Discussing the various authors and their upcoming efforts, she focused on their work until, after going through a roster that included Kate Millett, Letty Pogrebin, and Robin Morgan, she got to Gloria, whom she identified not by an employer or professional association but as an exemplar of the liberated, brainy beauty. As one author later noted, the presentation offered a clear contrast. The other writers were identified by their work, but Gloria was judged by her persona, a clear and ironic rebuke to her efforts to move society away from seeing women as things and judging them more on the basis of their work and accomplishments (Stern 1997).

In a keynote address at a November 2007 symposium held at the Bella Abzug Leadership Center at Hunter College in New York, Gloria asserted that the 1977 Houston Conference had taken feminism to the next level. It had, she declared, moved it from a small grassroots effort to a national movement, one that empowered a whole generation of feminists who were, in fact, barely familiar with the term before Houston. Gloria would later write that the Houston experience had been transformative. It was, she said, an event that made people recognize that the dreams they had long harbored could be realized. She added that while the conservative backlash that was developing had slowed some efforts, it could not stop the fundamental power that had been unleashed at the Houston gathering or through the efforts that had made it a reality. At the same time, in looking back, the clear-eyed Gloria also recognized that while the Houston Conference was the high watermark of the movement, it also offered a foreshadowing of the challenges ahead, ones that had already made their presence felt in the Stop ERA campaign (Spruill 2017).

In 1977, there was no denying the victory the Houston Conference represented. It was both a triumph in its own right as well as a sharp rebuke to those who, in the early 1970s—in the aftermath of Nixon's victory over a feminist-fueled McGovern campaign, amid reports of dissension in the feminist ranks, not to mention the slowing of the ERA ratification effort—believed the feminist movement was in decline. The *New York Times* had at one time referred to the movement as a "passing fad." And yet, while challenges remained, the movement had gained new energy, and the *Times* reports from Houston reflected a whole different view.

Following in the spirit of the United Nations' proclamation that 1975 was the International Women's Year (IWY), on January 9, 1975, U.S. president Gerald Ford had issued Executive Order 11832, which created a National Commission on the Observance of International Women's Year "to promote equality between men and women." In legislation sponsored by Hawaii congresswoman Patsy Mink, Congress had approved five million dollars to support a series of state conferences, an exercise that would culminate in the national conference in Houston. With representatives chosen at fifty individual state meetings coming together to produce a report on the state and aspirations of U.S. women, the event would offer a way to hear from the nation's women and bring them together, if only symbolically, under the tent of equality and opportunity that had been launched two centuries before.

While Gerald Ford appointed a broad-based, bipartisan commission, with his defeat in the 1976 presidential election, planning and preparations for the IWY Conference was delayed, and some aspects came to a halt. Happily, given the timetable of the original enabling legislation, most of the state planning as well as the selection of Houston as the site of the 1977 national conference had been completed by the time the new occupant, Jimmy Carter, arrived in the White House.

At the same time, the changing of the guard raised questions about the makeup of the IWY Commission itself. Relying primarily on Midge Costanza, a close friend of both Gloria and Bella as well as a liberal from Rochester, New York, who served as Carter's assistant for public liaison, President Carter reappointed several members of the Ford-appointed IWY National Commission. He also added Betty Ford and many new Democrats and others whose constituencies were of importance to Carter's political fortunes. Not surprisingly, given their close ties to Costanza, Carter also appointed Steinem and Abzug. As the Houston Conference approached, despite the objections and concerns of many (including his wife, Rosalynn), Carter went on to name Bella Abzug as the presiding officer of the National Commission on the Observance of International Women's Year.

Under Abzug's leadership, the effort moved forward, and state conferences began to gather and elect delegates for the Houston Convention. The peripatetic Gloria traveled the country in support of the effort, often speaking at state IWY conferences. Reflective of her singular star power, organizers of the Nevada conference noted that her luncheon address attracted a bigger crowd than had in fact registered for the conference. But despite her travels, neither Gloria nor her experienced New York allies left the home front untended. In fact, giving heed to the old adage that all politics is local, Gloria joined Bella, New York lieutenant governor Mary Anne Krupsak, and countless volunteers in an ultimately successful last-minute push to ward off a conservative-sponsored surreptitious campaign designed to catch the Empire State's feminist forces unaware and elect a decidedly more conservative delegation (Heilbrun 1995).

It was a necessary precaution, for as spring turned to summer in 1977, convention organizers found themselves facing unexpected opposition, and an expected celebration turned into a challenge that tested the nation's feminist leaders beyond expectations. The challenge came in part from the emergence of a strong, well-organized, and strategically astute opposition, one that built upon the existing conservative base. No one in the liberal or feminist camp was surprised by the opposition to the convention that was posed by the established right wing, fringe groups such as the Ku Klux Klan and the John Birch Society, and church groups such as the Mormons and the Baptists, which had historic, established gender roles that would clearly be threatened by the demands for equality and respect. But more problematic was the female-based movement led by longtime activist Phyllis Schlafly. Redirecting her Stop ERA forces, she mobilized a sizable cadre of experienced political activists and organizers who were concurrently showing their political might in the ERA ratification effort. In much the same way that the media had anointed Gloria the face of feminism, Schlafly, a tenacious if seemingly gracious upper-middle-class homemaker who also possessed a law degree, not to mention household help, was crowned the guardian of the effort to protect "family values" and the traditional American mores that her followers believed feminism was determined to destroy (Critchlow 2005).

After a series of battles at the state level, the feminist leaders gained control of the conference, which proved to be not only a showcase for the feminist cause but also for what, in many ways, Gloria, did best: work behind the scenes, supporting others. Yet it was a talent that the media often overlooked as they focused on the public celebrity. Congresswoman Bella Abzug's appointment by President Carter to preside over the National Commission on the Observation of International Women's Year made her the group's public face. Meanwhile, Gloria, also a member of the commission, worked quietly but effectively to move the feminist agenda forward. The Houston Conference gave Gloria the chance to assume her preferred position. Leaving the headlines and photo ops to others, she circulated among the hundreds of delegates troubleshooting and working to bridge some of the divides that threatened to upend the effort, something that could have been devastating given the Schlafly-led opposition that was already waiting at the gates. Photos of the conference seldom included Gloria, but friends and colleagues marveled at the way, out of the glare of the spotlight, she worked to get diverse groups to achieve consensus on some of gathering's most contentious issues.

Typical was her role in developing a statement from the minority groups at the conference. Respected, indeed admired, by all parties, Gloria was able to use her political skills to good effect. At one point, over the course of two sleepless nights, she served as the active go-between and facilitator during negotiations that resulted in an unprecedented collaboration between Native American, Hispanic, African American, and Asian contingents. Drawing upon her singular diplomatic skills as well as the respect, admiration, and trust she had engendered over the years, Gloria, along with a young California legislator Maxine Waters, IWY commissioner Carmen Delgado Votaw, and author Gail Sheehy played an important role during an all-night session that produced an eloquent and comprehensive statement that linked the shared concerns of the minority groups (Heilbrun 1995).

While each was concerned lest their own interest be sacrificed, under Gloria's leadership they were able to find common ground and produce a shared resolution, one that described the common experiences of women of color while retaining the distinctiveness of each group. In the end the groups produced a statement notable for its eloquence and comprehensiveness. And despite the controversy that swirled around a conference that brought together so many disparate groups, this resolution, which reached across strong and previously seemingly impenetrable barriers, was approved by acclamation when brought before the conference. It was a ringing triumph for the conference and for Gloria's approach, one based in respect for all participants and their interests. Almost two decades later Gloria would cite the experience as perhaps the emotional high of her years as a writer (Steinem 2015).

Leaving the Houston Conference, an event Gloria has since called the most important event that no one knew about, she was exultant. She believed that feminists had reached new heights, ones that, going into the conference, she feared were absolutely unattainable. In addition, in developing and proposing a national plan of action, they had achieved a new consensus, a new societal coalition, one that brought together Black, white, and Latinx participants, the young and the old, the radicals and the establishment figures such as First Ladies Betty Ford and Rosalyn Carter, as well as former first daughter, now political spouse Lynda Johnson Robb. It was inspiring. And yet, within months, things moved in a whole different direction, leaving many to view the Houston Conference as the beginning of the end, an event that triggered the conservative, family values backlash that would soon leave the feminist movement back on its heels and forced to reassess its goals and operations.

Following the conference, Bella, Gloria, and other leaders sought to build on the momentum. Working with Midge Costanza, they prepared a final report, a 220-page, lavishly illustrated document, titled *The Spirit of Houston: The First National Women's Conference: An Official Report to the President, the Congress and the People of the United States*. In addition, many of the Houston leaders began working with Costanza to develop plans aimed at implementing the proposals and guidelines the conference attendees had passed.

On March 22, 1978, the IWY Commission members presented *The Spirit of Houston* to President Carter at a highly publicized gathering at the White House. The President was effusive in his praise of the commission, its work, and the conference, but in fact those words masked growing tensions between the president and movement leaders. In the lead-up to the presentation, there were many questions about what came next. Finally, but only after much prodding, Carter agreed to create a new group to succeed the expiring IWY Commission. The new body, the National Advisory Commission for Women (NACW), included many of the members of the original commission. Amid competing political pressures, Carter again named Bella Abzug to chair the new advisory body, but this time, he paired her with Hispanic leader Carmen Delgado Votaw, who served as cochair (Spruill 2017).

The new structure ended up satisfying no one. While Bella and her fellow committee members believed they had a responsibility to serve as advocates for the plan of action that had been adopted by the Houston Conference, Carter saw the commission as an advisory group, one to which he could turn for guidance and counsel on women's issues.

In the meantime, the movement's uneven relationship with President Jimmy Carter had not been helped by the January 1978 *Ms.* cover that depicted a pregnant Carter with the caption, "Carter discovers 'life is unfair.'" The depiction was a fitting next step concerning an issue, abortion, that had bedeviled the relationship between Carter and feminists from the start. Candidate Carter had tried to straddle the line on abortion, making clear that he personally opposed the practice while also noting that as the nation's chief executive, it was his responsibility to uphold the law. During the campaign, he had not always included both sides of the equation before all audiences. However, when he assumed office it became clear that he was not willing to actively pursue federal efforts to equalize opportunities for rich and poor in this area. His comment that life is unfair, a response to questions about the administration's budget's failure to include funds to help poor people pay for abortions, was deeply resented by pro-choice advocates. Making matters worse was the fact that not only did *Ms.* put the president on the cover, but Gloria appeared with an almost life-size version of the cover for a photo op outside the White House fence. To say that relations between the movement and White House were frayed would have been an understatement (Spruill 2017).

Things came to a head in January 1979 when, in the aftermath of a meeting of the commission with Carter, the president announced that he was firing Abzug. The decision came as a shock, especially to the committee members who had attended the hour-long meeting, a gathering that lasted twice the scheduled time. Admittedly, Carter had expressed his dissatisfaction with their approach, noting that they could not be as effective as they all wanted to be if the committee continued to be as confrontational as he believed they had been. At the same time, when Abzug and cochair Carmen Delgado Votaw met with the press, Abzug declared that they had had a good meeting, noting that they had thanked the president for his good work in support of their most important goal: equality. Shortly afterward, however, things changed, as Abzug was called into the office of top Carter aide Hamilton Jordan and told that she was being replaced as cochair of the committee. He told her that the president believed that the committee needed new leadership to enhance its effectiveness. Some said that the president saw Abzug as the main force behind the confrontational aspect of the committee's approach and that he had grown tired of it.

It was reported that the firing was also tied to a press release that the White House learned was scheduled to be released at the end of the day and that criticized the president's economic policies, especially the continuing inflation, a fact that they noted was taking a particular toll on women. According to that report, the press release was the last straw for the beleaguered chief executive. But given the tone of the meeting and the fact that the decision was not shared with the committee members in attendance, the firing caught them all by surprise (Spruill 2017).

In the aftermath of President Carter's firing of Abzug as one of the cochairs of the NACW, Gloria and other commission members immediately called upon their fellow members to join them in resigning in protest. The majority, including Abzug's cochair, Carmen Delgado Votaw, did so. Harking back to a turning point in the Watergate saga, Gloria termed the incident the "Friday Night Massacre." While the decision was said to have had the support of Sarah R. Weddington, Carter's special assistant for women, it severely damaged the president's standing among liberal feminist leaders and for many, it would become an issue in the upcoming 1980 presidential campaign (Spruill 2017).

The 1980 election, in fact, presented major challenges for Gloria and her liberal allies. Ideologically, they were supportive of Massachusetts senator Edward M. Kennedy's challenge to incumbent Jimmy Carter. The firing of Bella Abzug as NACW cochair had alienated, once and for all, many of the leading feminist leaders, including Gloria, crystalizing as it did all the doubts they had harbored going back to Carter's carefully crafted 1976 campaign. And yet, beyond his ideology, Kennedy's behavior at the accident at Chappaquiddick and the death of Mary Jo Kopechne hung heavy. In the end, most feminists sat out the Democratic contest, and only when the campaign became a matchup between Carter and conservative former California governor Ronald Reagan did they pick a side. Indeed, as the campaign came down to its final days, with the gap supposedly having narrowed, Gloria joined Bella and others in placing a full-page ad in the *New York Times*, supporting Carter, or—perhaps more properly—opposing Reagan. But it was all for naught, as Ronald Reagan easily defeated Jimmy Carter to become the nation's fortieth president. Not long after the election, a disgruntled Hamilton Jordan observed that feminists had gotten the president they deserved (Spruill 2017).

6

Ms. Magazine

It was only two letters and a punctuation mark, but the adoption of "Ms." in 1986 by the *New York Times* as an appropriate title for women marked a major cultural shift. And yet the *Times*'s decision represented little more than jumping on the bandwagon, for by 1986 that seemingly insignificant title had already assumed an important role in the developing women's movement (Cohen 1988). Nowhere was that clearer than in its role as the title of the pioneering women's magazine, whose first stand-alone issue hit newsstands in early 1972. In real terms, the acceptance by the public of "Ms." in the early 1970s represented a modification of women's public identity based on marital status. At the same time, those same two letters on the cover of *Ms.* magazine marked the arrival of a new voice for those newly unencumbered women. The title was an outlet, a voice, and an affirmation for members of the population whose identity was based in themselves. Like the men for whom "Mr." had long been the one size that fit all, women could now boast an identity based in their character, their personality, and their accomplishments and not based on a relationship or the lack thereof. It was new, it was distinctive, and it was theirs.

By any account, the creation and development of *Ms.* magazine was a landmark event in the women's movement. But for Gloria Steinem, the founding of the first feminist magazine, a publication both created and operated entirely by women, was much more. It not only represented a return to Gloria's journalistic roots but also was the embodiment of her deep commitment to the empowerment of women. And like Gloria herself,

Ms. played both a substantive and symbolic role in the ongoing movement. *Ms.* was the bold voice for these people and their movement, and Gloria Steinem was the driving force behind *Ms.* It would become a centerpiece of Gloria's feminist legacy.

Few aspects of the feminist movement are more closely associated with Gloria than her work with *Ms.* She was deeply devoted to the magazine and to the idea that women should have a voice. To her, being heard was central to their liberation, and it fueled her deep commitment to the barrier-breaking publication. She was determined to make *Ms.* a magazine that was aimed at a female audience and run by a team of women. But Gloria soon learned that a publication for and by women faced challenges that made the whole enterprise a near-constant struggle. But in meshing her ideological commitment to the cause and her long-held professional ambitions as a journalist and writer, *Ms.* allowed Gloria to concurrently pursue two passions. Unhappily for the fledgling magazine executive, her desire to write was often overtaken by the business needs of the publication, needs that in some cases could only be addressed by the face of the movement: Gloria Steinem. And in fact, as a cofounder and the inaugural editor of *Ms.*, she assumed yet another role in the movement that sought to open the door to previously unimagined opportunities. No longer was she simply the media-designated face of an effort to "liberate"—the term of the era—over half of the nation's population. Yes, however reluctantly, she still carried that burden. But with the arrival of *Ms.*, she became the driving force behind a publication that sought to give that movement and the people it represented a voice.

Ms. emerged from humble beginnings. The early 1970s saw a wave of coverage of feminist issues in the mainstream press. Cover articles, including the one in *Newsweek* that had featured Gloria, were typical. The movement's leaders wanted to use the media's increased interest to spread the word to a population not only hungry for information but ready to act on it. From discussions about such a venture in the NWPC and its research and referral organization, the Women's Action Alliance (WAA), emerged the idea for a newsletter to distribute information ranging from setting up a campus women's center to rape counseling. The newsletter idea was appealing, if for no other reason than it was a low-cost venture that could be easily produced. At the same time, given the high-profile names associated with the NWPC, taking such a route seemed like a wasted opportunity, and in fact, there was a vocal group that believed a more ambitious undertaking should be mounted. Gloria's involvement in the start-up effort at *New York* meant she understood the challenges of starting a magazine, from dealing with staff to finding financial backers. In fact, Gloria was initially reluctant to get involved with what became *Ms.* She was not wholly convinced of the need for such a vehicle, and even if the need existed, she was by no means sure she should be involved. Her freelance career was starting to take off; she was at long last getting the kind of substantive assignments she wanted and had come to realize she found a certain security in the insecurity of the field, not to mention the independence and autonomy it provided (Thom 1997).

Patricia (Pat) Carbine, then the editor at *McCall's* and a longtime and well-respected figure in the publishing world, argued that if Gloria and her compatriots really wanted, as they professed, to create a public forum, a national venue for women to talk with each other, then a national magazine was what they needed. Despite the fact that she had only recently taken the reins at *McCall's*, she backed up her admonition by soon agreeing to join the fledgling publication, serving as the original publisher and editor in chief. And so it was that Gloria added a whole new chapter to her journalistic odyssey.

In fact, Gloria's involvement—indeed, her leadership—was obvious and logical, for her previous work made her the perfect person to lead the effort. Reflective of the collaborative and inclusive approach they wanted to take, the early days of the operation saw Gloria overseeing the editorial side, while Elizabeth (Betty) Forsling Harris and Brenda Feigen Fasteau headed the business side. Betty Harris was a well-connected, former journalist and public relations executive who also boasted an impressive roster of political connections based on a longtime relationship with Lyndon Johnson and Sam Rayburn. She also had close ties to Kennedy in-law Sargent Shriver, under whom she had served as the highest-ranking woman in the Peace Corps. Meanwhile, Brenda Feigen Fasteau, an accomplished attorney, and one of Gloria's old friends, had been the first to suggest to Gloria that she start a glossy feminist magazine. Both editorial and business operations were aided and abetted by numerous volunteers and well-wishers whose input and energies were appreciated, valued, and used. But while volunteers and enthusiasts were plentiful, money was not, and in fact, financial concerns would plague the magazine throughout its existence (Stern 1997).

As things started to develop, discussions began about Betty serving as publisher. However, from the start, she and Brenda had strong disagreements on important matters, and Gloria was forced to step in as peacemaker. While Brenda and Gloria were longtime friends, Gloria's interactions with Betty had been limited prior to the *Ms.* start-up. But as tensions grew, Gloria interceded, effectively brokering an accord under which Brenda headed back to her demanding legal practice as well as the WAA, the organization out of which the idea of *Ms.* as a voice for the movement had originally emerged. Meanwhile, Betty and Gloria moved the magazine forward (Stern 1997).

Gloria began to consult with Pat Carbine, who had long years of experience in the publishing world. Pat had begun in the industry as a researcher for *Look* straight out of college in 1953 and had worked her way up the ladder. By all accounts, it was only her gender that had prevented *Look*'s owner from naming her editor in 1969; she was already serving as executive editor, the highest-ranking woman of a general interest magazine in the country. In 1970 Pat become editor in chief at *McCall's*, a post that did make her the top-ranking woman in the magazine world. In the course of this climb, she had not only earned the universal respect of the industry but had also become a fan of Gloria's, twice putting her career on the line on Gloria's behalf. Once she had threatened to resign from *Look* when the advertisers were trying to kill Gloria's article on Cesar Chavez. Later, when Pat fought to get Gloria named *McCall's* "Woman of the Year," her threat to quit was all that stood between Pat Nixon and the honor. Throughout the period during which the idea for *Ms.* was moving toward reality, Gloria was meeting with Pat Carbine after hours, getting tutorials about aspects of the magazine business that a former freelancer had never before encountered. It was an eye-opening experience, one that not only made clear to Gloria how much she had to learn but also how important it would be to have Pat Carbine at the editorial helm as they sought to make *Ms.* a success (Stern 1997).

While Gloria was wooing the newly installed *McCall's* editor, Betty Harris was having trouble securing funding for the developing venture. With finances very much in a state of flux, but with a clear idea for the kind of magazine she wanted, Gloria went back to her old friend and mentor Clay Felker, whose *New York* magazine had become must reading in the city while inspiring numerous imitators across the country. Felker recognized the possibilities and offered to help with the venture. After discussing the magazine's plight, he agreed to finance a sample issue—an insert, consisting of 30 pages of content—that would be part of a year-end double issue of *New York*. It would then be followed in the spring by a single 130-page preview issue that would appear on newsstands sporting its own logo. The profits from the initial venture would be split between Felker and the magazine, and that would be the end of Felker's formal involvement in the endeavor (Heilbrun 1995).

With the plan in place, the founding members, Gloria, Betty, and Pat (who at this point was willing to back the venture but was not yet ready to leave *McCall's*) set up a company, Majority Enterprise, with each holding a third of the stock. Then, after much debate and consideration of names such as Everywoman, Sisters, Lilith, and Sojourner, among others, they decided to go with the title "Ms." While the title was new and not yet recognized by many public institutions, its status as an independent designation for women made it an appropriate label for a magazine that aspired to be the voice of a new movement, one that, like the term itself, was seeking to achieve greater acceptance for a wide audience (Marcello 2004).

In the early going, Gloria drew heavily upon her numerous friends and contacts for content, ideas, and psychic support. She was especially reliant on her colleagues at *New York*, a fact that only cemented the partnership that was so critical to the magazine's birth. In addition to Gloria and Betty, those present at the creation included Joanne Edgar, Nina Finkelstein, Mary Peacock, and Letty Cottin Pogrebin. The work they produced was a resounding success, with the year-end double issue setting a *New York* newsstand sales record. Meanwhile, the initial single issue, dated spring 1972 in order to allow for slow sales, went on open newsstands in late January. The three hundred thousand copies that had been distributed nationwide sold out in just over a week. All of this helped Gloria convince Pat Carbine to finally take the plunge and give up the financial security and income she had at *McCall's* in order to be part of something revolutionary (Stern 1997).

While Pat's decision to come on board represented both a validation of all they had already done as well as a promise of even better things to come, it had become apparent that Betty Harris was a liability to the magazine's success. She failed to raise money, leaving the magazine in difficult financial straits from the beginning. Betty also regularly clashed with the magazine's staff. So acrimonious, frustrating, and dispiriting were the discussions that at one point, Pat and Gloria told Betty that they would give her the magazine if she could find someone to buy their shares. But Betty proved no more successful in that effort than she had been previously. In the end, Gloria and Pat bought out her share, giving her the profits from the spring issue, and began the effort to build upon the tremendous start they had enjoyed. The financial side of the operation remained a major stumbling block. However, the content of the early effort, coupled with the incredible response from women across the country, gave the magazine's staff every reason to believe that they had created something that could play an important role in furthering the feminist movement and empowering women all over the United States (Heilbrun 1995).

With a more stable structure established, Gloria and Pat began to build upon the magazine's early success. Befitting her multiple roles with the magazine, when the inaugural issue, dated Spring 1972, hit newsstands in late January, Gloria was a one-woman public relations machine, traveling from coast to coast to raise awareness about this new vehicle for the women's movement. She appeared in markets large and small, on local television and radio as well as network outlets, and she interviewed with any newspaper that would talk with her. Her energy was contagious and the response was overwhelming (Marcello 2004).

The initial response to the magazine far exceeded anyone's expectations, as well as the fondest hopes of Steinem and company. Not only were there twenty-six thousand subscription orders, but *Ms.* received twenty thousand letters, an almost unimaginable response to the run of three hundred thousand copies. Indeed, Carbine noted that when she was at

McCall's, which had a circulation of seven million, they would typically receive about two hundred letters. In addition to the size of the response was its distinct nature. As letter writers responded to any number of articles, they referenced their own lives. From the very start, *Ms.* was clearly making a connection with its female readership, resonating in a way that other magazines just did not do (Stern 1997).

As unprecedented as the initial response to *Ms.* was, it did not reduce the pressure to build a successful magazine. The response to the initial subscription drive was exceptional, with the return on the subscription cards that had been included in the initial issues exceeding Gloria and Pat's wildest hopes as well as every industry-based expectation. Yet *Ms.* was no different from any other magazine. Subscriptions funded only a small part of the effort and were most important as something that could be taken to advertisers, not only the source of real money but also the guarantors of survival. It was there that the creators' singular mission clashed with reality. And with Felker's funding having ended and the profits from the inaugural solo issue having been used to buy out Betty Harris, it fell to Gloria and Pat to try to fill the money gap. The duo received early support from *Washington Post* publisher Katharine Graham. Her investment of twenty thousand dollars of her own money gave them a much-needed infusion of cash and, no less importantly, added credibility.

An even more important breakthrough came in May when, working through Letty Pogrebin's contact at Warner Communications, executive

---

KATHARINE GRAHAM

Katharine Graham was one of the most influential women in the United States in the 1960s and 1970s, and as the head of the *Washington Post* Company in 1972, she became the first woman CEO of a Fortune 500 company. While eschewing the term *feminist*, Graham set an example as a CEO, a leader in the publishing world, and a behind-the-scenes political power that made her a model for a generation of women. Guiding the *Post* through the controversies surrounding its publication of the Pentagon Papers as well as its coverage of Watergate, she oversaw the paper's transformation from a paper dedicated to covering the local business—government—to an industry leader whose influence rivaled that of the *New York Times*. At the same time her life story, that of a rich young heiress who lacked confidence and experience but nevertheless refused to give up control of the paper after her husband's suicide, offered inspiring life lessons for many. Indeed, not only did Graham rise to the occasion but she candidly and eloquently recounted her journey in her Pulitzer Prize–winning memoir, *Personal History*, providing an inspiring set of life lessons for generations to come.

Kenneth Rosen, Warner gave *Ms.* one million dollars in exchange for a 25 percent interest. The investment, Warner's first minority holding (not to mention a minimal amount for the communications giant), served as both a major triumph for *Ms.* and a public relations boost for Warner (Stern 1997).

While money would never stop being an issue, the Warner investment allowed Gloria and Pat to begin to map out the future. They began to expand the staff and put into practice the distinctive collaborative approach that would be central to the magazine's existence. *Ms.* was not just a forum for furthering the movement's agenda. It was also a place where a certain philosophy of operation and leadership were to be modeled and tested. While it may have mattered little to its audience, how *Ms.* operated and how the magazine developed its voice were no less important to its leaders than was what it offered its highly enthusiastic readers. From the start, Gloria and company sought to avoid formal leadership positions or titles, and originally they had a limited organizational hierarchy. While *Ms.* proved to be a launching pad for many ultimately influential writers and publishing figures, it was not the kind of place where people sought to burnish their resume. Rather, by working at *Ms.*, they were contributing to the cause more than they were climbing the career ladder. Collaboration—exemplified by open workspaces and seemingly everyone, including Gloria, sitting on the floor in meetings—inclusiveness, and a desire to hear from often overlooked quarters were at the heart of the process. At the same time, that approach could lead to challenges and debates over ultimate responsibility, not something that could be avoided if a magazine were to be produced. Not surprisingly, given her past experiences, Gloria once described the atmosphere at the *Ms.* office as similar to a political campaign (Thom 1997).

While Pat had come on board with the expectation of serving as editor in chief, with Betty's departure, she assumed the role of publisher. However, such titles were unofficial, and while her authority was fully acknowledged internally, the magazine masthead had only an alphabetical listing under the basic headings of "Editing," "Publishing," and "Advertising." But that aside, no one doubted that some employees were more equal than others. Pat was the publisher, and final editorial authority rested with her and Gloria. And anyone who may have had a problem with that was reminded gently, but directly, that Pat and Gloria were the owners. But given their devotion to *Ms.* as not only offering a different voice but a more egalitarian workplace, pulling the ownership card was an act of last resort (Stern 1997).

In their effort to make *Ms.* more than both a feminist-oriented magazine as well as a real and broad-based voice for women, Gloria and Pat determined that their operations could not mirror the norm for the publishing world. In the same way that the masthead reflected a different approach to leadership and authority, its fundamental operations and approach were also distinctive. The emphasis on a collaborative atmosphere was reinforced by the lack of formal and defined offices. Given its distinctive identity as both a workspace as well as a movement hangout, the *Ms.* office saw more than its share of interesting, if not crazy, people. In addition, given its role as the voice of the movement, the office was the not-infrequent object of pickets and protesters who sought to air their grievances against the magazine's basic existence, a recent article that had inflamed the conservative opposition, or just the concept of equality for women. Such efforts were not limited to the New York office. From the beginning, the magazine was a frequent target of those who sought to ban it from local and school libraries (Thom 1997).

While Gloria was the public face of the magazine much as she was the face of the movement, she was happiest inside the walls of the office. There, despite her many roles, formal and informal, she was able to connect with her *Ms.* colleagues on a personal level. At the same time, she served as the mother hen for the *Ms.* family she sought to develop. It was a role she relished. Attending to both the practical and philosophical, she viewed *Ms.* as both the product of the movement as well as an example of what women could do if they had the opportunity.

The meetings at which story ideas were pitched and ideas gathered included any employee who had something to offer, but there was no denying Gloria's stature as the leader. As she assumed her favored place on the floor, "directing traffic" in the middle of a freewheeling story session, she was nothing more than the first among equals. Yet her role was to facilitate the empowerment of countless others who did not realize just how much they had to offer. From those few with masthead titles to student interns and volunteers and everyone in between, the group reflected Gloria's vision and determination to have all voices heard, shared, and hopefully included on the pages of a publication that wanted to expand the idea of an inclusive human society. It wasn't always the most effective or efficient management, but it was inclusive in a business that had long excluded women (Thom 1997).

It would be years before Gloria and the *Ms.* Foundation would formally initiate the "Take Your Daughter to Work Day," but the *Ms.* office was regularly populated by children who played in corners of the wide-open art room or in any corner of the wall-less workspaces. Interestingly, one author observed that even though Gloria had intentionally avoided being a parent because she did not want to again assume the responsibility of caring for another that had marked her life with Ruth, in many ways she did exactly that with *Ms.* In its own way, the magazine was a constantly sick child, one whose struggles were a constant concern, if not a burden, for Gloria. Yet she never failed to try to nurse back to health her "baby," a task that sometimes was an all-consuming chore. *Ms.* became so much more than a job, but at the same time, the magazine and its impact were central to her life and ultimately her legacy.

In the office, Gloria and Pat were trying to change the prevailing culture of the workplace, seeking to put feminist principles into effect in the day-to-day operations of the magazine. But in the marketplace, in the never-ending effort to keep the magazine financially afloat, they found themselves battling age-old conceptions of the relationship between companies and the women's magazines in which they advertised. It was an uphill battle. Indeed, while finances would be a challenge throughout the magazine's existence, for *Ms.* it was further complicated by the fact that Gloria and company were determined to have the ads mirror the magazine's content. Consequently, much of the advertising that was central to magazines such as *Ladies' Home Journal* or *Good Housekeeping*, ads that focused on and furthered stereotypical roles, were problems for *Ms.* and not only required them to make a standard sales pitch but also forced them to educate potential advertisers (Marcello 2004).

For years, standard advertising in women's magazines sought to push fashion, beauty products, home furnishings, and a better, easier life at home. In addition to advertising items that made all this happen, the advertisers wanted their ads paired with content, articles that touted their important role in the ideal home and lifestyle. Clothing companies wanted to see fashion spreads that made what they were advertising on the adjoining pages all the more attractive. Cosmetics companies wanted articles on how makeup would enhance a woman's looks, while recipes and entertaining ideas were de rigeur for food companies. All of this was the norm in periodicals such as *Ladies' Home Journal, Good Housekeeping*, and even *Cosmopolitan*, although the emphasis differed from magazine to magazine. With *Ms.* seeking to be a showcase for articles about the challenges faced by working women, a venue where issues such as sexual harassment and equal rights could be aired, there were fewer of the natural connections between ads and content even if the editors had been willing to entertain that approach. And despite having the research to back up their assertions, Gloria and Pat struggled to convince potential advertisers that women, in fact, were potential customers for products such as automobiles, electronics, and even liquor and that the decisions about those items were not being made solely by their husbands. But their research notwithstanding, for the most part companies saw advertising their products in a magazine targeted to women as a risk, and it was not one they were willing to take (Stern 1997).

What became quickly apparent was that among the many challenges the magazine faced, *Ms.* was not just seeking advertising but was seeking to change the advertising landscape. The consciousness-raising that was such an important part of the movement at large was equally applicable to the many meetings Gloria and Pat had with advertising executives across the country. But the executives represented a bigger challenge, for they not only needed to be sold on advertising in *Ms.* but they also needed to be convinced that there was a whole market out there that they were ignoring. It was an uphill climb. Gloria and Pat went to countless meetings where they were left wondering if the executives had simply wanted to meet Gloria (something that was especially true when a meeting with only Gloria was demanded), since it became quickly apparent that the companies in question had no real interest in advertising in *Ms.* Equally dispiriting were the times when they left the meeting feeling they had done little more than allow the corporation to assuage its gender guilt. At the same time, those encounters were preferable to ones in which the males took the meeting as an opportunity to confront these leaders of the feminist movement and vent their spleen over the damage that they were doing to the nation, to their families, and to corporate America (Stern 1997).

With a calm and grace that earned the admiration and respect of all at the magazine, Gloria spent countless hours trying to convince advertisers of the market that *Ms.* could offer. Concurrently, she was trying to push corporate America past its preconceived notions and prejudices. Historically, the companies that saw women as their advertising targets were food manufacturers, makers of household products, and cosmetics companies. These included major corporations such as Procter & Gamble, Nabisco, Revlon, and Kellogg's, among others. But they tended to buy their advertising in bulk, so they were not likely to want to go with a new magazine whose audience and continuing existence were suspect. In addition, they were all examples of companies that wanted their ads placed alongside content that would enhance its appeal. *Ms.* was not going to be that kind of operation. It was a gender battlefield that, while little noticed, represented a crucial aspect of the effort to make *Ms.* a viable and profitable publication (Thom 1997).

Given her prominence as well as her identification with the magazine, *Ms.* used Gloria to promote it whenever it could. As she crisscrossed the country campaigning for pro-choice political candidates, appearing on a college campus, or headlining a fundraiser for, as an example, a battered women's shelter, the magazine's promotions department would seek to book her onto every radio and television station that would have her. They did not think twice about adding to her schedule the occasional drop-in at an advertiser's or another speech to a local civic organization. Her charisma and high profile made her a powerful draw, but while her efforts all benefited both *Ms.* and the movement, such efforts meant that, inevitably and through no fault of her own, Gloria was being promoted ahead of other feminist leaders. This reinforced and heightened resentment that had plagued the movement since Gloria had arrived on the scene (Marcello 2004).

It all became almost overwhelming for Gloria. In fact, so frenzied did the pace at *Ms.* become, and so much pressure did Gloria feel to make the magazine a success, that years later she admitted to having sometimes fantasized that the economy would kill the magazine or that the office would go up in flames. While such thoughts were certainly far-fetched, they were a reflection of the pressure Gloria felt to make the magazine a success (Stern 1997).

Beyond the ongoing battles that the magazine faced, from conservative groups who sought to keep it off newsstands and out of local libraries and from local school boards that sought to keep it out of their schools, there was skepticism from the national media. Nationally respected journalist Harry Reasoner declared that he gave the magazine six months before it ran out of things to say. Such comments raised fears that if the magazine failed, it would be a tremendous setback for the movement itself. Consequently, the pressure to succeed, the pressure to not have a failed *Ms.* be seen as a failed movement was almost crushing (Heilbrun 1995).

In response, Gloria and Pat did everything they could to make *Ms.* a success, even if one of the challenges of that effort was to redefine the very nature of that term. Feeling pressure from all directions, they struggled to secure appropriate advertising and funding. Their founding ideals, which focused as much on having the magazine serve as a voice for the nation's women, a provider of opportunities, and a forum for new talent as on ways to begin a dialogue on and raise awareness about previously unexplored issues, such as sexual harassment, were at the heart of the effort.

The financial pressures were many and constant, and they inevitably had an impact on every other aspect of the magazine. Salaries were not what they should have been, and in an ironic turn, they took advantage of the status of those staffers who were married, reasoning that they had two incomes and could survive on a lower *Ms.* one. Meanwhile, others simply took less out of dedication to the cause that the magazine represented. For her part, Gloria often did not draw her salary, and in fact, over her many years with the magazine, she frequently contributed parts of her speaking fees and outside income to the magazine's coffers. Of course, there was some flexibility in addressing certain kinds of costs, but when, over the course of the first year, paper costs rose by 20 percent, ink by 40 percent, and postage by 60 percent, the financial realities could not be ignored (Stern 1997).

At the same time, as financial challenges emerged, Gloria and Pat were determined to retain editorial control over *Ms.* while also keeping the magazine true to its mission and roots. However, after a conversation in which *Washington Post* publisher Katharine Graham, whose earlier personal investment had been important to launching the magazine, warned them that any investor who got control—including the *Washington Post*—would turn it into a conventional publication, they realized they needed to do something dramatic. After looking at numerous options and considering a range of possibilities, in 1977 Gloria and Pat determined that the best solution would be to have the magazine published by a nonprofit educational foundation; specifically, they would publish it under the auspices of the *Ms.* Foundation for Women (Thom 1997).

The idea of a nonprofit serving as the publisher of a magazine had already been pioneered with *Consumer Reports, Mother Jones,* and *Smithsonian,* although in those cases their publisher had been an attendant nonprofit from the start. The fact that *Ms.* had been created as a for-profit periodical did pose some additional, minor hurdles, but ultimately these were all surmounted. In 1978 *Ms.* began operating as the public information arm of the *Ms.* Foundation for Education and Communication, itself a subsidiary of the *Ms.* Foundation for Women, the organization that had been founded in 1972 with Gloria Steinem, Letty Cottin Pogrebin, Pat Carbine, and Marlo Thomas as its founders. The arrangement between the Foundation for Education and Communication and the magazine represented a critically important financial lifeline, for as the publication of the nonprofit foundation, it qualified for significantly reduced postal rates. The tie to the nonprofit did mean that the magazine could not actively support individual candidates for office, but that approach was, for the most part, in line with Gloria's desire to share information. In addition, the establishment of the foundation allowed for support of *Ms.* and its related endeavors through tax-deductible contributions to the foundation—something the *Ms.* Foundation for Women was already enjoying. The Ford Foundation had indicated that it would be very open to making a sizable contribution to the nonprofit organization. At the same time, while the postal rate break was important to the magazine's early efforts, from the beginning it was clear that the magazine and the foundation needed to maintain separate operations. Since 1987, when the magazine went through the first of its numerous ownership changes, they have been separate entities. At the same time, especially as both the magazine and the movement were still finding their legs, the relationship represented a logical connection between the goals of the movement and two of the institutions that were playing central roles in keeping the dialogue alive. The arrangement also enabled the survival of a voice for active women who remained dedicated to change (Thom 1997).

While the switch to nonprofit status in 1979 helped financially, advertising remained a challenge, as did the magazine's overall financial picture. *Ms.*'s demographics were tremendously appealing—the average age of readers was thirty, almost two-thirds had at least some college education, and over 85 percent were employed outside the home. In addition, *Ms.* readers were people active and involved in their communities, and the circulation was a healthy 450,000. But developing a healthy and enduring list of advertisers remained a struggle (Stern 1997).

In 1982, in an effort to jump-start a revival, the *Ms.* leaders decided to use their tenth anniversary to generate new publicity and interest for the magazine, which, despite its struggles, had still defied all expectations. Special mailings were sent to all of their distributors, and in typical fashion, Gloria hit the road, beating the drum for the voice of the feminist movement. Marlo Thomas's husband, talk show host Phil Donahue, one of the nation's leading male feminists, devoted a whole show to the magazine, while NBC's *Today* saluted the magazine for a whole week. The magazine's supporters held an anniversary party for over a thousand guests and capped the effort with a July-August double issue that featured Gloria on the cover. Despite the obvious connection, as well as her high visibility, getting Gloria to agree to be on the cover had been a struggle. However, she gave in when an outside consultant, Ruth Bower, whose many years in publishing included a longtime association with Clay Felker and *New York*, gave her the necessary credibility, convinced Steinem that her face on the cover was a necessity for generating the kinds of newsstand sales that the effort needed (Marcello 2004).

While the tenth-anniversary efforts injected a shot of energy and interest into the magazine, they did not change the financial realities. Postal rates continued to climb, and the magazine's editors were forced to raise subscription rates. In an impressive show of support, over one hundred readers donated at least $1,000 each and became *Ms.*'s Special Friends of Equality and lifetime subscribers. Meanwhile, Gloria convinced Sallie Bingham, who had received a 15-percent share of the earnings when her family sold their Louisville, Kentucky, newspapers for well over $400 million, to donate $1.2 million to *Ms.* (Stern 1997).

Meanwhile, creative ideas never stopped flowing as the staff worked nonstop to create and develop events that combined fundraising with consciousness-raising, all with an eye to publicizing the magazine and its efforts. In 1983, seeking to counter *Time* magazine's "Man of the Year" designation (a title that was finally switched to "Person of the Year" in 1999), *Ms.* began bestowing the "Ms. Women of the Year" award, with influential psychologist Carol Gilligan being the inaugural honoree. The next year the editors decided to honor more than one, with Congresswoman and vice presidential nominee Geraldine Ferraro, Olympic marathon gold medalist Joan Benoit, and singer Cyndi Lauper being feted at a breakfast whose guests included *Time* "Man of the Year" Peter Ueberroth. Over the years, the designation has served as something of a measuring stick of the year for women, with newsmakers and pioneers from a range of fields being featured in the year-end issue (Stern 1997).

From its first cover, which depicted an eight-armed woman juggling more tasks than was physically possible, *Ms.* addressed the challenges

American woman confronted on a daily basis, looking at issues through the distinctive, but too long ignored, lens of their impact on women. That first issue also included a powerful article on welfare as a woman's issue, addressing the reality that the hard times that could lead to being on welfare could happen to anybody but most frequently happened to women.

The list of issues that *Ms.* addressed over the years, always offering a distinctive perspective, represents a review of the nation's history over the last third of the twentieth century. Even articles that covered more familiar ground, such as its ratings of presidential candidates Richard Nixon and George McGovern in 1972, did so from a perspective that had too long been ignored. But more important were *Ms.*'s efforts to go where no periodical had gone before. The magazine's own name reflected a change in language and women, while the Spring 1972 article titled "De-Sexing the English Language" offered a thoughtful, eye-opening look at the way language influenced views on gender while also recommending changes that might help level the playing field.

And speaking of the playing field, *Ms.* was a solid supporter of the developing world of women's athletics. With the new opportunities afforded by Title IX arriving not long after the magazine began, *Ms.* featured articles on a number of sportswomen, including a cover piece on Olympic stars Florence Griffith Joyner (FloJo) and her sister-in-law, Jackie Joyner-Kersee. Meanwhile, athletes including basketball star Lynette Woodward have been among the magazine's "Women of the Year" honorees. Not surprisingly,

---

THE U.S. WOMEN'S NATIONAL SOCCER TEAM (USWNT)

No team or program has more fully exemplified the increased involvement and impact of women on the American athletic landscape than the U.S. women's national soccer team. The team's incredible international success—it won the 1991, 1999, 2015, and 2019 World Cup titles as well as the Olympic gold medal in 1996, 2004, 2008, and 2012—has been part of the equation, but no less important has been the way the team has done it. For three decades, the team and its players have exemplified what, given an opportunity, women can do. They have inspired a generation of young female players, while their distinctive personalities and their willingness to be more than "just" soccer players has allowed them to have an impact that transcends their sport. In stars ranging from Mia Hamm to Abby Wambach to Megan Rapinoe, the team has produced a whole new type of marketable athlete and role model. At the same time, the fact that despite their success, they have struggled to achieve the proper respect for their efforts, a fact highlighted by the ongoing lawsuit aimed at gaining them equal pay, points out the continuing gender imbalance that remains an all-too-real part of American culture in so many areas.

> **THE BATTLE OF THE SEXES**
>
> The Battle of the Sexes was a 1973 tennis match between tennis superstar and feminist pioneer twenty-nine-year-old Billie Jean King and fifty-five-year-old Bobby Riggs, a former world number-one and Wimbledon champion, then playing on the senior circuit. After belittling the quality of the women's game and saying any of the top senior men could beat the best of the women, the fiery Riggs defeated Margaret Court, the world's top-ranked woman, after King turned down Riggs's initial challenge. Following his victory over Court, an accomplishment that landed him on the cover of *Sports Illustrated*, King, concerned about the impact on the women's game, agreed to play. The prematch buildup turned the event into a media sensation. Internationally televised, played in the Houston Astrodome, with *Time* featuring Riggs on its cover, the match itself was almost anticlimactic. But especially after King overcame an early deficit to earn the victory, handily defeating Riggs in straight sets, 6–4, 6–3, 6–3, it became a point of triumph for women's tennis. It also served as an inspiration for a generation of young women who were just beginning to reap the benefits of the newly passed Title IX.

when in 1974, tennis star Billie Jean King, fresh off her "Battle of the Sexes" victory over Bobby Riggs, started a new magazine, *womenSports*, a publication she hoped would serve as a female counterpart to *Sports Illustrated*, Pat and Gloria were at the forefront of those providing assistance to the fledgling periodical (Thom 1997).

At the same time, while *Ms.* continued its efforts to change society, it also continued to sometimes be a victim of the society in which it operated. Few things better illustrated the challenges and the triumphs that *Ms.* experienced than the time that contributing editor Robin Morgan got an interview with four exiled feminist leaders from the Soviet Union. The interview not only broke the news of the populist peace movement that was developing in response to the Soviet Union's occupation of Afghanistan but it also offered a previously unseen window into the lives of the Soviet women. It struck a chord with *Ms.* readers and was also well received in the journalism community, earning a Front Page Award from the Newswomen's Club of New York. But in reflecting on the incident years later, Gloria could not help but remember how the article had undone the years of effort she, Pat, and the advertising team had undertaken in their efforts to get Revlon to buy an ad schedule in the magazine. The professed reason for the refusal: none of the four Soviet emigres pictured on the cover was wearing makeup. *Ms.* was never able to get better than periodic, issue-by-issue ads from the cosmetic giant (Steinem 1995).

From the very start, a central part of *Ms.*'s mission was to provide an outlet for female writers as well as a place to showcase and highlight female accomplishments in any number of fields. Yet despite these efforts and its professed goals to serve as a voice for the movement, it could not escape becoming embroiled in some of the personal feuds that marked the era. One example occurred after Gloria Steinem brought some of the best writers into the *Ms.* fold, an accomplishment that led her on-again, off-again antagonist Betty Friedan to accuse her of exploiting the movement for her own profit. Yet for those writers, including Alice Walker, Angela Davis, Barbara Ehrenreich, and Susan Faludi, all of whose work has graced the pages of the magazine, it has been a singular showcase. Similarly, cover articles shined a spotlight on luminaries as varied as Hillary Clinton, Angelina Jolie, Glenda Jackson, Jane Fonda, Lily Tomlin, Sally Ride, Beyoncé, Katharine Hepburn, Charlize Theron, Nancy Pelosi, and Cory Aquino, among others. In addition, frequently going where advertising-inhibited magazines have feared to tread, *Ms.* has shined an important spotlight on a range of issues, including overseas sweatshops, FBI surveillance, sex trafficking, date rape, and domestic violence. The magazine has also explored issues such as women priests, while offering a platform for male feminists such as Alan Alda to share their views (Thom 1997).

For Gloria, *Ms.* was the best and worst of all experiences. While she could take considerable pride in the voice for women that she had done so

---

NANCY PELOSI

Nancy Pelosi's election as Speaker of the House in 2007 represented a major step forward for women in the American political hierarchy. The Baltimore-born daughter of a former mayor of that city who also served in Congress, Pelosi not only crashed through a glass ceiling to achieve her office but then demonstrated a deft feel for power as she led the House from 2007 to 2011. During that period, she was the central figure in the passage of the Obama administration's signature legislative accomplishment, the Affordable Care Act. While the Republicans gained control of the House after the 2010 midterm elections, Pelosi demonstrated her political skills by maintaining an impressive command of the Democratic caucus while it was in the minority. At the same time, she was laying the groundwork for the 2018 election, when she led the stunning electoral reversal—one marked by the election of a record-setting number of new female members—that returned a Democratic majority while soon making her only the seventh Speaker to reclaim the gavel. In the aftermath of that triumph, she emerged as the face of the Democratic Party as she oversaw the House's controversial vote to impeach President Donald Trump in the waning days of 2019.

much to create, there were too many times when Gloria felt overwhelmed by the magazine's financial troubles. While she wanted nothing more than to support the efforts of others, she and the magazine she loved became a prisoner of her own celebrity. Indeed, to her everlasting chagrin, whenever it became necessary to increase newsstand sales or simply remind readers of the magazine's royal roots within the movement, Gloria was put on the cover. No one was more associated with the magazine in the public eye than she was, but it was a source of ongoing personal frustration. Still, it was also an apt reflection of her commitment from the beginning, when she had thrown herself into its operations at all levels.

Looking back over the magazine's history, observers realized how much Gloria had been all but consumed by the magazine and how it had become her "pride and joy" but also how closely she became identified with it (Stern 1997). In fact, before the concept was commonplace, *Ms.* had become Gloria's personal brand. However unintentionally, her involvement with the magazine seemed to have been previewed on the cover of the inaugural stand-alone issue with its portrayal of the eight-armed woman juggling her many—too many—roles and responsibilities. Early feminist leaders often complained about how Gloria seemed to have co-opted the movement, despite being a latecomer to the effort. But while she never denied being a late arrival to the party, she also noted that it was not her decision to be on the cover of *Newsweek* nor did she ask to do the countless media-based events that made her a celebrity—as well as a high-profile, dedicated, compelling, and successful advocate for the cause.

In contrast, there was never any confusion about Gloria's role with and devotion to *Ms.* It represented an intersection of her talent and her vision. It gave her a voice unfiltered by the outside media and it gave her a vehicle through which she could nurture and develop other voices and through which they could be heard. *Ms.* was an empowerment machine. It never compromised its standards. But it also recognized the changes—many of which it could count among its accomplishments—in both the feminist landscape and American society more broadly, and it responded accordingly. Meanwhile, its offshoots, the various products and programs sponsored by and developed by the *Ms.* Foundation, continued to resonate in American society.

In 1986 Gloria and Pat came to the painful decision that to save their *Ms.*, they would have to sell it. After much searching, by the summer they found who they believed were ideal buyers: a pair of Australian feminists who worked for a corporation with the resources needed to keep the magazine alive in its distinctive form. Sandra Yates and Anne Summers both worked for companies under the umbrella of John Fairfax Ltd. and were at the time working in New York. When Yates, who had been sent to the United States by Fairfax to start a magazine, *Sassy*, that was targeting teenage girls, learned that *Ms.* was looking for investors, she immediately decided that Fairfax should buy the magazine and that she and Summers should take over the reins. Summers, the author of a book often called the bible of Australian feminism, *Damned Whores and God's Police*, as well as the onetime head of Australia's Office of the Status of Women, jumped at the chance. In November 1987 the *Ms.* Foundation for Education and Communication sold the magazine for ten million dollars, part cash and part assumption of debt. After everyone had been repaid, the foundation was left with about three million. In addition, Gloria and Pat were given contracts under which they would serve as consultants for the next five years. Other staffers were rewarded with severance bonuses (Stern 1997).

To no one's surprise, when Yates and Summers took over operations in January 1988, they changed both the look and the content of the magazine. Meanwhile, Yates was preparing to use Fairfax's considerable resources to pursue the advertisers that would make the difference between the old and new versions of *Ms.* But the death of the elder Fairfax coupled with the October 1987 stock market crash left the company reeling. Desperate for funds while fending off bids, only months after the new start, the magazine was put up for sale yet again. But in an action reminiscent of the spirit of the magazine's earliest days, in just a short time Yates and Summers had become deeply committed to both *Sassy* and *Ms.* In an effort to keep them both alive in their current form, they formed a new company, Matilda Publications, which purchased them from Fairfax. Although *Sassy* achieved some immediate popularity, it was not enough to sustain their effort and in June 1989, Matilda Publications put both magazines back on the block, where they were quickly purchased by Dale Lang, the owner of both *Working Woman* and *Working Mother* (Thom 1997).

Upon taking control of *Ms.* in October 1989, Lang fired both the circulation and advertising departments and canceled both the December issue—despite the fact it was ready for the printer—and the January "Women of the Year" issue, which was almost ready for publication. From the beginning, it appeared that Lang had no real interest in the magazine, but simply wanted access to *Ms.*'s subscription list. Gloria, who was not only still receiving a salary as a consultant but also had an office and a salaried assistant, decided to leverage the power of her longtime connection with the magazine, as well as her public celebrity, to try to salvage her creation. She called Lang on his effort to get *Ms.* subscribers to shift to his other magazines, *Working Mother* or *Working Woman*. In response, he offered to publish a six-times-a-year, reader-supported newsletter, an offer he thought would at least satisfy the outstanding subscriptions for those who did not want to switch to his magazine. Gloria objected strenuously, asserting that such a publication was not *Ms.* (Stern 1997).

And then she went a step further. After almost twenty years of struggling to keep *Ms.* both alive and true to its mission, Gloria and her allies sought to undertake something almost as bold as their initial endeavor. Rather than continue to struggle to find advertisers whose products and approach were unacceptable for a publication rooted in the ideas and philosophy of *Ms.* they sought to go in a different direction. Gloria urged Lang to make *Ms.* an advertising-free, reader-supported publication, one that would be financed through subscriptions and newsstand sales. Lang balked, agreeing only after Gloria threatened to undertake a public campaign to urge subscribers to demand their money back rather than accept a switch of the subscriptions. After then publisher Ruth Bower determined that such a venture would need a $40 annual subscription rate and that it could be published only six times a year, she and Gloria decided to take 155,000 names off the magazine's old subscription lists, send out a mailing, and see what happened. It was, in the words of one observer, a referendum on *Ms.*'s survival. Based on standard industry practices, they believed that a return of 2 to 3 percent would be a strong response. In fact, they were overwhelmed, receiving a response of 19.8 percent. After seeing those numbers, Lang agreed to publish the reinvented magazine, and Gloria's longtime friend and associate, Robin Morgan, became the editor in chief (Thom 1997).

In 1990, while announcing the decision that *Ms.* would forgo advertising, Gloria took the opportunity to once again vent her longtime frustration with the cozy relationship between women's magazines and advertisers that had so long characterized the publishing world. She chastised the industry and the mission that centered on a product-based culture. She decried the way the magazines manipulated their readers, creating a need for the products, teaching those same readers how to use them, and in turn creating a mindset in which the effective use of the products was central to a life ultimately measured by the social and spousal approval they fostered.

Gloria's commentary was reinforced by the early success of the new approach. Reliance on subscriptions and newsstand sales was a bold experiment, and in the beginning, reflective of the deep commitment of its readers to the magazine, it worked, with the one-year anniversary issue showing a profit. It also won a number of awards and recognitions, including selection by *Library Journal* as one of the ten best magazines of 1990. Unfettered by advertising, *Ms.*'s content became more focused and hard-hitting than ever before. Indeed, front and center in the first issue was a scathing attack by Gloria on the advertising industry and their impact on women's magazines (Stern 1997). After years of living a hand-to-mouth existence, at least briefly the tables were turned, and Gloria's dream was back in operation. *Ms.* soon settled in with a circulation of approximately 150,000, double what analysts estimated it needed to break even (Thom 1997).

Lang was thrilled, although he seemed to play a little fast and loose with some of the financial figures in an apparent effort to lowball the magazine's profits. Then when his other publications began to falter, he began to siphon money from *Ms.*, stopping payments to workers and writers. Gloria urged them to sue. No less of a problem was the way Lang exploited *Ms.*'s name and longtime relationships in dealings with printers and other vendors. Determined to keep *Ms.* operating as it had originally been envisioned to, Gloria began looking for a buyer, but Lang played a form of financial blackmail, holding out for an inflated price. Then by 1996, on the verge of going bankrupt, Lang sold *Ms.*, *Working Woman*, and *Working Mother* to Jay MacDonald, a thirty-nine-year-old former advertising executive with a number of big-name magazines who was then publishing *Inc.* Although financed by Paxson Communications, MacDonald soon found himself overmatched, and in no time the finances again became an issue, although at least for the moment editorial control remained in feminist hands (Thom 1997).

Recognizing the potential peril faced by MacDonald's financial problems and determined to keep *Ms.* both afloat and true to its roots, in 1998 Gloria gathered together a group of investors that included leading businesswomen, philanthropists, and activists and created Liberty Media, which purchased the magazine, returning it to independent ownership.

Continuing to operate ad-free, it earned several honors, including an *Utne* award for social commentary. But financial problems continued, and

---

CARLY FIORINA

When she became CEO of Hewlett-Packard (HP) in 1999, Carly Fiorina became the first woman to head a Fortune 500 Top 20 company. She also brought a female presence to the top ranks of the male-dominated tech industry. Combining a personal charisma and a reputation as a fine strategist, she sought to energize a company known for its slow, if not plodding, corporate culture. Early in her tenure, Fiorina engineered what was at the time the largest technology merger in history, with HP acquiring rival personal computer maker Compaq. The merger made HP the largest seller of personal computers in the world. But she was not without her critics. Her ability to articulate her vision was a recognized strength, but she was not as good at executing and implementing her plans. And her connection to the managers who could do that was not strong. Extensive layoffs stemming from the merger only added to her challenges. Despite all this, Fiorina was, for a time, seen as a corporate rock star. However, problems arose and in February 2005 differences with her board led to her resignation. After leaving HP, Fiorina got involved in politics, unsuccessfully seeking a Senate seat from California in 2010 as well as the 2016 Republican presidential nomination.

in November 2001, with Liberty Media facing bankruptcy, the Feminist Majority Foundation purchased the magazine. The new owners dismissed the staff and moved the editorial headquarters from New York to Los Angeles, although the publishing operations were headquartered in Arlington, Virginia. The magazine also dropped back from bimonthly publication to quarterly (Marcello 2004).

With the celebration of its forty-fifth anniversary of publication in 2017, the magazine again featured Wonder Woman on the cover, just as it had on the *New York* insert and subsequent anniversary issues. It was a tribute to Wonder Woman's belief in "sisterhood and equality," central values to the feminist beliefs that were at the heart of the magazine and its founders' vision. Indeed, *Ms.* magazine has had a distinctive role in the movement since its beginning. It sought to serve the movement editorially as a source of information-sharing ideas relevant to feminism while also seeking to be a voice. Its founders had also hoped to contribute 10 percent of its profits to feminist causes. The magazine's relationship with readers has been extraordinary. Becoming the voice it had aspired to be, readers inundated the magazine with letters, unsolicited manuscripts, stories, and artwork as well as hundreds of contributions to its "No Comment" feature, which shared examples of ads and items whose offensive nature was so clear as to require "no comment." The magazine itself was not immune to such mistakes. In fact, despite its vigilant efforts to align its advertising with its mission, *Ms.* too, could fall victim to running ads that reflected the sexism it decried. One ad in *Ms.* for Lady Bic Shaver, featuring a white woman's backside and the title "Bikini Legs," so offended one reader that she offered it for inclusion in "No Comment." The sense of ownership and community was unprecedented and was part of why Gloria and company believed that it could make a go of it as a publication without ads (Farrell 1998).

Almost fifty years after its founding, *Ms.* remains a touchstone for American women. Trusted as an unrivaled source for feminist-based news and information, the magazine has empowered generations of women and helped change the face of society at home and abroad. And in an enduring recognition of her influence on the magazine, whose website proclaims, "More than a Magazine. *Ms.* is a Movement," Gloria, its founding mother, remains on the masthead as both a consulting editor and a founding editor.

No discussion of Gloria and *Ms.* the magazine would be complete without focusing on the *Ms.* Foundation. An offshoot of the magazine, originally created and developed to help further the movement's activist efforts, it would soon, as mentioned previously, become a critical force in helping address the magazine's always challenging finances. Seeking to create what might be called an activist arm of the magazine, in 1972 Gloria Steinem, Patricia Carbine, Letty Cottin Pogrebin, and Marlo Thomas founded the *Ms.* Foundation for Women. They hoped to provide funding and other resources that would help empower women and lift their voices across divisions of race and class in communities across the country. The foundation was established in the belief that women could find solutions to the problems facing the country and the world. It has been tremendously successful, becoming the embodiment of their dream, an organization dedicated to helping lift women's voices and create positive change, with the end goal of helping pursue gender equality and justice. The founders sought to develop a national organization that could provide the support and backing needed to create and further develop women's grassroots organizing efforts across the county (Stern 1997).

And over the years, the organization has taken the lead in countless feminist-oriented programs and issues, from spotlighting child sexual abuse to the disproportionate impact that economic bad times have on women. Reflective of its broad reach, the *Ms.* Foundation has been involved in campaigns that seek to counter the efforts to reduce and limit school-based sex education, and it created the Katrina Women's Response Fund to respond to the immediate needs of the victims of Hurricanes Katrina and Rita while also offering support for female leaders working to address the challenges faced in the storms' aftermath. The foundation has also become increasingly involved in raising consciousness and in helping combat the many important issues relating to women's health, as well as in the empowerment of girls and the protection of reproductive rights.

The foundation has recognized the interrelationship of the women's movement with the broader populace. In a controversial move in 2000, the foundation added men to its board in an effort both to diversify the group and highlight the importance of men and women working together in the effort to fulfill the group's mission. Controversial it may have been, but to anyone who had followed Gloria's career or witnessed an organizational evolution that had seen "Take Your Daughter to Work Day" morph into "Take Your Children to Work Day" recognized that it was another example of feminism as part of the wider tent of humanity. Similar changes followed when, beginning in 2007, the foundation began to fund programs that served women, girls, and coed groups in an effort to show the way boys and men could be allied with girls and women to achieve their shared goals.

Throughout their respective existences, there has been an effective partnership between the magazine and the foundation. The *Ms.* Foundation's work with the magazine has extended well beyond its early connection as a vehicle for achieving reduced mailing costs and allowing for an alternative source of funding for the magazine. It worked with the magazine, building upon some of its early sponsorships of feminist-themed events, such as a New York Philharmonic concert highlighting music composed by women and conducted entirely by a woman, Sarah Caldwell, in

> ### FREE TO BE . . . YOU AND ME
>
> *Free to Be . . . You and Me* was a multifaceted entertainment project created by actress Marlo Thomas. The idea stemmed from Thomas's desire to teach her young niece about life but in a way that transcended the gender bias common in children's records and books. The original record and the accompanying book, released in November 1972, included a range of nonsexist songs performed by an array of celebrities including football star Rosey Grier and pop superstar Diana Ross. The record was an immediate sensation, quickly going gold, while the book reached number one on the *New York Times* bestseller list. The reaction was so positive that it spawned a TV special that aired in 1974 and featured an all-star cast that included Michael Jackson, Alan Alda, and Dustin Hoffman, to name a few. The show won both an Emmy Award and a Peabody Award and has been rebroadcast on cable television. Meanwhile, the book remains in print. To commemorate its fortieth anniversary, a book titled *When We Were Free to Be: Looking Back at a Children's Classic and the Difference It Made* was published in 2012. All of the earnings from the book, the record, and the TV special have gone to the *Ms.* Foundation, where the book continues to have an impact.

1974. *Ms.* also produced a set of magazine-format programs for television, under the title *Woman Alive!* One of the most famous segments was on Crystal Lee Jordan, the labor organizer whose life was the basis for the later Academy Award–winning film, *Norma Rae*.

Reflecting its roots with the magazine, some of the foundation's most successful ventures have been in publishing. Producing books such as *The Ms. Guide to Health* and an anthology titled, *The First Ms. Reader* filled gaps in feminist literature. Their most successful undertaking was created and developed by Marlo Thomas. *Free to Be . . . You and Me* is an original record of nonsexist songs and skits for children that was adapted into a book and a TV special that won an Emmy.

Like the magazine, the foundation was a trailblazing organization whose impact continues to be felt, and as such both the magazine and the foundation are central parts of Gloria's feminist legacy (Stern 1997).

7

The Personal Is Political

As Gloria's prominence in the movement grew, it sometimes seemed as though every photo of her at a rally, march, or protest was matched by a more glamorous depiction of her on the arm of a well-known celebrity at a ball or opening night. Similarly, much to her dismay, articles about her style and beauty competed for attention with ones about her latest political initiative or statement. As much as she bemoaned the situation, Gloria's personal life and her personal appearance were no small part of the public fascination that was central to her role as a leader of the feminist cause. Her glamour was an undeniable part of Gloria's public image, but it was an image that made her an object of both admiration and vitriol. Indeed, in the increasingly divided American political and cultural landscape, how one responded to Gloria Steinem became something of a Rorschach test for an American's feminist versus nonfeminist beliefs. Gloria's looks and lifestyle resonated with both the media and the public in both positive and negative ways. As an experienced journalist, Gloria understood the dynamic at play. Her string of high-profile celebrity suitors made for a better story than did coverage of her trips spreading a message of female empowerment across the country.

Part of the appeal and interest in her social life stemmed from preconceived notions that dominated much of the debate about the women's movement. From the beginning, opponents of feminism contended the women's movement was made up of old maids and women so unattractive they could not get a man. Gloria offered a resounding rebuttal to those arguments. Her status in the movement demonstrated that given the opportunity, women could flourish. That fact alone enabled Gloria to make a distinct connection—both in fact and symbolically—with the nation's women. She became an inspiration to a generation of young, white, middle-class women who wanted to be Gloria. While the glamour attacked one set of assumptions and stereotypes, her Seven Sisters–minted intelligence, not to mention her countless books, articles, and media appearances, soundly refuted the stereotype that equated beauty with stupidity. Gloria was nobody's "dumb blonde." On the contrary, she represented the embodiment of the movement's promise. If the doors of opportunity were opened to women and the freedom to choose was secured, then all women could, like Gloria, write their own definition of success.

Gloria's love life and her social life, a combination that were necessarily one and the same, are the stuff of novels. And in fact, the longest lasting of her "mini marriages"—as the marriage-averse Gloria Steinem once termed her relationships—to attorney Stan Pottinger, did make its way onto the pages of one of the novels he wrote after they broke up. At the same time, the men in her life often received far more attention than they deserved (Stern 1997).

Indeed, the relationship between her sexual partners, social liaisons, and professional success has always been a complicated one for Gloria. And ever since she became a feminist leader, her relationships have been a source of public curiosity. Over the years, Gloria has been alternately coy and candid. On some occasions she adamantly maintained that her choice of lovers was unrelated to their ability to help her. Yet at other times she acknowledged that yes, given her ambitions, to be with the right man was important and something she sought–admittedly, for the wrong reason. In 1984 she told an interviewer that at one point she definitely sought out rich and famous men. She said that while she would not go out with someone she didn't like, she was definitely seeking a certain position and status in her relationships (Stern 1997).

A look at her list of high-profile relationships seems to confirm her own observation, and yet, in the beginning, the pattern was not so clear. Gloria's first New York–based relationship was with future acclaimed screenwriter and film director Robert Benton, whom she met in 1960 soon after she arrived in New York. At the time Benton was working as *Esquire*'s art director, and they first became acquainted when Gloria, while trying to scout up any kind of writing assignment, spent a lot of time hanging around *Esquire*. They immediately hit it off and soon began dating. By this point Gloria already boasted a lengthy list of former lovers, as well as a onetime fiancé, but she later said her relationship with Benton represented the first time she had truly been in love.

It was by all accounts a relationship that was right for both of them at that point in their lives. Gloria has recalled him as the first person with whom she could speak naturally about her experiences in Toledo, a product in part of his ability to give her a "sense of place." A native of Texas who had arrived in New York on a Continental bus, Benton impressed Gloria as a person totally at ease with himself. Meanwhile, for all the artistic talent that was evident in his work at *Esquire*, Gloria played a critical role in convincing Benton he could write. He saw her as one of the people who helped him become the man who would write *Bonnie and Clyde*, *Kramer vs. Kramer*, and *Places in the Heart*.

By 1962 they were talking about marriage. Not surprisingly, as things proceeded in that direction, it was Gloria who hesitated. Rather than rush things and risk a breakup, they decided to take it one step at a time. They first got a marriage license to see how it felt. But Gloria remained deeply conflicted, unable to explain her fear, especially since she admitted she adored Benton. She even saw a psychiatrist in an effort to address the issue, but in the end, she decided she could not marry him. With that decision, the relationship ended (Stern 1997).

In somewhat typical fashion, before beginning her next long-term involvement, Gloria had a brief affair with Paul Desmond, the saxophonist for Dave Brubeck's band. He lived only a block away from her, and he would frequently call to share a walk around the Museum of Modern Art, a walk he believed was enhanced by a dose of mescaline. While she tried the drug, she did not enjoy it. Similarly, whereas she experimented with marijuana with friends, the experience left her with a sense of doom. She also had limited experience with alcohol—it had made her sick when she was in college, and it left her drowsy as an adult. In fact, she was, for the most part, abstemious. She did smoke cigarettes and thin cigars but limited her intake. In general, her vices were in other areas (Stern 1997).

In the summer of 1962, while *The Beach Book* was in the works but before it was published, Gloria began seeing Viking publisher Thomas Guinzburg. Guinzburg, who was only thirty-four when he assumed leadership of the company after the death of his father in 1960, was concerned about dating a writer that Viking was publishing. When his marriage ended not long after his father's death, he took up with Gloria. Tom had spent a lifetime moving in exalted social circles while growing up among some of New York's leading families, including the likes of the Sulzbergers of the *New York Times*. He had been a roommate of conservative writer and social commentator William F. Buckley Jr. at Yale, and his best friends were songwriters Betty Comden and Adolph Green, who were part of an arts-based circle that included the parents of Gloria's former fiancé, Blair Chotzinoff. Occasional sightings of Gloria and Tom at social events only reaffirmed the elder Chotzinoffs' earlier belief that Gloria was a social climber, although Blair told his parents she and Tom would not marry. And of course, he was right but not because Tom wasn't interested. In fact,

Tom adored Gloria and showered her with impressive gifts, including a hard-to-find Cartier watch as well as a trip to Italy to meet his sister. Meanwhile, Gloria gave him a custom-made red blazer that he wore for almost thirty years (Stern 1997).

Yet for all of Tom's wealth and social connections, Gloria's ambition left him feeling threatened. In particular, he was both impressed and even a bit intimidated by her ability to deal with people, a talent that subsequently became a hallmark of her career but had not yet been on display on such a public stage. And in fact, while Tom headed one of the nation's leading publishing houses, he saw Gloria as more focused and confident in her writing ability as well as in where her career was heading. He noted that John Kenneth Galbraith was among her admirers, as were John Steinbeck and Arthur Miller. Looking back, he ruefully observed, "They all liked her. How could you not like her?" (Stern 1997).

As with virtually all of her relationships, Gloria Steinem's relationship with Tom Guinzburg ended amicably. Indeed, he was never anything but a great fan. In fact, in one instance Tom, seeking yet another special gift to bestow on his girlfriend, approached the owner of Reuben's Delicatessen in New York with a special request. The local eatery was known for the sandwiches it had named for famous people, including Jack Benny and Bob Hope. Tom asked what it would cost to have a sandwich named for Gloria. When the owner understandably responded that she wasn't famous, Tom countered, "Not now, but she will be" (Stern 1997).

Gloria's relationship with JFK confidant Ted Sorensen certainly seemed to embody her general approach, as the high-profile, if short-lived, liaison represented a perfect meshing of the professional and the social. Having gotten a freelance assignment to write about the Kennedy White House, she latched onto JFK's speechwriter Sorensen, whom she had met during the campaign. While Sorensen was not, by Steinem's own reckoning, a part of the glamorous Kennedy social circle, no one knew JFK's mind better than the Nebraska native, nor did anyone in the administration write better. When Gloria asked to spend time in the office as part of her research, he agreed and countered that she might be able to offer some help with a speech. It was an offer no starstruck, aspiring political journalist could turn down. Soon they were seeing each other socially, and Gloria had an insider's access to life in the White House. It was also how she got a final glimpse of the dashing young president on a day in late November 1963. Going through clippings in Ted's office, she looked out the window to see the speechwriter running out to the West Wing lawn with the final draft of the speech in hand. He caught up with JFK before the president hopped on the helicopter that would take him to Air Force One and ultimately to Dallas. It was the last time Steinem or Sorensen saw Kennedy alive. While they spent much of the next few weeks comforting each other in the aftermath of the president's death, the relationship quickly cooled afterward, and each moved on to a new chapter of their lives (Stern 1997).

In Gloria's case, that next chapter starred Mike Nichols. Half of the onetime hit-comedy team, Nichols and May, in 1963 he was emerging as one of the hottest directors on Broadway. Steinem began to see Nichols while his first Tony Award winner, *Barefoot in the Park*, was in rehearsals. She was by his side as the awards began to accumulate and he turned to films, making his directorial debut in 1966 with *Who's Afraid of Virginia Woolf?* starring Elizabeth Taylor and Richard Burton. It was a heady time, and Gloria reveled at the opportunity to sit in on meetings with Charles Webb, the author of *The Graduate*. In fact, Gloria was the one who suggested Smith College as an appropriate place for the film's faculty house and campus scenes (Stern 1997).

Given Nichols's ever-increasing prominence and Steinem's still-evolving career, the relationship brought to the fore some of the same issues she had experienced with Blair. She feared being seen only as the director's girlfriend and potentially his wife and mother of his children. She knew she projected the right image. She was educated, accomplished, but not too famous. She had a credible career during the postcollege, premarriage years, but at the same time, her beauty and educated polish would make her an appropriate helpmate to the great man. Increasingly, Steinem was feeling pressure to marry Nichols, and every doubt she had came rushing to the surface (Heilbrun 1995).

While she was with Nichols, Gloria also began to see writer Herb Sargent, who in 1964 hired her to work on the show *That Was the Week That Was*. The show was an adaptation of a British series for which he was the head writer and producer. She joined an imposing group of writers that included Buck Henry, who would write the screenplay for Nichols's *The Graduate*, as well as Alan Alda, who had a starring role in the show. While it was a highly collaborative undertaking, Gloria's primary responsibility on the show was a segment called "Surrealism in Everyday Life." Working under Sargent, who would later be one of the original writers when *Saturday Night Live* debuted in 1975, was a boon to Steinem's career, but it complicated her life socially and emotionally (Stern 1997).

Low-key Herb Sargent was a marked contrast to the former comic performer Mike Nichols. The contrast left her emotionally torn, and to make matters worse, she found herself undertaking a comparative analysis of how they would be as fathers. Further complicating things was the fact that Ruth particularly liked Herb, and the couple had taken her with them on a vacation to Curacao. For her thirty-first birthday, Herb gave Gloria a six-month option on Elie Wiesel's book, *Town beyond the Wall*, the story of a young man who had been so traumatized by his imprisonment by the Nazis that he was unable to speak but was ultimately helped through the kindness of others. The novel resonated with Gloria when she first read it, and she hoped to adapt it as a play. While in the end, she was unable to make the project a reality, the gift from Sargent reflected a central element of their relationship, one of critical importance to Steinem: his respect and professional encouragement.

Her series of relationships, as well as her seemingly endless list of contacts allowed Gloria to move effortlessly in the most elite social circles. Her stature was evident when she appeared on the guest list for Truman Capote's 1966 Black and White Ball. The gathering, whose five-hundred-person guest list the *Washington Post* called a "Who's Who of the World," featured cultural icons from Jackie Kennedy to Marlene Dietrich, from Alice Roosevelt Longworth to Frank Sinatra, with *Washington Post* publisher Katharine Graham as Capote's designated guest of honor. In addition to making the list, she also took pride in getting Sargent, whom Capote had not deemed important enough to include, added to the guest list. In typical fashion, Gloria would ultimately complete the circle by writing about the gala for *Vogue* (Stern 1997).

In the latter part of the sixties, at a time when a mixed-race couple would raise eyebrows in all but the most liberal social settings, Gloria had relationships with two of the nation's most celebrated Black athletes, Jim Brown and Rafer Johnson. Her 1968 affair with the football legend and film star Brown was short lived, coming after Steinem had interviewed him for a profile, "The Black John Wayne," which appeared in the November 11, 1968, issue of *New York*. While neither had any illusions about the relationship, its end was hastened when Brown's then girlfriend, Eva Bohn-Chin, suffered physical injuries in an incident that remains shrouded in mystery. The episode not only added to a long list of questions about Brown's treatment of women but also raised questions about Gloria's judgment (Heilbrun 1995).

Her relationship with Rafer Johnson was very different. She first met him at the 1968 Democratic Convention. A witness to his close friend Robert Kennedy's assassination—he was one of the people who wrestled the gun away from assassin Sirhan Sirhan—Johnson was still grieving over Kennedy's death when he met Gloria. In contrast to the ultramacho Brown, Johnson was a more sensitive, if no less competitive, individual. Determined to serve the greater public, he had been making his living as a sportscaster before he was fired by a local NBC affiliate, allegedly because of fears that his association with Kennedy might ruffle conservative viewers' feathers. In the aftermath of the Robert Kennedy assassination, he devoted himself to the Special Olympics (Stern 1997).

Gloria and Johnson saw each other for three years, but while their relationship was serious, both recognized that there was no marriage in their future. The East Coast-West Coast split represented a clear obstacle, but it was no more of a hindrance than Gloria's by now clear lack of interest in marriage. Besides, Johnson believed that an interracial marriage would hinder Gloria's career, something he was loath to do given his tremendous respect and admiration for her wide-ranging activism. In 1971 they ended the relationship, although, in typical Gloria fashion, they remained friends (Stern 1997).

In the aftermath of her breakup with Johnson, Gloria began to date Franklin Thomas. Gloria's relationship with Thomas began in 1971, although they first met in the late 1960s, when he was the head of the Bedford-Stuyvesant Restoration Corporation, an RFK-sponsored urban renewal initiative. Thomas was a Brooklyn native who had gone to Columbia, where he was the first African American basketball captain in the Ivy League. He served as an assistant U.S. attorney after law school. He soon caught RFK's eye and was approached about heading the Bedford-Stuyvesant project, which he did for the decade from 1967 to 1977. In 1979 he became president of the Ford Foundation (Stern 1997).

Despite their shared public profiles, the relationship, which lasted from 1971 to 1974, was certainly far less public than Gloria's usual attachments. When asked, as she so often was, about her social status, she said she was in a relationship but refused to say more, perhaps because Thomas was separated when the affair began. Out of the public eye, the relationship with Thomas seemed to be one that provided Gloria with great support and a safe space during the years when she was navigating the often-tricky waters that came with her emergence as a high-profile feminist figure.

Her time with Thomas was also a period of great stress because she was so deeply involved with the creation and development of *Ms.* By all accounts, Thomas was a source of critical support through all of that. It was, she recalled, one of the most fulfilling relationships she ever had, and after his divorce the two of them considered marriage. Ultimately, near what proved to be the end, Thomas suffered some major health setbacks that changed the relationship dynamic. Gloria began acting as Thomas's caregiver, a role she had undertaken during her long years with her mother in Toledo. In doing so, the emotional connection she felt with Thomas altered, and they parted on typically amicable terms (Stern 1997).

Those who were surprised or puzzled by Gloria's involvement with three Black men failed to understand two things. First, Gloria was not going to let her personal life be dictated or impacted by any outside influences. In fact, for committed activists, such relationships could also be seen as a way to thumb their noses at the conservatives whom they battled on so many levels. But more importantly, Gloria came to the issue of race from a very different place than many of her peers did. As a young child at Clarklake, she had lived among many musicians, who in the 1930s and 1940s represented one of the truly integrated groups in the United States. In that venue, she saw her parents treating entertainers—Black and white—the same. Leo housed them all in the band cottage while Ruth cooked for all. In addition, Gloria recalled being very influenced by her early reading of Louisa May Alcott, a staunch abolitionist whose Civil War stories sent clear messages about her views on race. And Gloria's experience lifeguarding at the segregated pool in Washington, coupled with her experience in India, had given her an expansive and open view of people and humanity (Heilbrun 1995).

Indeed, in later years, one of Gloria's few regrets about her early professional years was her failure to follow her instincts and her heart and get more directly involved in the civil rights work taking place in the South. She felt a strong urge to join the many who were marching, freedom riding, and working on voter registration efforts. But in the end, she acceded to the desires of Robert Benton, who was not similarly committed and feared such an experience, if not shared, might negatively impact their relationship. Instead, as she would later ruefully admit, she buried herself in her developing career and while her work reflected her commitment to civil rights, she regretted not being on the front lines in the 1960s. Those regrets aside, all of her experiences with people of color, as well as the attitudes those experiences reflected, informed her inclusive dating practices (Stern 1997).

Gloria also brought an additional perspective that helped overcome the social barriers of the period. By the early 1970s, as her celebrity status soared and she became the media-anointed face of the feminist movement, she had become an insider, albeit in an outsider's movement. Whether it was as a young girl living on the wrong side of Toledo or the blue jeans–clad girl amid her Bermuda shorts–attired Smith classmates, Gloria knew what it was like to be on the outside. And while she retained an outsider's viewpoint, she could feel empathy for many of the nation's outsider groups. She also never lost her ability to see things through that lens—and then when the picture was clear, she did all she could to open the door to all.

Gloria's next relationship holds the "record" as the longest of what the matrimonially averse Gloria referred to as her "little marriages." Stan Pottinger was arguably the one man in her string of relationships and lovers who offered her little beyond the relationship. While he was a high-ranking member of the Justice Department, the 1970s were a time when indictments rather than advancement were apt to be such an official's lot. By no one's standards did he have the professional profile or social cachet of the men in whose company Gloria could usually be found. Yet with an already bulging Rolodex and a public profile that was putting her in the crossfire of both the developing culture wars and a feminist movement, the low-key, supportive Stan was exactly what she needed.

They first met in the fall of 1974 when Pottinger, the assistant attorney general for civil rights, called Gloria to discuss sex discrimination. He wanted to get the Justice Department involved in such cases but needed to learn more about the issue. A Dayton, Ohio, native, he had earned degrees from Harvard and Harvard Law School, and, after marrying his high school sweetheart (also named Gloria), settled in San Francisco. A protégé of longtime Nixon confidant Robert Finch, Pottinger went to Washington in 1970. There he headed the Office of Civil Rights in the Department of Health, Education, and Welfare, which Finch headed. Following the 1972 election, he moved to the Justice Department, where he served under three presidents and seven attorneys general, from Nixon to Carter and John Mitchell to Griffin Bell. He was lucky in that his entry to the Justice Department came at a time when it was focused on Watergate, and so Stan was able to pursue his own agenda with little interference. Gloria put together a gathering in New York that included Brenda Feigen Fasteau as well as Ruth Bader Ginsburg, who was then teaching at Columbia, to educate Stan on sex discrimination

Smitten from his first encounter, Stan heard Gloria was going to Hartford for a speech and offered to drive her to the engagement. The pair bonded immediately, spending the ride comparing notes on their mutual Ohio roots as well as their shared love of Vernors ginger soda. He stayed for her speech and then drove her back to New York. He later said he was amazed at the way Gloria's efforts to address substantive issues were overridden by a press more interested in the length of her skirts and her latest boyfriend. After dropping her back in the city, he followed up by sending her a case of Vernors and within a few months, after she fully disentangled from Franklin Thomas, they became a couple.

With Gloria living in New York and Stan in Washington, their time together was usually limited to weekends, especially since Stan's two oldest children lived with him. Gloria got along well with his children, and the relationship flourished. After practicing law in Washington for a couple of years after leaving the government—a period that coincided with Gloria's fellowship at the Woodrow Wilson Center—he moved to New York in 1980.

Working in a fluctuating real estate market, he both made and lost considerable sums of money before his relationship with Gloria ended in 1984. When Gloria moved on to another lover, she and Stan remained friends. Stan seemed comfortable with the split and was seen with a string of high-profile women. A few years after the split, Stan undertook a career change, becoming a novelist. His first book, a medical thriller, *The Fourth Procedure*, earned a spot on the best-seller list while also piquing people's interest about the origins of one Gloria-like character. While Stan acknowledged that, like most authors, he had taken parts of his characters from real people, he made clear that he combined those elements with his own imagination, thus creating fictitious characters. At the same time, given her celebrity and the length of their relationship, readers could not be blamed for wondering where the line between fictional Victoria and real Gloria was drawn (Stern 1997).

In 1984 Gloria began a four-year relationship with Mortimer Zuckerman, a multimillionaire real estate developer. To her friends, the Canadian-born Zuckerman, who had earned degrees at McGill, Harvard Law, and the University of Pennsylvania's Wharton School, struck a wrong chord. In addition to developing projects all over the county, he also taught city and regional planning at both Yale University and Harvard's Graduate School of Design. Yet despite his affiliation with Harvard, his effort to develop a site next to the Boston Public Gardens met with nothing but opposition. He managed to alienate the city's establishment before he abandoned the project but not before spending almost two million dollars over seven years. As he accumulated his fortune, Zuckerman expressed a desire to move into the public arena, either in politics or journalism. When in June 1979 he was approached about investing in *Atlantic Monthly*, he jumped at the chance, buying the magazine and then firing editor Robert Manning, who had first offered him the opportunity to get involved. Zuckerman and Manning engaged in a lengthy legal battle, and none of it did anything to help Zuckerman's image. By 1983 he had made New York his primary residence and started to see Gloria at occasional social events. By 1984 they were a couple, if an odd one (Heilbrun 1995).

In typical fashion, the transition from Stan Pottinger to Zuckerman was a little awkward. While Stan accompanied Gloria to her big fiftieth birthday gala, Mort was also there. They had, in fact, been seeing each other for a while, although she had not yet cut ties with Stan. Zuckerman made clear that he did not like the clandestine nature of their relationship, and Gloria made a final break with Stan soon after the party. She then jumped into her relationship with Zuckerman with both feet. However, his relationship with Steinem did not alter his business approach, and that may have contributed to the reaction of her friends. In 1985, he embarked on a development project not unlike the Boston Public Garden imbroglio. He planned to develop a city-owned site next to Central Park, a proposal featuring a pair of buildings, one over fifty stories and the other over seventy, which would have cast an imposing shadow over the park. The proposed development was met with vocal opposition from high-profile figures including Jacqueline Kennedy Onassis, Walter Cronkite, and Henry Kissinger. Although he later scaled back the plan, the damage was done. At the same time, while Zuckerman's real estate efforts kept adding enemies to his ledger, he was also expanding his media holdings in an effort to increase his stature as an opinion maker. In 1984 he purchased *U.S. News & World Report*, and in 1993 he added the *New York Daily News* to his media portfolio (Stern 1997).

Gloria told friends that he was the most intelligent man she had ever met. She even told Bella Abzug she was obsessed with him. The effect of the relationship was stunning. The couple was seen all over, as they danced, socialized with friends, and spent weekends at his house in the Hamptons. The never-domesticated Gloria was seen walking his Labrador retriever Stockman, named for Ronald Reagan's budget director, and she was also a regular spectator while Mort played in some very competitive, celebrity-studded softball games in Sag Harbor. At the same time, while Gloria had made clear over the years that she had no interest in either marriage or children, Zuckerman made clear that he was eager to marry Steinem and have children. It seemed an irreconcilable situation and yet their many similarities—they were both hardworking, fun-loving, well-connected leaders, deeply concerned about their public images—fueled the relationship that would ultimately last for about two and a half years. The end appeared to come in 1986, but it proved to be short lived. After only a brief interlude, the pair reconnected. While this period did see each of them occasionally dating others, they were essentially a couple for another year and a half. Ultimately, increased acrimony, as well as a total lack of agreement over the issue of marriage and children, brought the relationship to an end. Among Steinem's many exes, Zuckerman is the only one with whom she has not remained friends (Stern 1997).

In 2000, after spurning countless proposals over the years, Gloria both shocked the world and reaffirmed her reputation for independence by getting married. In a September 3 ceremony performed at the home of Wilma Mankiller, the first female principal chief of the Cherokee Nation and a longtime Steinem friend and ally, the sixty-six-year-old Gloria married fifty-nine-year-old David Bale, a South African activist and father of actor Christian Bale. The couple met not long before, when he had approached her at a Los Angeles Voters for Choice benefit. While the marriage was in Gloria's words, a "green-card marriage" intended to resolve David's immigration status, Gloria said they would have been together anyway, and she did not use that status as the reason for ending her long-expressed personal opposition to marriage. Rather, while acknowledging that it was counter to much of what she believed, she noted that her life and the world had changed. She observed that the institution of marriage and the society in which it operated now made it possible for a woman to marry without giving up her fundamental self (Marcello 2004).

Ironically, after waiting so long to marry, and having what was by all accounts a happy marriage, Gloria's union with Bale was not a long one. Barely three years after they were married, on December 30, 2003, David Bale, whom Gloria once said, "had the greatest heart of anyone I've ever known," died of brain cancer. Gloria nursed him through his final days. The experience was reminiscent of Toledo and was something she had frequently referenced when expressing her desire for a life sans spouse or children.

While for a brief period she lost the autonomy that had always been so important to her, she saw "helping David out of life," as she put it, as a way to show her love. No less importantly, she recognized that David's illness forced her to live in the present, which in its own way helped her, indeed forced her, at long last, to chase away some ghosts from her past. In typical fashion, the princess of hope and optimism looked on the experience as a positive one, offering her a chance to redo something she had done before. While introspection is not her strong suit, she realized that caring as an adult for an adult was different from the earlier experience with her mother. No less importantly, when David Bale became ill, Gloria was ready to deal with it in the way he needed. That response represented a stark contrast to the events of 1974, when her relationship with Franklin Thomas foundered with regard to his illness and her emotional inability to be a full-time caretaker. David's death represented another chapter in a life that was always evolving and building upon previous experiences (Shriver 2011).

The whole experience with David Bale served to shine a renewed light on her views on marriage. Admittedly, she had said that she had many friends, as well as a sister, who had marriages that seemed to be fulfilling and right for them. At the same time, she had spent decades rebuffing such opportunities on a personal level, making clear that while it was OK for others, marriage was not for her. She reasserted that she had never been against marriage in the abstract, that it had simply never been right for her. And yet her often flippant comments over the years—most famously, the observation that a woman needed marriage like a fish needed a bicycle— seemed to belie a more deeply seated antipathy toward marriage. And yet in accepting it at that point, she seemed to be reminding people, close friends as well as those who knew her only as a feminist symbol, that her work—and that of a generation of fellow feminists—had created enough change so that it was safe even for Gloria Steinem to marry. She could marry without losing her name, abandoning her identity, or giving up the autonomy that she had long seen as central to an individual's life and to which she had so doggedly clung since escaping Toledo almost a half century before (Paquette 2015).

Over the years, admirers and critics alike have tried far too hard to find political meaning in each of Gloria's relationships. Indeed, at the same time that she was personifying the changing status of women, the glamorous Gloria, a trail of high-profile lovers in her wake, was still dogged by generations-old societal expectations. The media still wondered when she would settle down, get married, and start having children. The answer to her was clear: it was not their concern. Instead, in not behaving as expected, in continuing on an independent, career-oriented path, she was embodying a central tenet of the movement: a woman's right to make her own choices and to establish herself as an independent human being.

Once she had emerged as a major figure in the movement, she found herself consistently frustrated by the media's insistent focus on her personal life and her romantic affairs. She believed that it was not just intrusive. More importantly, she feared that it all came at the cost of recognizing, appreciating, and absorbing her feminist message. The apparent conflict between Gloria's desire and ability to sometimes simply enjoy the world and her place in it versus her determination to change that world reflected the competing pressures that dogged Gloria for the rest of her tenure in the spotlight. It frustrated her, too, that observers did not recognize that the list of high-profile figures she dated transcended all boundaries and labels. She dated artists, writers, and political leaders, among others. Gloria saw her male partners as the products of an approach that could be characterized as extralegal, serial monogamy. And for the most part, all of her former lovers became part of her extended family, a tribute to her ability to relate and connect with people. But that is not what got noticed by the media.

If only because of her visibility and celebrity, few of her relationships, especially those with high-profile men, were taken merely for what they were. There always seemed to be speculation about what the pairing indicated, with political opponents seeking to find ways that her choice of men or their faults could somehow be used to tarnish the movement, not to mention Gloria herself. It was a tricky business, living one's life under an almost constant spotlight. At the same time, as Gloria moved from relationship to relationship, while the transitions were sometimes awkward, in almost all cases her former beaus remained at least friends, sometimes confidants, and almost always people who spoke of her in the most glowing terms. Even when she sometimes engaged in more casual affairs, some more public than others, they never seemed to tarnish her image in her own circles.

Gloria's longtime close friend Letty Pogrebin marveled at the way Gloria managed her relationships. She observed that for years Gloria had been led around by her libido, a fact that complicated the relationship side of things as she moved from man to man. It also set her up to be pilloried by outsiders who continued to adhere to conservative sexual mores. It was an era that saw men demonstrating their virility and manliness by accumulating sexual conquests, while a woman who appeared to enjoy sex and taking control of her own social/sexual life was derided for having loose morals. Gloria's approach to sex and relationships was in many ways complicated, but it was also very much in line with the liberation and the choice-based lifestyle she advocated. At the same time, it made her an easy target for attacks by the conservatives who saw her lifestyle as a rebuke to the "family values" they held dear and were determined to defend. Interestingly, as Gloria later reflected upon the changes brought on by menopause, her once-raging libido dimmed, encouraging a more "enjoy it when it happens" approach to sex (Stern 1997).

While the romantic side of her private life regularly became public, Gloria worked hard to keep two major health scares private. The first involved breast cancer, and only with the 1992 publication of her book, *Revolution from Within: A Book of Self-Esteem*, did Gloria publicly address the diagnosis she had received in 1986. And even then, it was only in the context of larger issues. In fact, she discussed it primarily in the context of how she treated aging. Her first reaction upon hearing that the tumor doctors had removed was malignant, was, "So this is how it's all going to end," followed soon thereafter with, "I've had a wonderful life." She noted that only when faced with her own mortality did she think of how she had been in denial about the aging process. The cancer diagnosis forced her to face the changes she would have to make if she were fortunate enough to survive. She did not discuss these revelations in *Revolution from Within*, and the fact that she only revealed it in a later book was a disappointment to many, especially those who believed that given Gloria's prominence, a discussion of breast cancer could have had significant cultural meaning. In the end, of course, Gloria had every right to protect her limited privacy. In this case, her unwillingness to disclose her breast cancer only added to the disappointment many felt at *Revolution from Within* itself, a work seen by many as little more than another big-name author posing as a self-help guru. In addition, for many in the feminist community, the book was a distraction from the social activism they thought should be Gloria's primary focus (Stern 1997).

The backlash that greeted *Revolution from Within* surprised Gloria, because she believed a strong self-image and self-esteem were critical to an individual being able to pursue and create change. To her the book was an effort to address important issues that hampered her generation's efforts while also hoping to highlight—and preview—some of the challenges that the next generation could expect to face. She sought to both address the issues for her generation and offer some advice for the next wave. Indeed, in defending herself against those who felt she had sacrificed activism for new age self-help, she said she thought it was actually her most political book, because many institutions sought to undermine women's self-esteem in an effort to exert authority over them. In Gloria's mind, the book was a way to support women's independence (Stern 1997).

The second health scare came in the winter of 1994, when Gloria was slowed down by trigeminal neuralgia, a nerve disorder that left her housebound for several months. Forced to cancel a speaking tour tied to her recently released book of essays, *Moving beyond Words*, she observed that she had been fortunate to have good medical care and insurance, without which she said she might well have been misdiagnosed, as are many who have trigeminal neuralgia. It was, she said, a sobering experience.

Meanwhile, commenting on aging, Gloria says that as she approached sixty, she felt that she entered a new phase in life, one that was free of the "demands of gender" that she had faced from adolescence onward. As she had done so many times before, she helped others adjust to the changing landscape of aging. For Gloria and her peers, even the journey into old age represented a pioneering effort, one that prepared the path for those who came after them, unaware of how much progress had been made but benefiting from it nonetheless.

The media reports surrounding her many high-profile liaisons have often left the impression that such couplings were her only interpersonal relationships. But they are the only ones the celebrity-focused media has found interesting. In fact, Gloria has long had a close-knit group of friends who were a source of support and strength throughout her life. Given the total mix of her life and her work, virtually all of these friends were involved in some way with the women's movement. At the same time, one of the distinctive aspects of these relationships was the way they often moved Gloria in a different direction, expanding her perspective and her agenda.

Gloria's list of friends is lengthy, but at the heart of the group is a small, unwavering band led by Letty Cottin Pogrebin, herself an accomplished author. A founding editor at *Ms.*, she had sat at a desk barely ten feet from Gloria in the early days of the magazine. After the Woodrow Wilson Fellowship failed to result in a book, Letty vowed that Gloria's next effort would yield a book—and she would help make it happen. After first negotiating an advance, Letty sifted through the many pieces Gloria had produced over the years, culling them into a collection that, with some slight revisions and explanatory notes, would ultimately hit bookstores as *Outrageous Acts and Everyday Rebellions*. The book's commercial success added a whole new dimension to Gloria's influence. Meanwhile, Gloria and Letty's relationship evolved into a potent partnership that has served both of them as well as the movement.

Longtime ally Robin Morgan was a fellow author and *Ms.* editor too. An activist who helped organize the 1968 Miss America protest, Morgan's writings were a critical part of the early part of the movement, particularly her 1970 anthology *Sisterhood Is Powerful*. Robin's writing underwrote a broader-based activism and included a special emphasis on feminism as a global issue. This made her and Gloria obvious allies, and they worked side by side for decades on numerous projects. In 2005 she and Gloria joined with their friend, actress-activist Jane Fonda, to create the Women's Media Center.

No less important was Pat Carbine. Succumbing to Gloria's entreaties to join the *Ms.* team, Pat was critical to establishing the magazine's early credibility. Her determination to make it work as a feminist periodical true to its mission and roots matched Gloria's and heavily contributed to making it a reality. But as with others, as the years went on, what began as a professional relationship transcended those roots, yielding a comfort that suited them both (Stern 1997).

Another of the inner circle is Marlo Thomas. The actress, whose portrayal of Anne Marie in the iconic show *That Girl* represented the first time that television had dared make a single, independent woman the lead character in a show, was an early friend with whom many partnerships developed. Not only was Thomas one of the founding mothers of the *Ms.* Foundation but her *Free to Be ... You and Me* was the Foundation's greatest commercial success, one that added huge amounts to the Foundation's coffers, all of which in turn went to support countless feminist causes. Marlo Thomas and her husband, talk show host Phil Donahue, were the hosts of Gloria's fiftieth birthday party, which doubled as a *Ms.* Foundation fundraiser. That event was a fitting testament to Gloria's work while also providing clear testimony to the extent of Marlo Thomas's connections and influence (Stern 1997).

Also in the inner circle was Wilma Mankiller, the first woman chief of the Cherokee Nation. While Wilma came to the party a bit later than some of Gloria's friends, her impact and the relationship itself were no less important. In bringing a spiritual approach to much of what she did, Mankiller drew upon her Native American heritage for distinctive lessons in leadership. Gloria found these lessons central to her work and well-being. Steinem would later call Mankiller "chosen family" (Stern 1997).

Over the years Gloria's inner circle expanded to include disparate individuals whose support and friendships were critical parts of Gloria's life

---

DREW GILPIN FAUST

Drew Gilpin Faust was the first woman president of Harvard University, taking office in 2007. Faust's appointment was a symbol on many levels. Her predecessor, former Treasury secretary and well-respected economist Lawrence Summers, had made remarks that seemed to disparage women's abilities, and the ensuing uproar contributed to his decision to resign. Faust's appointment seemed designed to show what a woman could do, and do she did. During her tenure, Faust oversaw the most successful university fundraising campaign in the history of higher education, easily surpassing the $6.5 billion goal of a campaign intended to benefit the whole university. Much of that money was aimed at achieving two of the primary goals of her presidency: increasing both the school's sustainability and its financial aid. A self-described rebellious daughter of the South, Faust went north for her education, graduating from Concord Academy in Concord, Massachusetts, and then from Bryn Mawr College, near Philadelphia. She went on to earn her PhD from the University of Pennsylvania, where she taught history and was an award-winning scholar of the American South from 1975 until 2001. She then moved to Harvard, where she served as the first dean of the Radcliffe Institute for Advanced Study. She retired as Harvard president in June 2018.

and work. These included women such as attorney Brenda Feigen Fasteau, who supported Gloria's Harvard Law address, a milestone on many levels, and her speaking partners Flo Kennedy, Dorothy Pitman, and Margaret Sloan. Given her wide-ranging travels and her countless personal and organizational connections, Gloria's list of friends is ever expanding, although the friends most closely tied to a specific project or cause tend to be less enduring and more utilitarian (Stern 1997).

Regardless of the length of their association or the exact nature of the relationship, each friend played an important role in Gloria's very private life. It remains one of the paradoxes of this woman that she is a major public figure who also remains, on many levels, a private enigma—shy and unknown. Perhaps it is rooted in the young actress who honed her skills dancing on the boardwalk of Clarklake, or perhaps in the teenager who put on her practiced face as she made the transition from caregiver to carefree teen among her peers in Toledo. Even into her eighties, Gloria has professed to dislike the public side of her life. And yet she recognized that celebrity—however distasteful it may have been—was important to her work as an organizer and advocate. And to observers it all seemed like second nature. But after all the years on the road, after the countless meetings with previously unknown people, knowing that there was a group who had known her through the years, who had seen the ups and the downs, and for whom the scoreboard had long stopped counting, provided a support and comfort whose value was incalculable.

One evening a month, a particularly special set of friendships is celebrated when the group of *Ms.* veterans join with Gloria in sessions that are nothing more than reunions of friends who have a history. While Gloria calls the gatherings "group therapy sessions," they are more noteworthy for the relaxed warmth of dedicated activists who once proudly stood shoulder to shoulder in battle, women who can now take pride not just in what they did but in the people with whom they did it.

From her Rolodex associates to the friends who would frequently crash on her floor, the range of Gloria's connections and friends illustrate a central aspect of her organizing philosophy. They also represent a meshing of the personal and political. While she is known as a feminist leader, she has long seen that as only a part of her larger role as an advocate for human rights. Perhaps it is a product of the fact that before she plunged into the women's movement she had already been involved, at least tangentially, in the civil rights movement, the antiwar movement, and the dump Johnson movement. And all of that was complemented by her time in India and with the ISI, not to mention her experience as a reporter. From the outset, she seemed to have a broader perspective on the movement and, perhaps even more importantly, was able to see the ways it intertwined with so much of the changing society of which it was a part.

Those interests were based in people and their human experiences. Despite its power, Betty Friedan's suburban middle-class perspective had inherent problems, while elected officials such as Bella Abzug were hampered by the limits of the electoral process. But lacking any real institutional constraints and drawing upon a distinctive set of experiences, Gloria Steinem was able to frame the issues in ways that often resonated with a broader audience. And for all of her celebrity, she was a low-key, empathetic revolutionary picking up one recruit at a time. She understood that each new story shared added an additional square in the quilt of humanity she was assembling.

At the same time, despite her many years as a public figure, certain contradictions never disappeared. While in many respects, her life was the embodiment of her message—freedom and equality to allow people to make their own choices—for many there was a disconnect, as Gloria's drumbeat for equal pay and for childcare centers for poor workingwomen clashed with her often glamorous social life. While she obviously had no control over what aspects of her life and work the media did or did not cover, the end result was often a mixed message in an era when nuance and thoughtful exposition were increasingly rare. However unintended, to many outsiders, the personal became political.

For all the glamour that seemed to define her nonworking life, Gloria never forgot her roots or her family. Despite wildly different lifestyles, Gloria and her sister Sue were supportive and close—but for the most part, it was a private, family-based relationship. While Gloria did make a point at her fiftieth birthday party of publicly thanking Sue for all she had done, going back to her days as a surrogate parent, it was one of the few public acknowledgments that either of them had ever made. Sue, for her part, appreciated how despite her extensive travel and countless public commitments, Gloria still made Ruth a part of her life. She noted that Gloria would have their mother come to visit in New York once Gloria had settled there. In addition, once Gloria was established, she annually took Ruth on a vacation, treating her again to some of the benefits that came from having a world-renowned daughter. In many ways, Ruth reveled in the reflected glory that Gloria's celebrity offered (Stern 1997).

Advances in medication allowed Ruth to live on her own, for the most part, in her later years, with few of the outbursts and incidents that had so characterized her life with Gloria. Gloria's time with Ruth also did much to reduce Sue's burden when she had to balance the demands of raising six children with returning to law school. It was a challenge that often saw Sue retreating to her parked car in an effort to find a quiet place to study. Near the very end, when Ruth was moved into a nursing home not far from Sue's home, Gloria visited frequently, and both sisters were at the hospital when she died. And they both sat with her for a while afterward, fulfilling a long-held promise to their mother, who was fearful that hospital attendants might mistake a coma for death (Stern 1997).

Interestingly, for all the criticism Gloria suffered over the years for her support of reproductive rights as well as her apparent disdain for the institution of marriage, she chose to never use Sue and her family as a defense. A ready-made, close-to-home example, they could have easily buttressed Gloria's contention that she was not looking to mandate a way of life but only trying to expand individual options. But while Sue could have been the poster child for Gloria's support for and understanding of the "family values" approach, she had far too much respect, admiration, and appreciation for her sister to exploit her life as a part of a public relations gambit. When it came to Sue, a woman married to the same man for over a half century, a proud mother of six (to whom Gloria was an equally proud aunt), and a respected career woman, Gloria refused to be anything but a grateful and loving sister.

At the same time, the sisters could not prevent the occasional reporter from investigating. And yet despite the stark contrast in their lives, it was not something that drew much attention. One of the few times that Sue was deemed a newsworthy partner of her sister was when an article entitled "Gloria Steinem's Sister: She Took Another Road" appeared in the February 18, 1978, issue of the *New York Times*. In the piece, Sue made clear that Gloria had never changed, and she noted that she always came to their home for Christmas and usually for Mother's Day, where Ruth would join them. She added that they also talked frequently on the phone. But they had their own lives. In the end, perhaps that said it all, for while Gloria had to become a public figure to pursue the cause to which she was so devoted, in private, and in her own way, Sue had lived that effort, with all the daily challenges it entailed. And Gloria was happy to let her do so. In the end, it was probably not an accident that when Sue died in 2007 at the age of eighty-two, Gloria warranted only a brief mention in the obituary, the last-named survivor, "a sister, Gloria Steinem of New York," right before "and 12 grandchildren."

In its own way, the passing mention was a fitting reflection of one important aspect of Gloria's life. Notwithstanding the headlines, photos, and mentions in the "style" section of periodicals, the high-profile Gloria Steinem has always been comparatively closemouthed about her private life. Yes, she has been frequently photographed, but she has been known less for the quantity of her comments than for the pithy nature of the ones she has made. Nonetheless, the never-retired journalist has preferred to be judged on the totality of her actions and not on a collection of one-liners. Similarly, she has felt no need to use her private life to refute the observations or perceptions of others. Whether it was failing to share her own story, declining to defend herself against Pat Nixon's frustration-inspired assertion that "she [Gloria] had it easy," or refusing to use Sue and her family as a defense against the countless accusations about Gloria's views on family, Gloria made no apologies and offered no excuses. She simply advocated for her cause.

8

The Good Fight in a Conservative Age

Ronald Reagan's election as president in 1980 changed everything for the women's movement. In fact, his victory was as much a product of the developing forces against the movement as it was a harbinger of the future. Jimmy Carter's presidency had, by all accounts, been something of a rollercoaster ride for feminists, but for all the disappointments, they could point to tangible triumphs such as the Houston Conference as well as the less easily defined, but no less real, attitudinal and societal changes that it represented. However, the election of Ronald Reagan, coupled with the defeat soon afterward of the ERA, brought the movement to a crossroads. Confronted with a new and well-organized opposition, Steinem and her allies had to reassess their approach, given the shifting social and political landscape. It was not easy.

Part of the problem was that conservatives, led by Phyllis Schlafly and aided by Jerry Falwell's "Moral Majority," had co opted the discussion. The conservative opposition had, for the most part, emerged on the national scene in response to both the Houston Conference and the effort to ratify the ERA. Schlafly, Falwell, and their allies framed their arguments in the context of "family values" and used that to attack feminists and their agenda. What the women's movement had touted as opportunities were presented by conservatives as the elimination of long-granted protections for women. For example, they argued feminism took alimony rights from women and threatened them with draft registration, particularly if the ERA were passed.

The Schlafly-led effort was certainly not new, nor was its strategy. The St. Louis lawyer and her allies had made their presence felt at the Houston Conference and in their ongoing effort to prevent ratification of the ERA in the 1970s. But those efforts had occurred when both the Congress and the presidency were controlled by the Democrats. The Republican victories in 1980 gave Republicans a majority in the Senate and created opportunities for the conservative agenda. Schlafly was no long an outsider relegated to simply putting up obstacles. Instead, she was able to work side by side with her fellow 1964 Goldwater supporter, Reagan, in an effort to roll back some of the advances for women that had marked the 1970s (Spruill 2017).

With his declared opposition to the ERA and abortion as well as his announced intention to cut social programs, Reagan represented a substantive rebuke to women's rights and the advances of the previous decade. And while this new challenge required the movement to rethink its direction and strategy, Gloria's commitment never wavered. Nor, by all appearances, had her influence waned. In fact, in an ironic twist, at the end of 1982 Gloria tied with Phyllis Schlafly for fifth place in *New York* magazine's list of the nation's most influential women, a list topped by Justice Sandra Day O'Connor, who had just completed her first full year on the High Court. Indeed, O'Connor's appointment reflected the growing political power that the women's movement had helped foster. Similarly, while the ERA was stopped dead in its tracks in 1982, the Democratic Party's nomination of

---

GERALDINE FERRARO

The 1984 selection of Congresswoman Geraldine Ferraro as the Democratic nominee for vice president not only guaranteed the New Yorker a place in history but also reflected the growing influence of women in American politics. The first in her family to graduate from college, she first worked as an elementary school teacher. Attending Fordham Law School part time, she earned her degree in 1960, the same year she married John Zaccaro, a realtor and businessman. While raising three sons, she worked as an attorney in her husband's real estate firm and got involved in local Democratic politics. In 1978 she was first elected to the House of Representatives. There she caught the eye of House Speaker Thomas P. (Tip) O'Neill. She quickly began climbing the ranks, being elected secretary of the House Democratic Caucus, a role that gave her a seat on the influential Steering and Policy Committee. While her selection for vice presidential candidacy by Walter Mondale was a surprise, she proved to be a successful candidate, although her effort was undermined by controversy surrounding her husband's business dealings. Although President Reagan cruised to an overwhelming victory over Mondale, Ferraro served as an inspiration to a generation of girls and young women who saw new doors opened with her nomination.

New York congresswoman Geraldine Ferraro for vice president in 1984 was a major, if symbolic, step forward. And even though her candidacy was undermined by allegations concerning her husband, not to mention being a victim of Reagan's overwhelming reelection victory, she reached a political height never previously scaled by a woman (Collins 2009).

Ferraro's selection was particularly sweet for Gloria, who had predicted that 1984 would be the year people talked seriously about putting a woman on the ticket. She was happily surprised when they actually did it. She celebrated the precedent-shattering choice by writing an article about Ferraro for *Ms.* and then featuring her on the cover. That symbolic triumph complemented a string of earlier Supreme Court decisions that had removed many long-standing, gender-based inequities, including women's exclusion from jury duty, unequal Social Security survivor benefits, and unequal military spousal benefits. In addition, society had begun to see the Title IX–based advances that would ultimately revolutionize sports for women and open new doors in academia.

Gloria's mother Ruth died in July 1981, less than a month before her eighty-third birthday. After all the pain of her years with a young Gloria in Toledo, advances in medication as well as a true understanding of her condition had combined to allow Ruth to live a more enjoyable and generally independent life in her later years. She was able to work part time, and whether she was living with Sue or out on her own, she was a doting grandmother. Ruth was also a proud mother who not only basked in the glow of Gloria's celebrity but also enjoyed the occasional perks that accompanied her daughter's status.

Title IX

Title IX of the Education Amendments Act of 1972 (known simply as "Title IX") is the federal law that prohibits discrimination based on gender in any education program receiving federal financial aid. With its passage, the door to college athletics was opened to women across the nation. Title IX was not just about sports, but admission to college as well as scholarships can rely upon an individual's athletic talent, and now talented female athletes could share in these benefits. That represented a major step forward in more than sports. But Title IX also became a source of controversy when its implementation began to have an impact on the number of men who could compete, a controversy based as much on the realities of football's overwhelming numbers as anything else. And yet, the high-profile success of American women in the Olympics as well as the national soccer team, not to mention the massive increase in female participation in the college ranks, demonstrate clearly the multidimensional impact of Title IX and its promise of equal opportunity.

Ruth's funeral service was at an Episcopal church in Washington, DC, that she had enjoyed attending (Marcello 2004). Unlike with Leo, Gloria had a sense of closure with Ruth, and she would later honor her mother's memory in print.

With the political winds blowing in an increasingly conservative direction, Gloria shifted much of her focus away from an unresponsive political process. Instead she pursued an approach designed to bring greater respect and dignity to all people. Gloria believed that the defeat of the ERA as well as the rise of the conservative movement was a product, in large part, of political naïveté. Liberals and feminists had underestimated not so much the Schlafly forces, although they were real, but also the opposition posed by real estate interests, insurance companies, and numerous other, similar special interests who believed that their worlds would be significantly altered by its passage. It was, she believed, those forces that turned their attention to politics and directed their resources to the state legislatures and in those efforts became cultural cousins of the problems she had encountered in countless advertiser meetings at *Ms.* (Cohen 1988).

In addition, the feminist movement stalled because even at its best, it had never been pitched or presented as a mainstream movement. Rightly or wrongly, it was seen by many Americans as a bunch of elite white women making a fuss, and Gloria appeared to fit that profile. None of these perceptions was easily broken, but Gloria recognized the problem needed addressing. Gloria also believed that the ERA failed because, while it as well as the movement had initially ridden the reform spirit of the sixties and earned a place in a changing American consciousness, by the time the first wave of ratifications had been achieved, the nation was in turmoil. The momentum for change that had characterized the previous decade had been lost. The Watergate scandal had eroded faith in government, and the way the Vietnam War ended in 1975 had diminished the nation's status around the globe. The gas shortage of the mid-seventies left drivers waiting in line at gas pumps, while the economy was experiencing a previously unknown phenomenon called "stagflation." The United States seemed at a loss, experiencing, in the words of President Carter, a "national malaise." All of this, coupled with the seizure of the U.S. Embassy in Iran in November 1979, set the stage for a major change in government.

For Gloria, the way to respond to that change was to continue to organize in an effort to reform a culture. She tackled issues such as pornography, feminism in the arts and literature, and women's studies programs, both in college and out. She also sought to broaden the consciousness-raising approach that had long characterized her speaking engagements, in an effort to empower women in ways unrelated to their politics but important to their everyday life. These grassroots efforts were particularly important at a time when high-profile advances obscured the continuing

> ### SANDRA DAY O'CONNOR
>
> When Ronald Reagan appointed Sandra Day O'Connor to the Supreme Court in 1981, he not only fulfilled a campaign promise but also provided new inspiration for a generation of female lawyers. With the ascension to the high court of a woman who, despite graduating near the very top of her Stanford Law School class, was only offered positions as a legal secretary, young female attorneys could now envision a whole new range of opportunities. For O'Connor, the appointment was not the fulfillment of a dream but, rather, simply the latest in a series of unexpected opportunities for public service. From the county district attorney's office to the state attorney general's office, she served the state's legal system with distinction, and a stint in the state legislature revealed exceptional political skills. In all these posts, she demonstrated an impressive devotion to public service, serving the people of Arizona in an admirable manner. Her appointment to the Supreme Court guaranteed her place in history. Yet it was her work over the course of her almost twenty-five years on the Court where O'Connor made her real mark. There, judiciously wielding her swing vote on issues ranging from abortion to affirmative action to the election of an American president, O'Connor left a distinguished legacy.

second-class citizenship of the average woman. Indeed, as the nation moved into the 1990s and Ronald Reagan was succeeded by George H. W. Bush, each passing day offered evidence of progress. In addition to appointing Sandra Day O'Connor to the Supreme Court, Reagan had also appointed three women to the cabinet while also naming Jeane Kirkpatrick as the first female U.S. ambassador to the United Nations. Meanwhile, George H. W. Bush followed with three women cabinet appointees of his own. These appointments tended to obscure the GOP's staunch opposition to the ERA and the fact that it ignored the continuing disparities for women in income and opportunities (Spruill 2017).

Gloria had spent much of the 1970s traveling the country spreading the gospel of feminism and seeking support for the ERA, but in many respects, her many travels during the conservative renaissance were even more important. She was an evangelist for a movement whose heyday had passed, but whose message needed to be spread to a new generation in the midst of political and cultural opposition that often seemed to have the upper hand. In her travels, Gloria encountered a United States that only a very few are privileged to see, but it was the kind of distinctive experience that allowed her to remain a self-proclaimed "hopeless hopeaholic."

Gloria was uniquely positioned to see the diversity of the nation, and she came to relish the characters she encountered, the stories she heard, and the lessons she learned. She fondly recalled the woman she met after a particularly difficult session at a boys prep school. The woman shared with Gloria her frustration with an executive husband and two sons who believed that boys were superior to girls, an opinion the student body had apparently shared. Inspired by Gloria's talk, the determined wife and mother expressed her desire to change opinions, and seeking to mount her own everyday rebellion, she inquired of Gloria about how she might volunteer at Dorothy Pitman's childcare center—something she would ultimately do for many years thereafter (Steinem 2015).

Gloria recalled with disbelief the northern white train conductor, who blithely allowed Gloria to proceed into the parlor car before trying to direct her African American traveling companion Dorothy to the cheaper seats in the rear, as well as the flight attendant who termed Dorothy's nursing of her baby aboard a plane "obscene" (Steinem 2015).

She also recalled the man in one audience, who vehemently voiced his objections to Dorothy and her message by shouting that Dorothy should go back home to Russia, only to have his comment met with derisive and dismissive laughter. And there was the young Latinx college student, the daughter of undocumented immigrants, who handed Gloria her card, which declared simply, "Candidate for U.S. President 2032" (Steinem 2015).

Gloria later noted the time after a radio interview when the female station manager gave her a studio tour. She asked if Gloria remembered the time, years before, when an airline pilot had put one of the flight attendants, a Black woman, off the plane for reading Eldridge Cleaver. Gloria recalled the incident and was surprised when the station manager revealed that the pilot had been her husband—whom she had divorced before going back to school and ultimately getting the job at the radio station. There was also the time when, traveling through the Bible Belt of the Southwest, she saw a set of paired billboards along the road—one promised everlasting life through Jesus while the other offered services to reverse a vasectomy. The combination, she thought, was simply surreal (Steinem 2015).

Gloria also remembered the 98-year-old former Ziegfeld dancer who was on her way to dance at an AIDS benefit on Broadway, accompanied by her 101-year-old friend. The two women told Gloria that events such as this one had been a regular part of their lives since the AIDS crisis began. When Gloria asked the nearly century-old woman how, after all these years, she remained herself, she answered impatiently, "You're always the person you were when you were born. You just keep finding new ways to express it" (Steinem 2015). Each encounter, each observation, enhanced Gloria's understanding and strengthened her commitment.

Throughout her career as an activist organizer, Gloria struggled with the impact of her celebrity status on her efforts. An experienced journalist and publicist, she well understood that before you could do anything else, you had to get people's attention, and yet she remained frustrated with the inevitable questions about her love life or the latest red carpet event. But she also understood her celebrity made it possible to talk about equality, reproductive rights, or the other issues of the day to a wider audience than if she were an anonymous activist. Her celebrity undoubtedly served as a draw for the countless local events that she did. But after years of experience Gloria knew that those in attendance, especially the women, wanted—in fact, needed—something more than a status report on her social life. Sitting in a talking circle, Gloria was stripped of celebrity and instead connected on a human level. Looking her audience in the eye, getting an understanding of their lives, helping facilitate discussions, she helped each individual make personal discoveries that furthered their growth, as attested to by the letters she and *Ms.* received. Whether the audience was college students, unwed mothers, aspiring professionals, or established ones whom others sought to emulate, each person had a story she wanted to hear.

In 1983 Gloria published her first book since 1963's *The Beach Book*. *Outrageous Acts and Everyday Rebellions* was primarily a compilation of twenty-six previously published works, including "I Was a Playboy Bunny" and "Campaigning." The book also featured two original pieces, one an introductory essay about Gloria's years as an organizer, and the other, "Ruth's Song (Because She Could Not Sing It)," a tribute to her mother. One critic called the essay about Ruth the most moving piece Gloria has ever written (Stern 1997). Despite the emotional toll the tribute took, it was, Gloria recalled, one of the quickest things she ever wrote. In looking back, with over a decade of feminist activism under her belt, Gloria saw in Ruth a life that was the embodiment of the challenges that women faced, challenges that in Ruth's case were too much to bear. To her daughter, years removed from the dank Toledo existence they had shared, Ruth was a victim of a society that had robbed her of the opportunity to write and have a career. Ruth's enforced housewifery had taken away her sense of self. As a result, a life had been lost. In reviewing her mother's life, Gloria gratefully remembered her sale of the house that allowed Gloria to go to college. She remembered the support and the encouragement that Ruth gave her two daughters as they made the kinds of lives that she would have relished. It was a poignant essay. Notwithstanding the frequent and almost overwhelming challenges Ruth had represented to Gloria as well as the burden she had often been, Gloria had a strong and distinctive bond with her mother. "Ruth's Song" was an opportunity for Gloria to express both her appreciation for her mother's sacrifices and her sense of her mother's loss. The essay was also a self-examination, for the piece made clear that in their own way, all her organizing efforts were aimed at ensuring that other women would not have to suffer the way that her mother had. Gloria Steinem, activist, organizer, humanitarian, was Ruth Steinem's legacy and song (Steinem 1983).

Outrageous Acts and Everyday Rebellions added another dimension to Gloria's reputation. Ultimately selling over a half million copies (with a third edition being released in 2019), it was a phenomenon that fueled Gloria's desire to return to writing. In the aftermath of the defeat of the ERA and the ascension to power of the conservatives, Gloria looked for other ways to develop the movement. Writing, which she had once characterized as the one thing she did that did not feel like work, fit the bill. While her commitment to *Ms.* never wavered—and depending upon the magazine's financial crisis of the moment, it often forced itself to the forefront—she now turned to books. Her marketability as an author was confirmed by the strong reviews and great sales that *Outrageous Acts* had received, and after an extended book tour that had only enhanced her celebrity and star power, Gloria began looking for another project.

In 1985 she decided to do a book on Marilyn Monroe, and it became the central activity of her summer. Gloria had previously written an article about the iconic actress for *Ms.*, and the piece was included in *Outrageous Acts*. Consequently, when its publisher contacted her about writing the text to accompany some photographs that photographer George Barris had taken shortly before Monroe's death, Gloria jumped at the opportunity. Given that *Ms.* had used copies of *Outrageous Acts* as a renewal gift for subscribers, she was able to use her work on Marilyn to pay off the debt caused by the giveaway. Gloria originally thought that she was writing little more than captions for a book's photographs, but the project turned out to be more extensive. In the end the book became an extended essay that looked not at Monroe's films but rather at her personality, which in addition to her distinctive looks and appearance was what Gloria believed made Monroe a cultural phenomenon (Steinem 1988). The response to the book was generally favorable, with many appreciating the way Gloria avoided sensationalism while exploring the actress's sensitivity. However, there were some who said that the work betrayed Gloria's superficial knowledge of psychology. In the end, the pairing of the icons of femininity and feminism garnered lots of public attention while selling moderately well (Stern 1997).

Gloria's return to writing did not represent a withdrawal from the political battlefront. Reagan's 1987 nomination of federal appeals court judge and conservative scholar Robert Bork to the Supreme Court galvanized the liberal opposition that had been on the defensive throughout the 1980s, and Gloria joined the fray. Recognizing the threat that Bork replacing centrist Lewis Powell posed to *Roe v. Wade* and other recent legal advances, Gloria, NOW, and their feminist allies were in the forefront of the opposition that made the confirmation hearing one of the most contentious in Court history. Allying with civil rights groups that feared Bork's impact on race-based litigation, their broad-based equality coalition was able to help beat back the nomination by a 58–42 vote. It was an important victory and a reminder of the political power that both Blacks and women could still wield.

Four years later, they were tested again when, with the retirement of civil rights icon Thurgood Marshall, President George H. W. Bush nominated federal judge Clarence Thomas, an African American judge on the U.S. Court of Appeals. Thomas's race complicated the politics of the effort, but his record as the assistant secretary for Civil Rights at the U.S. Department of Education and later as chairman of the EEOC made clear that the avowed conservative posed a threat to Roe and many other liberal causes. Recalling their success with Bork, feminists jumped into the battle. When law professor Anita Hill alleged that Thomas had sexually harassed her when they worked together in the Department of Education as well as at the EEOC, the hearing took on a whole different dimension. The charges and Thomas's subsequent response almost derailed the nomination, although he was ultimately confirmed by a 52–48 vote (Collins 2009).

To no one's surprise, Gloria had been in the forefront of the feminist leaders who voiced their support for Hill amid the doubts and challenges she faced. Despite taking and passing a polygraph test, Hill was demeaned and verbally abused by the all-male Senate Judiciary Committee. But at the same time, her poise and steadfast integrity made her a symbol and inspiration for countless women, and her testimony would reverberate decades later with the advent of the #MeToo movement. Meanwhile, in typical fashion, beyond giving Hill her support, Steinem seized the opportunity to shine a spotlight on the issue of sexual harassment. Reflecting her original vision of *Ms.* as a vehicle for highlighting such issues, in the aftermath of the Thomas hearings, the January/February 1992 issue of *Ms.* ran an article that traced the evolution of the sexual harassment up to the case of Anita Hill (Collins 2009).

The whole episode proved to be a precursor for a year of heightened female political activity and success. The 1992 elections, became known as the "Year of the Woman," an effort highlighted by the election of four new female U.S. senators, who joined the two incumbents. Meanwhile, the House of Representatives saw forty-seven women win election, twenty-four of them for the first time (Spruill 2017).

These political efforts represented only one element of Gloria's multifaceted campaign to expand the reach of feminism. In fact, she sought to transcend it and instead put the focus on humanism. In doing so, she could not help but put a more direct spotlight on areas in which women were singular victims. Two areas that symbolized this concern were pornography and sexual harassment. In typical Gloria fashion, in attacking the issue of pornography, she put a human face on it when she discovered actress Linda Lovelace's story and became her champion.

Gloria's long-established opposition to pornography dated back to her role as a founding member of the New York branch of Women Against Pornography, which emerged in the late 1970s. The group was particularly concerned with the violence against women that pornography often featured. The group, whose founders included Andrea Dworkin, Lois Gould, Shere Hite, Robin Morgan, Grace Paley, Letty Cottin Pogrebin, and Adrienne Rich, helped raise consciousness about the issue. However, it had a limited impact in the ongoing debates about an issue that raised questions about the nature of obscenity, erotica, female autonomy, and censorship. Indeed, those debates showed a split in the feminist ranks, as issues and groups were said to be either pro- or anti-sex, not to mention being more or less supportive of the long-hallowed protections of the First Amendment. Suddenly, the very question of what exactly women's liberation meant came under fire.

No aspect of the pornography industry of the 1970s and 1980s had a higher profile than the film *Deep Throat*. The film, one said to have ushered in the "Golden Age of Porn" was different from the standard pornographic films of the time. Released in 1972, it offered a plot, some character development, and was of significantly higher film quality than was the norm at the time. It also got more a more mainstream reaction, helping, in the view of some, to move porn from tawdry to chic. At the same time, the film's high profile also made it the subject of a celebrated federal obscenity prosecution that galvanized the film community and heightened the political debate that had long surrounded discussions of pornography. In the middle of it all was the film's female star, an actress whose screen name was Linda Lovelace but whose real name was Linda Boreman Marchiano.

Gloria first saw Marchiano in an interview with talk show host Phil Donahue in 1980, discussing her recently released memoir *Ordeal*. After hearing Marchiano's story of being raped and pimped by her husband as well as being forced at gunpoint to make *Deep Throat*, Gloria reached out to the actress. It was an inauspicious pairing, as Marchiano had never heard of Gloria and was not sure what feminism was. But in offering Marchiano a helping hand and then writing about her, Gloria exposed the violence of pornography and gave it a human face. Her association with Marciano and her presentation of the issue as one that was based on the objectification of women and that furthered their victimization helped alter public attitudes about pornography. Marchiano herself recognized Gloria's efforts, noting that upon the publication of Gloria's article on the actress in the May 1980 *Ms.*, people suddenly looked beyond her *Deep Throat* character and instead began to take her and her story seriously. Perhaps most importantly, the onetime porn actress gratefully noted that for the first time, people began to treat her with respect. All that she attributed to Gloria's efforts (Steinem 1983).

> **SALLY RIDE**
>
> When Sally Ride became the first American woman to go into space in 1983, she broke through more than a glass ceiling. Indeed, in going where no American woman had gone before, she sent an important message to the many who came after her that they could soar in whatever field they chose in the same way she had. A trained physicist with a PhD from Stanford, she joined NASA in 1978 after a tremendously competitive selection process. Only thirty-two at the time of her first space flight, she is the youngest American to have traveled in space. Ride did two flights on the Challenger, spending almost 350 hours in space, and she had completed training for a third flight when the Challenger disaster occurred in 1986. Ride left NASA in 1987, returning to Stanford to work at its Center for International Security and Arms Control. Then in 1989 she joined the faculty at the University of California, San Diego, as a professor of physics. Ride served on the committees that investigated both the Challenger and Columbia Space Shuttle tragedies. She was the only person who served on both investigative panels. Forever a symbol of the literal heights to which women could rise, Ride died of pancreatic cancer in 2012.

With television taking on an increasingly prominent role in the world of news, and given her obvious good looks, it was inevitable that Gloria would eventually gravitate toward television as a venue where she could both further her career and expand the impact of her activism. Gloria had long been a frequent guest on a range of news and interview shows, and in 1984 she hosted a show on the Lifetime cable network called *A Conversation with . . .*, where her celebrity guests had run the gamut from Walter Cronkite to Bianca Jagger and Sally Ride.

Two years later, in 1986, she began to appear regularly on *Today*. Working with producer Carla Morgenstern, whom she had gotten to know while helping with the Geraldine Ferraro vice presidential campaign, Gloria did a series of freelance interviews and reports. The segments, which ranged from interviews with Robert Redford, Cher, and Marlo Thomas to such subjects as a Texas AIDs center and a childcare center in Minnesota, began to air in May 1986. For a week in September that same year, she agreed to serve as *Today*'s cohost, while Jane Pauley was on maternity leave. Prior to that stint, concerned about her appearance, she had a procedure to remove some excess fat from her upper eyelids. She would later say that it had taken her twenty years to take the short, two-block walk from her apartment to the office where the procedure was done. The procedure was a simple one. However, for the most recognizable face in the feminist movement, a woman who had struggled throughout her time in the public eye with the effect of her looks on her status and message, the decision to have

> **BARBARA WALTERS**
>
> In the days before cable news and 24/7 news coverage, few people were a more constant part of daily American life than the anchors of the evening newscasts. Indeed, the moniker of "Most Trusted Man in America" that 1960s CBS anchor Walter Cronkite carried was a testament to his stature. Consequently, it was no small thing when in October 1976 Barbara Walters assumed the role of coanchor with Harry Reasoner on the *ABC Evening News*. Walters's ascension to the anchor chair after years of cohosting the softer NBC *Today* was both a step forward for women and a bow to the changing audience that included more women. While hosting *Today*, Walters had earned a reputation as a tough interviewer, which network executives hoped could become an asset on the news. Ultimately, the pairing did not work and despite the fact that Walters had been given a five-year contract, after two years ABC made a change, with Reasoner returning to CBS and *60 Minutes*. Walters became a regular on ABC's newsmagazine *20/20*, where her interviews became a staple. It was another fifteen years before another woman occupied the anchor chair, with Connie Chung teamed with Dan Rather at CBS.

such surgery, however small, was not simple. Nor was it wholly personal—for her or the political world in which she operated. As was true of many issues, Gloria dealt with her own operation as well as the broader issue of cosmetic surgery for all women only later in her book *Revolution from Within* (Steinem 1993). At the time she shrugged it off, noting that she would probably not have undergone the procedure but for her appearance on *Today*. Specifically, given the early morning hours that the show involved and her desire to wear contact lenses, the procedure allowed her to wear sleep-in lenses (Stern 1997).

Meanwhile, during that same period, Gloria was forced to deal with a far more important health issue. On the Friday before her stint on *Today*, Gloria was diagnosed with breast cancer. Despite the news, she did the week on *Today*, and when one producer pronounced that her performance was "not bad" she thought to herself, "Yes, especially since I have just been diagnosed with breast cancer."

The diagnosis was a surprise, especially since she had detected a small lump in her breast the previous November, but a mammogram had detected nothing and subsequent check-ups also revealed no problems. Once discovered, the surgeon and Gloria decided to remove the whole lump just to be sure. Injected with Novocain, Gloria watched the whole procedure, after which the tumor was sent to the lab, where it tested malignant (Stern 1997).

Suddenly, the woman who spent most of her life looking out for and looking after others had to take care of herself. It was not something that came easily. But when she told close friends about the situation, all the while assuring them that everything would be fine, they responded. They helped finance the hiring of an assistant who would care for Gloria. Initially, Gloria kept the news of the cancer private, tightly limiting the number of people she told. Not only did she not want to have to answer the question before she had answers of her own, but she feared the impact on advertisers or creditors of *Ms.* if word leaked out that the face and force behind the magazine was battling cancer. While she had to cancel numerous appointments and readjust her schedule, the official reason was that she had an inner ear infection, an ailment that made flying particularly problematic. Throughout this time Gloria investigated treatment options. In the end, she opted for a lumpectomy at Boston's Beth Israel Hospital. Typical of the Gloria network, Stan Pottinger helped find the surgeon. Meanwhile, Mort Zuckerman, who she knew hated hospitals, stayed away at Gloria's urging. He did fly her home on his corporate jet after the surgery and visited her while she underwent radiation treatments, which she did under her grandmother's name, to protect her privacy. She did this all while making the final preparations for a long-planned book tour to tout her newly released work on Marilyn Monroe. It was another Herculean Gloria effort, albeit one experienced out of the public eye (Stern 1997).

While tangible political progress in women's rights may have slowed in the Reagan years, from the start Gloria knew that change had to continue. The talking circles, organizing, and barnstorming around the country were all a part of Gloria's approach, one that made her a singular leader among the nation's reformers. Her longtime interest in politics certainly made her attuned to the electoral and legislative side of reform and change; her efforts on behalf of numerous legislative campaigns as well as the ERA are evidence of that. At the same time, Gloria understood that real change was less about structural or legal change than it was about attitudinal change, the kind that allowed women to realize that they did not have to be second-class citizens and that helped men to see that their world would not collapse if women were accorded equal legal rights. True change needed to be aimed at the nation's hearts and minds (Steinem 2015).

For Gloria, the determination to engage with women, wherever they were, stemmed from her understanding of the critical importance of engaging with people if the process of change were to happen. She understood that the enactment of legislation to prohibit race-based discrimination would not wipe hate from the snarling faces that had lined the streets of Birmingham. Nor would it stop the taunting of the marchers on the road from Selma to Montgomery. Similarly, neither the prohibition on gender-based discrimination in the Civil Rights Act nor the ratification of the ERA would erase the pay gap. Nor would either end the assumption that the office coffeepot was to be tended by the women in the office. All of the legal support was critical, but true equality of race and gender was going to be based in attitudes. And it would only come after getting people to shed the ideas of the past as they moved into the future. It was the pursuit of that kind of change that was at the center of every talking circle, every speech in a school gym or auditorium, and every encounter on a picket line.

This is why Gloria preferred to be referred to as an "organizer." It was a term that reflected the process that has been so satisfying for so many years. For all her reported glamour, at the core of Gloria's efforts have been the countless trips she has taken over the course of decades to help local groups raise funds, develop plans, and fight back against repression. In meetings featuring talking circles and shared stories—whether in auditoriums, school gyms, civic meeting halls, or family living rooms in the nation's largest cities and its smallest hamlets—she has sought both a human connection and a refuge from political frustration. She has been a cheerleader, a storyteller, a talent scout, and an inspiration. And through it all she has sought to raise and publicize the voices of women at the local level, for they embodied the empowerment that the movement was all about. Those efforts have been the real weapon in the course of the many years that followed the glory days of the 1970s (Steinem 2015).

In the end the most important part of Gloria's leadership was her willingness to listen. It made her accessible to those she sought to reach and it disarmed those who either resented, feared, or suspected her—of what was hard to know. She would never claim to reach them all, but the efforts she made and the empowerment that came from allowing women and men to tell their stories was central to the change she sought to achieve. It also was tremendously interesting and educational for her. Over the course of her traveling thousands of miles, cabdrivers, flight attendants, random seatmates, and anyone in between became a source of news and of insights. All of it enabled her to better understand what people wanted. The countless conversations and Gloria's ability to connect were critical to her ability to organize. It was there that she found common ground and helped others find it as well. Indeed, her own awakening was based on just such a personal discovery when the Red Stockings abortion meeting made her realize that her experience was not unique. From then on, she realized that there were so many others with comparable experiences that needed to be addressed. And so she set out to share that message (Steinem 2015).

That approach had gotten her through the lean years of conservative power holding, and like many feminists she greeted the election of Bill Clinton with considerable optimism. Yet the Clinton presidency presented

> ### Ruth Bader Ginsburg
>
> While she became a pop culture icon in her eighties, Supreme Court Justice Ruth Bader Ginsburg's contributions to the women's movement began many years before she became a judge. From her earliest days, the young woman, whose mother died the weekend before she was to graduate as valedictorian of her high school class, possessed a passion for equality and for helping people achieve their potential that would fuel her future endeavors. Ginsburg's pioneering efforts as a law professor and as the head of the ACLU's Women's Rights Project led one commentator to call her the "Thurgood Marshall of the Women's Movement." Using the equal protection provision of the Fourteenth Amendment, Ginsburg the lawyer carefully chose cases that presented the Court with the opportunity to overturn laws based in unsupportable assumptions about gender roles and abilities. In choosing cases where the law sometimes discriminated as much against males as against females, but always because of a distinction based in nothing other than gender, Ginsburg made major strides and was able to convince the Supreme Court to remove numerous barriers to the achievement of legal equality for women—and men. Those efforts continued as a jurist, first on the U.S. Court of Appeals and then on the Supreme Court.

its own set of problems. The political center had shifted to the right, and the women's movement was one of the shift's many victims. First Lady Hillary Clinton was seen as a strong symbol of the modern woman that the movement had sought to empower. And yet even she was compromised. She returned to her married name in the 1980s after her husband lost a gubernatorial reelection campaign and she learned that her use of her maiden name was identified as a major political flashpoint. And the "bimbo factor" that dogged Bill Clinton's political history, a factor that she seemingly tolerated, made Hillary a less-than-perfect advocate for the feminist cause. From the awkward handling of potential female cabinet appointments to the affair with intern Monica Lewinsky that ultimately led to his being impeached, Bill Clinton all too often strained relations with what should have been a loyal feminist core group. In addition, his politically pragmatic approach on such issues as welfare, an approach that seemed to take a tougher stand on issues central to the daily lives of women than women would have preferred, only added to the tensions. On the other hand, feminists could take solace in Clinton's appointment of Madeline Albright as the first female secretary of state and Janet Reno as the first female attorney general. And, of course, his appointment of Ruth Bader Ginsburg to the Supreme Court would only grow more significant as the years passed.

All of these actions, among others, served as reminders of the changes in the culture that feminists had achieved while continuing to move the ball forward. And yet, as the United States entered the twenty-first century, feminists such as Gloria knew that much remained to be done (Spruill 2017).

9

An Eye on the Future

Gloria reached the traditional retirement age of sixty-five with no signs of slowing down. Rather, she continued to move her agenda forward while educating and collaborating with the next generation of activists. Election politics was one area in which she remained active. While at one time a self-proclaimed radical, the ever-pragmatic Gloria increasingly put a greater emphasis on electing women and men who could turn her political ideas into policy.

Take, for example, her approach to the 1980 and 2000 presidential elections. While the women's movement's differences with Jimmy Carter had been evident throughout his term, with the specter of a Ronald Reagan presidency hanging over the election, the third-party candidate John Anderson represented a philosophically enticing option for activists. And yet, in the end, believing that the liberal Republican congressman from Illinois would in fact only detract from Carter's chances to defeat the conservative Reagan, Gloria joined together with a group of friends to take out a full-page ad in the *New York Times* in support of Carter (Spruill 2017).

Similarly, in 2000, despite longtime ties and many alliances with Ralph Nader—he had even been a guest at her fiftieth birthday gala—Steinem wrote an op-ed piece explaining that despite her philosophical compatibility with Nader, she could not support the longtime reform activist. Her objection to Nader's campaign was not about ideology or platforms but rather about electoral viability. She was concerned that support for Nader could split Democrats' votes and lead to the election of the conservative

George W. Bush, a candidate whose stances on issues such as reproductive rights and affirmative action were distinctly antifeminist.

Despite her occasional claim to being a radical, Gloria has always taken a pragmatic view of politics. From the beginning, a central element of Gloria's pursuit of the feminist agenda has been her work on behalf of candidates who support women's issues and who could further her social agenda. No less central was her long-held view that the women's movement was part of a broader humanistic movement, one that could be furthered through the political process. Thus, she continued to campaign for candidates who could do so, regardless of the candidate's gender or her personal feelings. To this end, she has always campaigned as a volunteer, a status that left the autonomous Gloria able to operate unencumbered by the constraints of a payroll or a party line. For Gloria, the freedom of being a campaign volunteer was also the freedom to engage in policy conversations, and while most of her volunteer efforts involved advocating for a candidate or cause, they also allowed for the dialogues she believed were essential to democracy (Steinem 2015).

Her battles with the Phyllis Schlafly forces of the 1970s and 1980s made clear the potential power of conservative women, but Gloria Steinem recognized the irony in the emergence of conservative, Tea Party firebrands such as Alaska governor and 2008 Republican vice presidential nominee Sarah Palin and Minnesota congresswoman and 2012 presidential aspirant Michelle Bachman. Both women were products of the advancements women had achieved because of the efforts of Steinem and her peers. And so, in spite of, or perhaps because of, the conservative resurgence, Steinem continued a political involvement that dated back decades to the NWPC and the campaigns of the late 1960s and early 1970s.

While the list of people she has campaigned for is lengthy, Gloria's efforts have reflected no focused or considered strategy; they all, however, have reflected a central lesson that she traces back to her experience in the 1980 Missouri U.S. Senate race. There she campaigned in support of Harriett Woods's insurgent effort against incumbent Senator John Danforth. Steinem cites that election as an object lesson for two very important political principles. First, who won mattered. It was a point she consistently pounded home to feminist audiences, reminding them that in the aftermath of his victory, Danforth brought the young attorney Clarence Thomas to Washington to serve on his staff. That appointment started Thomas's climb through the Republican ranks, a journey that culminated with his 1991 appointment to a seat on the Supreme Court—and to take it even further, to his being one of the votes that elected George W. Bush president over Albert Gore Jr. The rest was history. Second, the Woods campaign illustrated all too clearly the importance of money in electoral politics. In 1980, in the final weeks of the campaign, Woods ran out of money. Consequently, in addition to being outspent almost 2–1 over the course of the campaign, in the final weeks Woods had to pull a set of effective television ads. Wood's loss would ultimately be a major motivating force behind the establishment of Emily's List, a feminist fundraising operation that would provide critical financial support for countless feminist candidates in the following decades (Steinem 2015).

Year after year Gloria has made countless appearances on behalf of lesser known, underfunded candidates. An appearance by Gloria Steinem and the local buzz it could create or the added funds it could raise could change the whole tenor of a campaign. Those were in fact, the more comfortable and rewarding efforts for Gloria, especially since she disliked being overly tied to a party line. Consequently, appearing on behalf of candidates running in local races where she could take a more personal approach was far more appealing, and such events came to increasingly dominate her calendar.

A prime example was the experience of Sharon Sayles Belton, for whom Gloria initially campaigned in 1983 when Belton won her first race for a seat on the Minneapolis City Council. Gloria's efforts helped mark the beginning of a political career that would see Belton elected City Council president in 1990 and mayor in 1993, the first African American and the first woman in the city's history to achieve that office. Similar efforts continued year in and year out. Typical of her efforts was 1996, a presidential election year and one in which Gloria appeared in support of over twenty-five candidates in races unrelated to the presidential contest. That year also revealed one of the unintended consequences of the NWPC's increasing success: the need to choose between two strong women candidates (Steinem 2015).

That year, respected judge Renee R. Roth, completing her fourteen-year term on the Manhattan Surrogate's Court, was challenged by longtime political figure and local officeholder, respected feminist Karen S. Burstein, who had abandoned a seat on Family Court two years before to make an unsuccessful run for state attorney general. Gloria and many of her friends were unhappy with Burstein's challenge, as it could split the feminist community. Nonetheless, Gloria (and most others) backed Roth, the ultimate winner, citing her experience as the reason for the support. While a difficult situation, it was evidence of women's increased political success.

The 2008 presidential campaign also put Gloria in an uncomfortable position after she wrote an op-ed piece for the *New York Times* in which she announced her support for then senator Hillary Clinton over Barack Obama, asserting that gender was probably the most restricting force in American life. The op-ed and her decision were met with criticism in some quarters, with readers arguing that she had made a knee-jerk feminist decision. Given her longtime sympathy for the civil rights movement and the quest for Black equality, she was hurt by the attacks and she responded in part by noting that she believed that Clinton was the more experienced candidate (Steinem

2015). Ultimately, the whole incident served as a reminder that even at her age, wading into the political waters was not without its risks. Of course, when Obama beat Clinton for the nomination, Gloria proved an active and enthusiastic supporter of his campaign. In an allusion to the fact that she was not an automatic female supporter, she noted that the choice of Alaska governor Sarah Palin as the Republican candidate for vice president was in no way enough to earn her support for that ticket.

During the 2016 campaign, Gloria was in typical campaign travel mode. At the outset of that contest, Gloria already had a relationship with Senator Bernie Sanders, a candidate from Vermont, one that illustrated her individualized, election-by-election approach to support. Sanders got off to a rough start with feminists when, as mayor of Burlington, he saw his 1986 independent campaign for governor foundering and desperately claimed that he would better serve women than the incumbent Madeline Kunin, the state's first female chief executive and a vocal supporter of the ERA. However, a decade later, things had changed. While the opponent in his 1996 bid for reelection to the House was a woman, Republican Susan Sweetser, Steinem made a point of traveling to Vermont to endorse Sanders. She even joked that she had come to the Green Mountain State to make the congressman "an honorary woman" (Murphy 2016).

However, his strong feminist credentials aside, Steinem was something less than happy when Sanders challenged Hillary Clinton for the Democratic

---

HILLARY RODHAM CLINTON

No woman represents the gains that women have made in the political arena more than Hillary Clinton does. From first lady to U.S. senator to secretary of state and then finally to being the first woman nominated by a major party to run for president, she has had an unparalleled public career. Her political career ended when she lost the presidency in the Electoral College, after winning the popular vote by just under three million votes. Yet over the course of a lifetime, Hillary Clinton has seen highs and lows and with each step has embodied the dreams and disappointments of a large swath of the American populace. She has been an object lesson for a life in politics and especially of the distinctive challenges a woman faces. With all the triumphs and disappointments, she represents clearly how far women have come—and still have to go. A 1969 graduate of Wellesley, a Seven Sisters member, in the era just before the Ivy League went coed, Clinton's life, as well as her public career, which began when she worked for the House Judiciary Committee during the impeachment proceedings of President Richard Nixon, offers a clear picture of the evolving role of women in American government over the past half century.

presidential nomination in 2016, for as the campaign began, former senator and secretary of State Clinton was the undisputed front runner for the nomination and could possibly have become the nation's first woman president. But as the campaign unfolded and Clinton was challenged by Sanders, two of Gloria's core beliefs came into conflict. Gloria had a long history with the Clintons and supported Hillary Clinton instead of Barack Obama in 2008, when the issues of race and gender were seen by many as being in conflict. Now the issue was women versus economic populism, and while Gloria's political history would have made Sanders an easy choice in a contest with another male, Hillary Clinton was a different story. Her years as a senator and in the cabinet coupled with her proximity to power as former first lady made the choice a comparatively easy one to make. But Gloria muddied the waters when she seemingly scolded the young women who were supporting Sanders over Clinton, glibly asserting that younger female campaign volunteers were joining Sanders's camp in order to meet young men (Weller 2016).

Although Steinem's comments were echoed by former secretary of state Madeline Albright, they created a firestorm. And yet in their own way, they were a reflection of the progress that an American society fueled by Gloria and her colleagues had achieved. Having never had to confront the barriers and obstacles that their mothers had, the generation of young people, one that had been impacted by the Great Recession more than by gender discrimination, was more receptive to Sanders's economics-based arguments than they were to Clinton's gender-based ones, especially given her ties to Wall Street. Indeed, analysts also found that for that generation of young women, the question was not whether a woman could be elected president, but when. There was an inevitability in their view that Gloria's generation had never experienced. As a result, they were less concerned about electing a woman, and especially this particular woman, than they were about supporting someone who would help provide them with economic opportunities. The fact that economics, rather than gender issues, was in the forefront of young women's decision making was, in its own way, a good indicator of just how far the nation had come over the four decades that Gloria had been preaching the feminist gospel.

Once Clinton had won the Democratic nomination, Gloria campaigned actively on her behalf in the effort to make the long-held dream of a woman president a reality. Gloria also campaigned for a range of local candidates, such as Democrat Deborah Ross in North Carolina, who sought election to the Senate against incumbent Richard Burr. In many ways, the 2016 presidential election should have been a victory lap for the nation's leading feminist. But of course, it was not.

Instead, all of those efforts were a prelude to a general election contest that seemed to fly in the face of the emerging #MeToo movement—not to mention feminist progress in general. Despite vigorous efforts by feminists across the country who were determined to see the first woman in the White House, Clinton, while triumphing in the popular vote, was defeated in terms of electoral votes by the Republican nominee, businessman Donald Trump. The triumph of the notoriously misogynist Trump, a man whose disrespectful behavior toward women has been a hallmark of his career, represented a slap in the face to countless women across the country. A known womanizer who has been accused by numerous women of sexual harassment and assault, he has even been caught on tape bragging about how he could sexually assault women without concern, since he was famous. But to too many people, none of that seemed to matter. His election served as a stark and painful reminder that for all the progress the women's movement had fostered, it still had a very long way to go.

To no one's surprise, Gloria was ready for the challenge, and she made that clear through her lead role in the Women's March on Washington, part of a nationwide protest that took place on January 21, 2017, the day after Donald Trump's inauguration. Deemed the largest single-day protest in U.S. history, the marchers advocated for policies fostering human rights, including racial equality, women's rights, immigration reform, reproductive rights, and religious freedom. The march, a hallmark of the opposition activism that would mark his presidency sought to send a message to the Trump administration that the marchers would not retreat from their goal of a nation committed to greater equity and justice. An honorary cochair of the march as well as one of the speakers, Gloria reminded the new president, as well as the thousands of onlookers that the American Constitution begins not with "I, the President" but rather "We, the People." It was a message she and the movement would continue to share over the coming years (Hess 2017).

In 2018 Gloria hit the road again for the midterm elections. Gloria first tweeted her support and then later appeared on behalf of Rachel Cooks, a candidate for the Ohio state legislature. Cooks was a former Trump Tower receptionist who, during the 2016 presidential campaign, had come forward and accused Donald Trump of sexual harassment. While her candidacy was unsuccessful, Gloria shared Cooks's frustration that Trump had not suffered any consequences for his harassment of multiple women. In another 2018 effort, Gloria returned to Toledo, where she campaigned on behalf of state representative Teresa Fedor, a Toledo Democrat who successfully won a return trip to the Ohio state senate. Gloria had first met Fedor two years before, when she was in Toledo as part of a book tour sponsored by the city's public library.

The 2019 Chicago mayoral election pitted two female candidates in the runoff, a situation that provided some measure of satisfaction for Gloria, whose memories of the Windy City included having her glasses broken in the midst of the melee that was the 1968 Chicago Democratic Convention. Over the years, Gloria had often returned to the city, offering support in 1979 for its first female mayor, ERA backer Jane Byrne, and in 2010 for former senator Carol Moseley Braun in her mayoral campaign against Rahm Emanuel. Her 2019 endorsement of the victorious Lori Lightfoot, the city's first female African American mayor, again reflected her independent choice of candidates.

As the 2020 presidential election ratcheted up and President Trump made clear his intention to seek a second term, Steinem did not remain on the sidelines. While she offered no early formal support, in January 2019 she was reported to be one of the twenty influential women whom New York senator Kirsten Gillibrand met with in advance of launching her candidacy for president. There were other women in the race, but early indications were that Gillibrand, with whom Steinem had worked previously, intended to make feminism and issues of particular concern to women a central focus of her campaign. Later in the campaign, in May 2019, Gloria announced that New York mayor Bill de Blasio was the only male among the four contenders she was considering backing. Her support of the liberal New York chief executive represented a change from the 2013 mayoral race when she had initially backed Christine Quinn, then the Speaker of the New York City Council. However, since de Blasio took office, Gloria has offered support for a number of his initiatives, offering particular praise for his efforts to secure a guaranteed paid parental leave for some of the city's workers. Reflecting his appreciation of her efforts, he named her an honorary commissioner of his Commission on Gender Equity. Ultimately neither Gillibrand nor de Blasio's campaigns gained any traction, and they were among the early withdrawals.

Gloria's continuing activism was not limited to politics and elections. In fact, when two issues—pornography and sexual harassment—with which she had been deeply involved during the Reagan and Bush years reemerged, Gloria again stepped into the fray. In 1997 she again entered the pornography wars. She wrote an op-ed piece criticizing the way the film *The People vs. Larry Flynt* turned publisher Larry Flynt into a First Amendment hero when, in her view, he was simply a fortunate beneficiary of the protections offered by the hallowed part of the American Constitution. Gloria suggested there would not have been a similarly laudatory response had the film been about someone who exploited and tortured animals or Jews the way that Flynt did women. However, a dwindling box office for the film coupled with less award recognition than had been anticipated led many observers to decry Gloria's actions as censorship (Stern 1997).

Meanwhile, as noted, Gloria had met actress Linda Marchiano in 1980 and had become a supporter and champion of her cause. Their involvement continued until Marchiano's death in 2002. In the aftermath of their initial meeting back in 1980 and Gloria's article in *Ms.* on Marchiano's experiences, Gloria and feminist attorney Catharine MacKinnon had begun to investigate the legal options Marchiano might have, and while MacKinnon initially thought there might be grounds for Marchiano to file a civil suit for damages under federal civil rights laws, they soon recognized that the statute of limitations prevented such an effort. However, Marchiano's experiences did serve as a partial inspiration for the effort that MacKinnon and Andrea Dworkin later undertook to bring pornography under the umbrella of the Civil Rights Act. Their efforts culminated in an antipornography ordinance that was adopted in 1984 by the city of Indianapolis, although the legislation was later ruled unconstitutional.

In 2013 the release of the film *Lovelace* reintroduced the public to Gloria's often overlooked involvement with the former porn actress when the credits for the biopic revealed that Gloria and MacKinnon had served as consultants on the film. This led to a new round of stories about their involvement with the late actress and the issue of pornography. It was because of their earlier association with Marchiano that the feminist allies initially became involved with the movie, for when producers wanted to do a film based on her life, they went to MacKinnon, who had served as the actress's attorney, for permission. She obtained it from the family, but in an effort to protect Marchiano's interest and be sure that the filmmakers did justice to her life and struggles, MacKinnon arranged for her and Gloria to serve as consultants on the film. Beyond a desire to ensure fair treatment of Marchiano, Gloria saw the film as another vehicle for raising awareness about pornography. Concerned about the way that the Religious Right's "Family Values" campaign had reduced the number of school-based sex education programs, she recognized that for too many young people, pornography had become a form of sex ed and that the messages it offered about the treatment of women were both dehumanizing and dangerous. Consequently, Gloria saw *Lovelace* both as a way to educate people about the ways pornography was dangerous to women while also serving as a valued and honorable part of Marchiano's legacy.

Similarly, sexual harassment became an ever more politically charged issue with the onset of the #MeToo movement. Indeed, with roots in the 1970s, it was very much on Gloria's radar in the 1980s and 1990s, highlighted by the explosive 1991 confirmation hearing of Supreme Court nominee Clarence Thomas. Given her distinctive perspective, in 2017 Gloria noted that the roots of the #MeToo movement could be found forty years earlier, in the successful filing of sexual harassment lawsuits by three Black women, two against the federal government and one against a bank. All of these laid the foundation for the unanimous 1986 Supreme Court decision that brought sexual harassment under the umbrella of the Civil Rights Act of 1964—and declared it a violation.

At the same time, sexual harassment, like pornography, split feminists while also leading to some after-the-fact mea culpas when revelations about previous actions often collided with longtime political loyalties. It was easy when Donald Trump's rhetoric and record, coupled with his programmatic priorities in the area of reproductive rights and funding for Planned Parenthood, made him an obvious villain. Meanwhile despite having been on the Supreme Court for over twenty-five years, Clarence Thomas remained both a symbol and a reminder of previous hard times. However, when #MeToo led to a reconsideration of the Bill Clinton-Monica Lewinsky affair and accusations against liberal stalwarts such as Minnesota senator Al Franken, feminist veterans like Gloria had to do some serious thinking: Where did one draw the line? Who was deserving of a second chance? The intersection of politics and feminism became complicated. How did one measure a man's inappropriate behavior against a full career of politically progressive action? It all made for a tricky terrain and one Gloria had to navigate.

In fact, Gloria had already walked this tightrope during the Clinton years. At that time, in a March 22, 1998, *New York Times* op-ed titled "Feminists and the Clinton Question," she had not challenged the accounts of the president's accusers, but she did conclude that what they described was not, in fact, sexual harassment. Her conclusion pleased no one, and she was the object of considerable criticism by publications ranging from the *Times* itself to the *Harvard Crimson*.

Decades later, Gloria expressed immediate respect and admiration for the #MeToo movement, noting with great excitement the increased level of engagement and activism it represented. It also led her to share some of her own experiences, memories from a time when such actions were, if not accepted, certainly unremarked upon, and definitely a part of the landscape that a working woman had to navigate. In an interview in early 2018, Gloria recalled that when she, as a freelance writer, delivered articles to the magazine's office, the editors would occasionally follow up by asking if she wanted to go to a hotel room in the afternoon. She also recalled an incident when at age thirty, shortly after the publication of "A Bunny's Tale," which had, of course, documented more than a few such indignities, she and author Terry Southern were sitting on a couch waiting for the man whose office it was to arrive. Suddenly Southern turned toward her, grabbed her wrist, and moved in to kiss her. In response, Steinem bit his cheek, drawing blood. She recalled not giving it a second thought. She said her reaction was instinctual and reflected the way she had been brought up. At the same time, it made her realize that most women had been acculturated to be obedient and submissive to male advances, even unwanted ones. She noted that Southern, who would, in fact, remain a longtime acquaintance, would for years afterward joke about the resulting scar. And yet the lesson she learned there resonated with Gloria as #MeToo emerged (Collins-Hughes 2018).

Ironically, in areas where Gloria had been in the forefront of efforts to achieve change, those efforts came back to haunt her. Suddenly in an altered landscape, she was viewed in a different light. While Gloria had been in the forefront of the effort to highlight sexual harassment after the testimony of Anita Hill and had pushed *Ms.* to conduct one of the earliest public investigations of the issue at a time when, as Gloria put it, the problem had no name, she too got caught in the shifting sands of the cultural landscape. In fact, as the #MeToo Movement assumed center stage and major public figures such as Franken and New York attorney general Eric Schneiderman were forced to resign, the 1998 *New York Times* op-ed piece she had written in defense of President Bill Clinton with regard to his relationship with White House intern Monica Lewinsky, as well as in view of the charges from Paula Jones and others, proved embarrassing. Despite her expressed support for the movement, Gloria was left in an uncomfortable, defensive position. And yet, confronted in 2017 with questions about her previous support for the president—the spouse of a woman Steinem had twice enthusiastically supported for president—Gloria remained resolute. She refused to apologize or to condemn Clinton for the affair with Lewinsky. At the same time, she essentially ignored the sexual harassment allegations made by onetime Arkansas state employee Paula Jones—a treatment that some modern female commentators have charged was a classic case of "slut-shaming" and blaming the victim. It was not a position that could be easily squared with Gloria's rhetoric (Redden 2017).

Although vehement in her denunciation of President Donald J. Trump, whom she called the "Harasser in Chief," and outspoken in her assertions that the women who have accused Trump must be believed, her support for Bill Clinton seemed, at best, hypocritical. Indeed, while her support of Anita Hill in 1991 had put her in the forefront of the sexual harassment issue, and despite speaking out forcefully against the Supreme Court appointment of Judge Brett Kavanaugh, believed likely to vote to overturn *Roe v. Wade* and accused of the sexual assault of a high school classmate, Gloria's credibility was undercut by the Clinton defense of long ago.

The whole situation was particularly ironic given that a November 5, 2017, article in the *New York Times*, addressing the rise of the #MeToo movement, referenced the trailblazing 1977 *Ms.* cover story on sexual harassment. The *Times* called the article as relevant in 2017 as it had been when it was first published. And yet Gloria's standing was damaged by her refusal to apologize for her Clinton defense. She has said only that she would probably not write the same thing today, adding that how things are construed at one time are not necessarily construed the same way at another. Ultimately, as was often the case for someone who has been on the battle lines as long as she has and, especially in Gloria's case, who has always been all about moving forward, she refused to revisit the past. Instead, she trained her eyes on the current state of things, where she was vehement about the need to address President Trump's harassment of women.

Gloria's late career activism was not limited to electoral politics or responding to public controversies. She continued to pursue new initiatives. As the world changed, Gloria became even more insistent on expanding the feminist tent. In an increasingly interconnected world, she was deeply engaged in international issues related to women. She has also made clear that issues of war and peace cannot be ignored, given their obvious impact on all people. Consequently, she has become more and more involved in organizations and efforts addressing issues of war and peace and international human rights.

To reiterate, over the years Gloria has never wavered in her determination to have people understand that the women's movement was part of a broader one that, like the civil rights movement before it, came under a bigger umbrella of human rights. She was particularly gratified when, in the mid-1990s, then First Lady Hillary Clinton, speaking at a United Nations conference in Beijing, declared, "Women's rights are human rights." Meanwhile, that same motivation led Gloria to greater involvement in other humanistic areas, especially those relating to war. She was outspoken in her opposition to the 1991 Gulf War as well as the incursion against Iraq launched in 2003. Changing world conditions coupled with her longtime global perspective led Gloria to only greater involvement in such issues in the twenty-first century. Barely a week after the September 11 attacks, she joined a long list of luminaries including Harry Belafonte, Ruby Dee, Ossie Davis, Barbara Ehrenreich, Mike Farrell, Danny Glover, Randy Hayes, Michael Lerner, Bonnie Raitt, Edward Said, and Martin Sheen in issuing a statement titled "Justice not Vengeance." The statement called on President George W. Bush to show restraint in his response to the attacks, arguing that a military response would not solve the problem but would only begin a cycle of violence, while urging him to pursue justice as sanctioned by the rule of law. Give this stance, it was no surprise that she was deeply disturbed by the American incursion into Iran and was an active backer of Senator John Kerry in the 2004 presidential election. At the same time, her support for Kerry was also a product of her ongoing concerns about the Supreme Court, where potential replacements for an aging group of jurists raised fears about the long-term safety of the decision in *Roe v. Wade*.

Also reflective of her global interests, Gloria helped found Donor Direct Action, the fundraising arm of the think tank Sisterhood Is Global Institute that was founded in 1984 by Simone de Beauvoir and Robin Morgan. In addition, she was a cofounder of Direct Impact Africa in 2008. The organization seeks to address the challenging wildlife-human conflict in Zambia while also fostering economic self-sufficiency as well as individual empowerment among rural African villagers in the region. In addition, since its founding in the early 1990s, Gloria has been actively involved with Equality Now, an international organization whose network of activists, lawyers, and other supporters have worked to hold governments across the globe responsible for ending legal inequality, sex trafficking, and sexual violence and other harmful, sex-related practices, such as female genital mutilation and "child marriage." A longtime board member, she holds the title of "Board Chair Emerita."

Another important undertaking was a collaboration with Robin Morgan, with whom Steinem served as the curator of the October 2017 Festival Albertine, a French-American cultural gathering in Manhattan. Sponsored by the Sisterhood Is Global Institute, the festival examines and celebrates feminism around the world (Ryzik 2017).

Ever concerned with the rights of men and women, in the summer of 2005, Gloria joined a coalition made up of individuals as well as groups, including the Center for Constitutional Rights, the Culture Project, Code Pink, Eve Ensler, Not in Our Name, and United For Peace and Justice; the coalition was created to demand the shutdown of the American Guantánamo Bay prison camp. The group's demands were in response to reports that in the aftermath of 9/11 and the U.S. War on Terrorism, American interrogators had engaged in abusive behavior and torture of their prisoners at the facility.

In 1993 Gloria had helped launch the first "Take Our Daughters to Work Day." The educational program sponsored by the *Ms.* Foundation sought to highlight the role of women in the workplace while raising the consciousness of future working women (Stern 1997). Further reflecting the changing societal landscape as well as Gloria's commitment to equal opportunity for all, the event's name was changed in 2003 to "Take Our Daughters and Sons to Work Day."

Gloria has long recognized that organizational structure is critically important to social justice movements' success. Consequently, over the course of the years and across the issues spectrum, she has been actively involved in the creation and operation of numerous groups, organizations, and institutions. While Gloria's many and wide-ranging activities and organizations have sometimes seemed disjointed and disparate, in fact they are all pieces that she has worked to stitch together into a patchwork quilt of causes. Typical of these was the creation of the Women and AIDS Fund, an organization supported by the *Ms.* Foundation to support women living with HIV/AIDS. Another was the founding in 2005, with Jane Fonda and Robin Morgan, of the Women's Media Center, an organization aimed at helping to raise the profile and political power of women in the media by securing broader distribution of their work (Steinem website). But in addition to helping get women's work into circulation, the center also provides the media with names of female experts for commentary or analysis, a practice that helps further raise their profile and awareness of their work. What is more, the center also monitors the media, offering periodic reports on both the status and the presentation of women in the media, collectively an institution that has long influenced the perception of women in society.

Gloria's efforts over the years have been so widespread that it is difficult to label her. For example, Ai-Jen Poo, the executive director of the National Domestic Workers Alliance, remembers Gloria involved in a vigil conducted by domestic workers in front of the governor's office in an effort to get him to push for the ultimate passage in 2010 of the New York State Domestic Workers Bill of Rights. Poo sent Steinem a last-minute note seeking help; not only did she appear at the event, joining the women in the picket line, but she also brought friends, all of whom joined the effort while sharing stories about previous efforts. Poo recalled that Gloria's presence did much to make the domestic workers feel valued while affirming the justness of their cause.

Gloria also became increasingly sensitive to the particular issues of African Americans. Her ongoing efforts were recognized in the spring of 2018, when she appeared along with former vice president Al Gore and Congressman John Lewis, a civil rights icon, as one of the speakers at the opening of the National Memorial for Peace and Justice and the associated Legacy Museum in Montgomery, Alabama. The memorial and museum were intended to renew American awareness of the nation's historic struggle to achieve racial justice, a cause that has been at the forefront of Gloria's continuing activism (Steinem website).

A major factor in Gloria's opposition to President Trump was his stance on reproductive rights. Consequently, as conservatives have undertaken a new campaign to limit abortion rights, passing new restrictive laws while also appointing judges who appear open to overturning *Roe v. Wade*, Gloria has been outspoken in her support of the Roe decision and reproductive rights generally. She was unflinching in her criticism of groups that sought to implement restrictive laws and policies that limit women's reproductive choices. Such concerns made her particularly appreciative of the appointments of women to the Supreme Court. Her friendship with Ruth Bader Ginsburg predated Ginsburg's judicial career, going back to a time when she was a New York–based litigator establishing a record that would lead one prominent legal observer to call her the "Thurgood Marshall of the Women's Rights Movement." Gloria was also pleased by the appointment of Sonia Sotomayor, the Court's first Latinx Supreme Court member and a strong advocate of women's rights on the increasingly conservative court.

Sonia Sotomayor

Sonia Sotomayor, the third woman and the first Latinx person to be appointed to the Supreme Court, is a poster child for Gloria Steinem's big-tent approach to feminism. The daughter of Puerto Rican natives, she was born and grew up in the Bronx. Despite being diagnosed with diabetes at age seven, she compiled a stellar academic record, earning admission to Princeton, where she graduated summa cum laude in 1976. Inspired at an early age by watching *Perry Mason* on television, she was determined to pursue a career in the law, and she graduated from Yale Law School in 1979. Sotomayor then spent over four years in the New York District Attorney's office. After a brief time in private practice, in 1991 she was appointed to the federal district court, where she gained fame as the judge who saved baseball, issuing a ruling that ended the 1994 strike. She joined the U.S. Court of Appeals in 1998 and was appointed to the Supreme Court by President Obama in 2009. There she has embraced the symbolic power inherent in being the Court's first Latinx member, being an active public role model. On the Court she has been a probing questioner, a forceful dissenter, and a passionate defender of the rights of the poor and disenfranchised.

Elena Kagan

As the fourth woman appointed to the U.S. Supreme Court, Elena Kagan might be seen as little more than a footnote in women's history, but as the first of the generation inspired by the appointment of Sandra Day O'Connor—Kagan graduated from Princeton the month before O'Connor was appointed—she represents the generation impacted by the fruits of the movement. At the same time, her career path and the road to the High Court is littered with the barriers she has broken through, including being an early female Supreme Court law clerk, the first female dean at Harvard Law School—where Ruth Bader Ginsburg once had to justify her place in the class—as well as the first female solicitor general of the United States. On the Court, she has written important opinions dealing with the Sixth Amendment right to counsel as well as gerrymandering. Considered a member of the Court's liberal wing, she is renowned for her ability to work across partisan lines and find common ground, skills she used to great advantage at Harvard Law School. Only fifty when she was appointed, Kagan has the potential to serve for a long time and make an impact on the law and society for years to come.

And the politically astute Gloria supported the appointment of former Harvard Law School dean Elena Kagan to the Supreme Court as well. She hoped that Kagan's reputation as a consensus builder would help her reverse the Court's turn to the right.

Throughout her years as a celebrity, Gloria has always been reluctant to be the center of attention. Consequently, it was only on the condition that they make the event a fundraiser that she would allow friends to throw any kind of birthday party. But acceding to that restriction, actress and feminist ally Marlo Thomas led an effort that turned Gloria's fiftieth into just that, a gala that not only celebrated the activist but also raised thousands of dollars for the *Ms.* Foundation. The event, which included a guest list estimated at 800 and dinner tickets starting at $250 per person, resembled a Broadway or Hollywood opening and was both a massive fundraising triumph and a reflection of Gloria's influence and status. Feted by influential and powerful figures from politics, show business, and the world of feminism, the event highlighted the wide-ranging reach of her efforts while helping fund their continuation. And in the aftermath, she indicated that it would not be the last such event. In fact, as she has gracefully aged in public, adding updates a decade at a time to her earliest rejoinder, "This is what 40 looks like," she has regularly used her birthdays as fundraisers with the most recent being a "This Is What 80 Looks Like" celebration that benefited the Shalom Center in Philadelphia. Such efforts will come to an end only when her celebrated life does, for she has made clear that she expects her funeral to be a major fundraiser too (Leland 2016).

Despite her continued activism, Gloria's status as an elder stateswoman of the movement has afforded her the opportunity to return to her writing. Having always been conscious of the changing social and political landscape, in 1992, reflective of her increased sensitivity to the changing nature of women's status, she published *Revolution from Within: A Book of Self-Esteem*. The work addressed issues that had arisen with women's greater opportunities and the resulting impact on their lives as they have struggled to balance work and home (Stern 1997). Although the book received mixed reviews, its commercial success had publishers clamoring for another work and in fact, before *Revolution from Within* was published, Gloria had contracted with Simon & Schuster to do a book on rich women, an expansion of her June 1986 *Ms.* piece, "The Trouble with Rich Women." However, with that idea having lost its appeal for her and with the original deadline long past—a not atypical scenario for the always overbooked and overcommitted Gloria—she sought to return the advance and move on. But Simon & Schuster was adamant; it wanted a book and threatened to simply invoke a clause in the original contract that gave them the rights to her next book.

Ultimately, after negotiations by her lawyer Bob Levine, an agreement was reached. Gloria agreed to include the piece on rich women in a collection of six essays, three written just for the book and three that had previously been published in *Ms.* The 1995 release, *Moving beyond Words*, was dedicated to her sister Sue and included reworked pieces on bodybuilding champion Bev Francis, "The Strongest Woman in the World," as well as one based on the original *Ms.* piece on rich women, which she titled "The Masculinization of Wealth" (Stern 1997). The final, adapted version of "Sex, Lies and Advertising" offered insight into the world of advertising and especially the challenges *Ms.* had faced in trying to stay true to its mission. The original works included "Revaluing Economics," a look at the way women were adversely impacted by traditional economic practices. Meanwhile, "Doing Sixty" offered thoughts on aging, seeing it as a liberating experience free from expectations about youthful beauty, not to mention a no longer demanding libido. The book opened with a creative look at Freud and how his work had been detrimental to women. Titled "What if Freud Were Phyllis; or the Watergate of the Western World," the "biographical" look at Dr. Phyllis Freud left few stones unturned in explaining how Freud reinforced women's suffering in a patriarchal society (Steinem 1995).

The critique of Freud was also a reflection of some long-standing grievances Gloria had with the male-dominated psychiatric profession. In the early 1980s, she had been asked by the Psychiatrists for Equal Rights to help persuade the national American Psychiatric Association (APA), to more fully support ratification of the ERA. The less-than-encouraging reception her appearance garnered at the 1983 APA convention, where she addressed the problem of psychiatrists sleeping with their patients, did little to enhance her view of the profession. Nor did their continued reliance on what she saw as the male-centered and Freud-dominated approach to analysis. With much of her approach to feminism rooted in attitudes and at least in part to psychology, Gloria's tensions with the formal psychiatric world would continue beyond her portrayal of the so-called Phyllis Freud. But that piece was at the center of the positive response to the book. Meanwhile, its strong sales were a testament to Gloria's celebrity status as much as to her writing, but in her view, the circulation of the ideas was the most important consideration (Stern 1997).

Gloria recognized that the generation that fought alongside her was now in a very different place and dealing with very different issues than their daughters and granddaughters were. Consequently, in 2006, she published *Doing Sixty and Seventy*, a short work intended to provide guidance in the golden years. The book was intended to provide something of a road map to the thousands of women who were trying to navigate through the changed landscape of being a senior citizen, a world now markedly different from the one their mothers had experienced. The bulk of the book, "Doing Sixty," was a reprint of the essay she had written for the earlier collection *Moving beyond Words*, but in addition, with another decade behind her, she offered a new array of thoughts about aging and opportunity and how to approach these years. Women of her generation could not learn these things from their mothers, because the terrain was so different from anything anyone had previously experienced. At the same time, how women in Gloria's generation handled aging would serve as a model for later generations and might help define parameters for the future (Steinem 2006).

Reveling in having greater opportunities to write, in the summer of 2009, Gloria escaped the daily turmoil that was her life as a feminist advocate and traveled to Hedgebrook, a renowned women writers' retreat on Whidbey Island, in Washington State. There she enjoyed a six-week retreat to work on a developing work, one that would eventually be released in 2015 as *My Life on the Road*. Interestingly, when it was announced that she would be at Hedgebrook, the book's working title was announced as *Road to the Heart: America as if Everyone Mattered*, and it was presented as a book that would highlight her work as a feminist organizer. The nurturing atmosphere she found at Hedgebrook represented a marked contrast with her last writers' retreat, the ill-fated fellowship at the Wilson Center. The book she would ultimately produce focused on how her years of travel were central to her efforts to forge a common bond in the pursuit of what she would often refer to as her humanist agenda (Gwinn 2015).

A look back on her career as an activist, most reviewers treated *My Life on the Road* as the closest thing to a memoir that Gloria would ever write. Fleshing out and illuminating some of her earlier work, it provided some interesting backstories to some of her journalistic pieces, both the well-known ones and others that were special to her. It pulled together what often seemed like singular episodes or vignettes, showing how they all related to her lifelong quest for a society and world marked by human equality and opportunity. From her piece "Ho Chi Minh in New York," which appeared in the first issue of *New York* magazine, to her delivery of a homily in a Catholic church in Minnesota, an undertaking that earned her a clear, if veiled, rebuke from the Pope, she had poked the bear and watched the impact thereof on the society she sought to change (Steinem 2015).

The book also pulled together and provided some overarching coherency to five decades of seeming nonstop advocacy across a country that she learned was by no means the singular "one" that people sometimes like to say it is. Rather, the book made clear that through the years, the miles, and the visits to all fifty states, she reveled in the differences she discovered while at the same time seeing evidence of her belief that all people were joined by a desire to be free and to pursue their own individual dreams. In its own way, Gloria's *My Life on the Road* was an organizer's manual, something of a cross between activist Saul Alinsky's *Rules for Radicals* and *Aesop's Fables* as Gloria shared the countless lessons she learned in her travels, lessons that could still be used to fuel future efforts to advance the causes to which she had had committed her life.

While reflection and introspection have not been Gloria's strengths, she is nevertheless conscious of her place in history. Indeed, with the passing of time, Gloria, who was always protective of her image, worked hard to make sure that history recognized her place and role in the movement in an appropriate and accurate manner. She worked with her alma mater, Smith College, where she had deposited her own papers, seeking to ensure that Smith's archives of the movement reflected the diverse nature of modern feminism.

At the same time, despite her own reluctance to reflect on her role, as the years passed, others looked back on her efforts and she became the subject of a number of dramatic portrayals and historical retrospectives of a kind usually reserved for those long dead. In August 2011 HBO premiered the documentary *Gloria: In Her Own Words*, a presentation that offered Americans, young and old, a new look at the feminist icon. Meanwhile, in 2013 Gloria was one of the subjects profiled in the PBS documentary *Makers*, which presented the stories of women who had "made America." In a nation that has long suffered from a limited historical memory, those productions helped introduce Gloria and her sister second-wave feminist leaders to the generations that were the most immediate beneficiaries of their efforts.

The off-Broadway production, *Gloria: A Life*, written by Emily Mann, directed by Diane Paulus, and starring actress Christine Lahti, Gloria's friend, premiered in the fall of 2018. Given the range of things that made up Gloria Steinem's life, the play could only offer snippets, portraying highlights and recreating vignettes, most of which were familiar to readers

---

Kathryn Bigelow

When Kathryn Bigelow won the 2009 Academy Award for Best Director for *The Hurt Locker*, it represented a major step forward for women in the film industry. Bigelow's becoming the first woman to win Best Director in the Academy's eighty-second year highlighted the fact that women, who had played a prominent role in front of the camera for as long as movies had been made, had long struggled to be recognized for their work either in the boardroom or behind the camera. Bigelow, a California native, earned an MFA from Columbia University, where she worked with famed director Milos Forman, who was teaching there at the time. Her first full-length feature film was the 1981 release *The Loveless*, which she codirected with Monty Montgomery. The biker film starred Willem Dafoe in his first starring role. Her biggest hit before *The Hurt Locker* was the 1991 film *Point Break*. Starring Keanu Reeves, it has become a cult classic and is the biggest moneymaker of her career. In addition to the Academy Award, she won virtually every other directorial honor, while the film, for which she was also a coproducer, won the Oscar for Best Picture.

of her work or followers of her career. But for those for whom the play was an introduction, it was a powerful reminder of a time long past as well as the story of the effort to make things that later became taken for granted a reality. Adding to the power of the play was the way it concluded, with a twenty-minute talking circle, in which members of the audience were invited to share their responses to the play. Sitting on Persian rugs just like those one found in Gloria's own apartment, the talking circle mirrored the countless circles in which Gloria participated over the years. Each night a different special guest kicked off the circle, and one early audience was treated to the arrival of an extra-special guest—Gloria herself, dressed in the same outfit Lahti had worn in that night's show—who undertook to lead the discussion. It was a powerful case of life and art coming together, and for that audience it was an opportunity to be a part of history. Another retrospective, renowned director Julie Taymor's film, *The Glorias*, based on *My Life on the Road*, was previewed at the Sundance Film Festival in January 2020 and released in the fall of 2020 (Collins-Hughes 2018).

Such attention was complemented by the fact that Gloria was increasingly singled out, honored, and celebrated for her lifetime of activism. In 1993 she was inducted into the National Women's Hall of Fame. Two decades later, on November 20, 2013, President Barack Obama presented Gloria Steinem with the Presidential Medal of Freedom, the nation's highest civilian honor (Steinem website). None of her many accolades caused her to slacken her pace, and in fact she saw some as opportunities to move her agenda forward. Whether it was the 2019 honorary degree she received from Yale University, an institution that first began admitting women only months after Gloria had her feminist awakening, or the one she received from her alma mater, Smith, in 1988, for Gloria each ceremony represented an opportunity to reach a new audience. While the Yale honor was on a lengthy list that included degrees from Southern Methodist, Columbia, Simmons, Washington, Hofstra, Hobart and William Smith, Tufts, and Wheaton, it was another opportunity to showcase the historic efforts of Gloria's generation of feminists (Steinem website). While graduates were often young enough to be her granddaughters, each ceremony introduced Gloria and her accomplishments to a new set of potential activists, and each commencement address was an opportunity to share a little history while challenging the next generation of leaders to pick up the banner. Issuing a call to arms, she has never tired of calling upon them to take the next steps in the continuing effort to achieve human equality.

Timeline

1930s

March 25, 1934 — Gloria Marie Steinem is born in Toledo, Ohio to Leo and Ruth Steinem.

1940s

1945 — Leo and Ruth Steinem divorce. Ruth and Gloria relocate to Toledo.

1948–1951 — Gloria attends Waite High School in Toledo.

1950s

1951 — Gloria moves in with her sister, Sue, in Washington, DC, and enters Western High School.

June 12, 1952 — Gloria graduates from Western High School, in Washington, DC.

November 4, 1952 — Dwight D. Eisenhower is elected the thirty-fourth president of the United States.

1954–1955 — Gloria, based in Geneva, spends her junior year studying and traveling in Europe.

Spring 1956 — Gloria becomes engaged to Blair Chotzinoff; she will later break it off as she plans to depart for Europe once again.

June 3, 1956 — Gloria graduates from Smith College, with a degree in government, having earned Phi Beta Kappa honors.

January 1957 — Gloria gets an abortion in London.

1957–1958 — Gloria studies in India on a Smith College–sponsored Chester Bowles Fellowship.

1958–1959	Gloria serves as co-executive director of the National Student Association (NSA)–sponsored Independent Service for Information (ISI), at the Vienna Youth Festival.

1960s

1960	Following her move to New York City, Gloria begins to work at *Help!* magazine.
November 8, 1960	John F. Kennedy is elected thirty-fifth president of the United States.
April 21, 1961	Leo Steinem dies.
December 14, 1961	President Kennedy issues an executive order establishing the President's Commission on the Status of Women.
January 1, 1963	*The Feminine Mystique*, by Betty Friedan, is published.
Spring 1963	Gloria works undercover as a "Bunny" at the Playboy Club in New York and then writes an exposé about the experience in *Show*.
November 15, 1963	*The Beach Book* is published.
November 22, 1963	President Kennedy is assassinated; Lyndon B. Johnson becomes the thirty-sixth president of the United States.
July 2, 1964	President Lyndon Johnson signs into law the Civil Rights Act of 1964, which includes a prohibition against sex-based discrimination.
November 3, 1964	President Johnson is elected to a full term as president.
June 30, 1966	The National Organization for Women (NOW) is founded.
April 8, 1968	*New York*, for which Gloria writes the "The City Politic" column, publishes its first issue.
November 5, 1968	Richard Nixon is elected as the thirty-seventh president of the United States.
March 21, 1969	Gloria attends a Red Stockings–sponsored abortion speak-out, which she later identifies as her feminist epiphany.
Spring 1969	Gloria works for the New York City mayoral campaign of Norman Mailer.

Timeline 181

April 7, 1969	"After Black Power, Women's Liberation," Gloria's first feminist piece, appears in *New York*.

1970s

May 6, 1970	Gloria testifies before the U.S. Senate on behalf of the Equal Rights Amendment (ERA).
1971	Gloria cofounds *Ms.* magazine, whose first stand-alone issue appears on newsstands in January 1972.
July 10–11, 1971	The National Women's Political Caucus (NWPC) holds its organizing conference.
March 22, 1972	The Senate passes the ERA and sends it to the states for the required three-fourths ratification.
June 23, 1972	President Richard Nixon signs Title IX of the Education Amendments of 1972 into law.
January 22, 1973	The Supreme Court issues its ruling in *Roe v. Wade*, establishing a woman's legal right to choose to have an abortion.
August 9, 1974	Richard Nixon resigns the presidency, and Gerald R. Ford assumes office as the thirty-eighth president of the United States.
1976	The first groups of women are admitted to the U.S. Military Academy, the U.S. Naval Academy, the U.S. Air Force Academy, and the U.S. Coast Guard Academy.
November 2, 1976	Jimmy Carter is elected the thirty-ninth president of the United States.
November 18–21, 1977	The National Women's Conference is held in Houston, Texas.

1980s

November 4, 1980	Ronald Reagan is elected the fortieth president of the United States.
July 1981	Ruth Steinem dies.
July 7, 1981	Sandra Day O'Connor is nominated as an associate justice of the Supreme Court.
June 30, 1982	The effort to ratify the ERA reaches the legally established deadline, falling three states short of ratification.
January 1, 1983	*Outrageous Acts and Everyday Rebellions* is published.

July 19, 1984	Geraldine Ferraro is nominated to be the Democratic Party's candidate for vice president.
February 25, 1985	The TV movie, *A Bunny's Tale*, based on Steinem's 1963 *Show* magazine articles, airs for the first time.
January 1, 1986	*Marilyn* is published.
November 8, 1988	George H. W. Bush is elected forty-first president of the United States.

1990s

January 1, 1992	*Revolution from Within: A Book of Self-Esteem* is published.
November 3, 1992	Bill Clinton is elected forty-second president of the United States.
March 11, 1993	Janet Reno assumes office as attorney general.
June 14, 1993	Ruth Bader Ginsburg is nominated as an associate justice of the Supreme Court.
February 1, 1995	*Moving beyond Words: Age, Rage, Sex, Power, Money, Muscles: Breaking the Boundaries of Gender* is published.
January 23, 1997	Madeline Albright assumes office as secretary of state.

2000s

September 3, 2000	Gloria marries David Bale, who dies of cancer in 2003.
November 7, 2000	George W. Bush is elected forty-third president of the United States.
September 11, 2001	The United States is rocked by a coordinated sets of terrorist attacks.
2005	Together with Jane Fonda and Robin Morgan, Gloria cofounds the Women's Media Center.
September 1, 2006	*Doing Sixty & Seventy* is published.
January 4, 2007	Representative Nancy Pelosi is elected Speaker of the House.
November 4, 2008	Barack Obama is elected forty-fourth president of the United States.
May 26, 2009	Sonia Sotomayor is nominated as an associate justice of the Supreme Court.

2010s

May 10, 2010	Elena Kagan is nominated as an associate justice of the Supreme Court.

August 11, 2011	HBO first airs the documentary *Gloria: In Her Own Words*.
February 26, 2013	PBS first airs the documentary *Makers*, a look at six famous women, including Gloria.
November 20, 2013	President Obama awards Gloria the Presidential Medal of Freedom.
October 27, 2015	*My Life on the Road* is published.
May 10, 2016	Steinem's television show *Woman* premieres on the Viceland network.
July 26, 2016	Hillary Rodham Clinton is nominated to be the Democratic Party's candidate for president.
November 8, 2016	Donald J. Trump is elected forty-fifth president of the United States.
October 29, 2019	*The Truth Will Set You Free, but First It Will Piss You Off!: Thoughts on Life, Love, and Rebellion* is published.

2020

November 3, 2020	Joseph R. Biden is elected forty-sixth president of the United States.

PRIMARY SOURCE DOCUMENTS

Equal Pay Act (1963)

Although the passage of the Equal Pay Act predated Gloria's involvement in the women's movement, it coincided with the early stages of her career as a journalist. It was fortuitous timing, for the law offered a particularly valuable form of protection for a young career woman working in a male-dominated discipline. Gloria was able to see the way the law and its subsequent implementation reflected the realities of the working world as well as the challenges that would become central to Gloria's future activism. Despite the legal mandate, and well into the twenty-first century, women were still being paid less than males for ostensibly the same job. Gloria worked to address such discrepancies, which became fodder for countless lawsuits and as well as the target of numerous political efforts. All of it reinforced Gloria's long-held belief that legal and political efforts were only one part of the change process and that they would need to be supplemented and complemented by efforts to change attitudes and cultural norms if true change were to be achieved.

An Act to prohibit discrimination on account of sex in the payment of wages by employers engaged in commerce or in the production of goods for commerce.

Be it enacted by the Senate and House of Representatives of the United States of America in Congress assembled. That this Act may be cited as the "Equal Pay Act of 1963."

Declaration of Purpose

Sec. 2. (a) The Congress hereby finds that the existence in industries engaged in commerce or in the production of goods for commerce of wage differentials based on sex—

(1) depressed wages and living standards for employees necessary for their health and efficiency:

(2) prevents the maximum utilization of the available labor resources;

(3) tends to cause labor disputes, thereby burdening, affecting, and obstructing commerce;

(4) burdens commerce and the free flow of goods in commerce; and

(5) constitutes an unfair method of competition.

(b) It is hereby declared to be the policy of this Act, through exercise by Congress of its power to regulate commerce among the several States and with foreign nations, to correct the conditions above referred to in such industries.

Sec. 3. Section 6 of the Fair Labor Standards Act of 1938, as amended (29 U.S.C. et seq.), is amended by adding thereto a new subsection (d) as follows:

(d) (1) No employer having employees subject to any provisions of this section shall discriminate, within any establishment in which such employees are employed, between employees on the basis of sex by paying wages to employees in such establishment at a rate less than the rate at which he pays wages to employees of the opposite sex in such establishment for equal work on jobs the performance of which requires equal skill, effort, and responsibility, and which are performed under similar working conditions, except where such payment is made pursuant to (i) a seniority system; (ii) a merit system; (iii) a system which measures earnings by quantity or quality of production; or (iv) a differential based on any other factor other than sex: Provided, That an employer who is paying a wage rate differential in violation of this subsection shall not, in order to comply with the provisions of this subsection, reduce the wage rate of any employee.

(2) No labor organization, or its agents, representing employees of an employer having employees subject to any provisions of this section shall cause or attempt to cause such an employer to discriminate against an employee in violation of paragraph (1) of this subsection.

(3) For purpose of administration and enforcement, any amounts owing to any employee which have been withheld in violation of this subsection shall be deemed to be unpaid minimum wages or unpaid overtime compensation under this Act.

(4) As used in this subsection, the term labor organization means any organization of any kind, or any agency or employee representation committee or plan, in which employees participate and which exists for the purpose, in whole or in part, of dealing with employers concerning grievances, labor disputes, wages, rates of pay, hours of employment or conditions of work."

Sec. 4. The amendments made by this Act shall take effect upon the expiration of one year from the date of its enactment: Provided, That in the case of employees covered by a bona fide collective bargaining agreement in effect at least thirty days prior to the date of enactment of this Act, entered into by a labor organization (as defined in section 6(d) (4) of the Fair Labor Standards Act of 1938, as amended), the amendments made by this Act shall take effect upon the termination of such collective bargaining agreement or upon the expiration of two years from the date of enactment of this Act, whichever shall first occur.

Approved June 10, 1963

Source: Equal Pay Act of 1963. Public Law 88-38, *U.S. Statutes at Large* 77 (1963): 56.

Gloria Steinem: Excerpt from ERA Testimony (1970)

Gloria appeared before the Senate's Subcommittee on Constitutional Amendments of the Committee on the Judiciary on May 6, 1970. The appearance, coming little more than a year after she had had her feminist epiphany and over a year before she appeared on the cover of Newsweek *as the symbol of the new American woman, presents a different Gloria and a different approach. While she had a reputation as a journalist, she was not the celebrity that she would become. Rather, the statement is more reflective of her role as an interested and politically active citizen. In that way the tone is different from later speeches, where she was not just a voice but a leader. And yet the issues are the same, and in the course of her presentation, she clearly articulates what she sees as the way that all of society can benefit if the equality promised by the amendment is achieved. In addition, looking back at the statement from the vantage point of five decades later, the sizable number of challenges and the long-standing list of inequities women then faced come to light. In that way, it offers a starting point for understanding the challenges Steinem was about to dedicate the rest of her life to addressing. Little could she have known that fifty years later, she would still be advocating for the ERA's passage.*

"My name is Gloria Steinem. I am a writer and editor, and I am currently a member of the policy council of the Democratic committee. And I work regularly with the lowest-paid workers in the country, the migrant workers, men, women, and children both in California and in my own State of New York. . . .

During 12 years of working for a living, I have experienced much of the legal and social discrimination reserved for women in this country. I have been refused service in public restaurants, ordered out of public gathering places, and turned away from apartment rentals; all for the clearly-stated, sole reason that I am a woman. And all without the legal remedies available to blacks and other minorities. . . . Most important to me, I have been denied a society in which women are encouraged, or even allowed to think of themselves as first-class citizens and responsible human beings.

However, after 2 years of researching the status of American women, I have discovered that in reality, I am very, very lucky. Most women, both wage-earners and housewives, routinely suffer more humiliation and injustice than I do.

As a freelance writer, I don't work in the male-dominated hierarchy of an office. . . . I am not one of the millions of women who must support a family. Therefore, I haven't had to go on welfare because there are no day-care centers for my children while I work, and I haven't had to submit to the humiliating welfare inquiries about my private and sexual life, inquiries from which men are exempt. I haven't had to brave the sex bias of labor unions and employers, only to see my family subsist on a median salary 40 percent less than the male median salary.

I hope this committee will hear the personal, daily injustices suffered by many women. . . . We have all been silent for too long. But we won't be silent anymore.

The truth is that all our problems stem from the same sex based myths. . . . Like racial myths, they have been reflected in our laws. Let me list a few.

That women are biologically inferior to men.

Man's hunting activities are forever being pointed to as tribal proof of superiority. But while he was hunting, women built houses, tilled the fields, developed animal husbandry, and perfected language. Men, being all alone in the bush, often developed into a creature as strong as women, fleeter of foot, but not very bright.

However, I don't want to prove the superiority of one sex to another. That would only be repeating a male mistake.

What we do know is that the difference between two races or two sexes is much smaller than the differences to be found within each group . . . [and] the law makes much more sense when it treats individuals, not groups bundled together by some condition of birth. . . .

Another myth, that women are already treated equally in this society. I am sure there has been ample testimony to prove that equal pay for equal work, equal chance for advancement, and equal training or encouragement is obscenely scarce in every field, even those—like food and fashion industries—that are supposedly "feminine."

A deeper result of social and legal injustice, however, is what sociologists refer to as "Internalized Aggression." Victims of aggression absorb the myth of their own inferiority, and come to believe that their group is in fact second class. . . .

Women suffer this second class treatment from the moment they are born. They are expected to . . . function biologically rather than learn. A brother, whatever his intellect, is more likely to get the family's encouragement and education money, while girls are often pressured to conceal ambition and intelligence. . . .

I interviewed a New York public school teacher who told me about a black teenager's desire to be a doctor. With all the barriers in mind, she suggested kindly that he be a veterinarian instead.

The same day, a high school teacher mentioned a girl who wanted to be a doctor. The teacher said, "How about a nurse?"

Teachers, parents, and the Supreme Court may exude a protective, well-meaning rationale, but limiting the individual's ambition is doing no one a favor. Certainly not this country; it needs all the talent it can get.

Another myth, that American women hold great economic power. Fifty-one percent of all shareholders in this country are women. That is a favorite male-chauvinist statistic. However, the number of shares they hold is so small that the total is only 18 percent of all the shares. Even those holdings are often controlled by men. . . .

The constantly repeated myth of our economic power seems less testimony to our real power than to the resentment of what little power we do have.

Another myth, that children must have full-time mothers. American mothers spend more time with their homes and children than those of any other society we know about. . . .

The truth is that most American children seem to be suffering from too much mother, and too little father. Part of the program of Women's Liberation is a return of fathers to their children. . . . Women's Liberation is Men's Liberation too.

As for psychic health of the children, studies show that the quality of time spent by parents is more important than the quantity. . . .

Another myth, that the women's movement is not political, won't last, or is somehow not "serious."

When black people leave their 19th century roles, they are feared. When women dare to leave theirs, they are ridiculed. We understand this; we accept the burden of ridicule. It won't keep us quiet anymore.

Similarly, it shouldn't deceive male observers into thinking that this is somehow a joke. We are 51 percent of the population; we are essentially united on these issues across boundaries of class or race or age; and we may well end by changing this society more than the civil rights movement. That is an apt parallel. We, too, have our right wing and left wing. . . . But we are changing our own consciousness, and that of the country. . . . The new family is an egalitarian family.

Gunnar Myrdal noted 30 years ago the parallel between women and Negroes in this country. Both suffered from such restricting social myths. . . . When evaluating a general statement about women, it might be valuable to substitute "black people" for "women"—just to test the prejudice at work.

And it might be valuable to do this constitutionally as well. . . .

Neither group is going to be content as a cheap labor pool anymore. And neither is going to be content without full constitutional rights. . . .

Women are not more moral than men. We are only uncorrupted by power. But we do not want to imitate men, to join this country as it is, and I think our very participation will change it. Perhaps women elected leaders—and there will be many of them—will not be so likely to dominate black people or yellow people or men; anybody who looks different from us."

Source: Congress, Senate, Committee on the Judiciary, The "Equal Rights" Amendment: Hearings before the Subcommittee on Constitutional Amendments of the Committee on the Judiciary, 91st Cong., 2d sess., May 5, 6, and 7, 1970.

Equal Rights Amendment (1972)

The effort to get the Equal Rights Amendment passed and ratified was one of the constants in Gloria's career as an activist. From her appearance before the Senate Judiciary Committee's Subcommittee on Constitutional Amendments on May 6, 1970, barely a year after her feminist epiphany, to her continued advocacy of the proposal into the twenty-first century, Gloria worked unceasingly to secure the guarantee of legal equality for women that the amendment would provide. She recognized that the ERA represented one of the foundations upon which all subsequent efforts could be based, and there could be no denying that, with the achievement of legal equality, society would be one step closer to reaching the full human equality to which Gloria aspired.

Section 1. Equality of rights under the law shall not be denied or abridged by the United States or by any State on account of sex.

Section 2. The Congress shall have the power to enforce, by appropriate legislation, the provisions of this article.

Section 3. This amendment shall take effect two years after the date of ratification.

Source: Congressional Record, 92nd Cong., 2nd sess., March 22, 1972. Washington, DC: Government Printing Office, p. 9598.

Roe v. Wade (1973)

Over the course of her five decades as a feminist activist, no issue has been more important to Gloria than that of reproductive rights. She has worked ceaselessly to protect the freedom of choice articulated by the Supreme Court in Roe v. Wade. *Gloria never stopped wondering how different her own life would have been had she not had an abortion in 1957. That was certainly part of the reason she pursued a lifetime of activism and advocacy for all women. Her insistence on a woman's right to choose has been at the heart of many of her political efforts, including her decisions as to which candidates to support.*

MR. JUSTICE BLACKMUN delivered the opinion of the Court.

This Texas federal appeal and its Georgia companion, *Doe v. Bolton*, present constitutional challenges to state criminal abortion legislation. The Texas statutes under attack here are typical of those that have been in effect in many States for approximately a century. The Georgia statutes, in contrast, have a modern cast and are a legislative product that, to an extent at least, obviously reflects the influences of recent attitudinal change, of advancing medical knowledge and techniques, and of new thinking about an old issue.

We forthwith acknowledge our awareness of the sensitive and emotional nature of the abortion controversy, of the vigorous opposing views, even among physicians, and of the deep and seemingly absolute convictions that the subject inspires. One's philosophy, one's experiences, one's exposure to the raw edges of human existence, one's religious training, one's attitudes toward life and family and their values, and the moral standards one establishes and seeks to observe, are all likely to influence and to color one's thinking and conclusions about abortion.

In addition, population growth, pollution, poverty, and racial overtones tend to complicate and not to simplify the problem.

Our task, of course, is to resolve the issue by constitutional measurement, free of emotion and of predilection. We seek earnestly to do this, and, because we do, we have inquired into, and in this opinion place some emphasis upon, medical and medical-legal history and what that history reveals about man's attitudes toward the abortion procedure over the centuries. We bear in mind, too, Mr. Justice Holmes' admonition in his now-vindicated dissent in *Lochner v. New York* (1905):

[The Constitution] is made for people of fundamentally differing views, and the accident of our finding certain opinions natural and familiar or novel and even shocking ought not to conclude our judgment upon the question whether statutes embodying them conflict with the Constitution of the United States.

The Texas statutes that concern us here are Arts. 1191–1194 and 1196 of the State's Penal Code. These make it a crime to "procure an abortion," as therein defined, or to attempt one, except with respect to "an abortion procured or attempted by medical advice for the purpose of saving the life of the mother." Similar statutes are in existence in a majority of the States.

Texas first enacted a criminal abortion statute in 1854. This was soon modified into language that has remained substantially unchanged to the present time. See Texas Penal Code of 1857; G. Paschal, *Laws of Texas* (1866); Texas Rev. Stat. (1879); Texas Rev. Crim. Stat. (1911). The final article in each of these compilations provided the same exception, as does the present Article 1196, for an abortion by "medical advice for the purpose of saving the life of the mother."

Jane Roe, a single woman who was residing in Dallas County, Texas, instituted this federal action in March 1970 against the District Attorney of the county. She sought a declaratory judgment that the Texas criminal abortion statutes were unconstitutional on their face, and an injunction restraining the defendant from enforcing the statutes.

Roe alleged that she was unmarried and pregnant; that she wished to terminate her pregnancy by an abortion "performed by a competent, licensed physician, under safe, clinical conditions"; that she was unable to get a "legal" abortion in Texas because her life did not appear to be threatened by the continuation of her pregnancy; and that she could not afford to travel to another jurisdiction in order to secure a legal abortion under safe conditions. She claimed that the Texas statutes were unconstitutionally vague and that they abridged her right of personal privacy, protected by the First, Fourth, Fifth, Ninth, and Fourteenth Amendments. By an amendment to her complaint Roe purported to sue "on behalf of herself and all other women" similarly situated.

James Hubert Hallford, a licensed physician, sought and was granted leave to intervene in Roe's action. In his complaint he alleged that he had been arrested previously for violations of the Texas abortion statutes and that two such prosecutions were pending against him. He described conditions of patients who came to him seeking abortions, and he claimed that for many cases he, as a physician, was unable to determine whether they fell within or outside the exception recognized by Article 1196. He alleged that, as a consequence, the statutes were vague and uncertain, in violation of the Fourteenth Amendment, and that they violated his own and his patients' rights to privacy in the doctor-patient relationship and his own right to practice medicine, rights he claimed were guaranteed by the First, Fourth, Fifth, Ninth, and Fourteenth Amendments.

John and Mary Doe, a married couple, filed a companion complaint to that of Roe. They also named the District Attorney as defendant, claimed like constitutional deprivations, and sought declaratory and injunctive relief. The Does alleged that they were a childless couple; that Mrs. Doe was suffering from a "neural-chemical" disorder; that her physician had "advised her to avoid pregnancy until such time as her condition has materially improved" (although a pregnancy at the present time would not present "a serious risk" to her life); that, pursuant to medical advice, she had discontinued use of birth control pills; and that if she should become pregnant, she would want to terminate the pregnancy by an abortion performed by a competent, licensed physician under safe, clinical conditions. By an amendment to their complaint, the Does purported to sue "on behalf of themselves and all couples similarly situated."

The two actions were consolidated and heard together by a duly convened three-judge district court. The suits thus presented the situations of the pregnant single woman, the childless couple, with the wife not pregnant, and the licensed practicing physician, all joining in the attack on the Texas criminal abortion statutes. Upon the filing of affidavits, motions were made for dismissal and for summary judgment. The court held that Roe and members of her class, and Dr. Hallford, had standing to sue and presented justiciable controversies, but that the Does had failed to allege facts sufficient to state a present controversy and did not have standing. It concluded that, with respect to the requests for a declaratory judgment, abstention was not warranted. On the merits, the District Court held that the "fundamental right of single women and married persons to choose whether to have children is protected by the Ninth Amendment, through the Fourteenth Amendment," and that the Texas criminal abortion statutes were void on their face because they were both unconstitutionally vague and constituted an overbroad infringement of the plaintiffs' Ninth Amendment rights. The court then held that abstention was warranted with respect to the requests for an injunction. It therefore dismissed the Does' complaint, declared the abortion statutes void, and dismissed the application for injunctive relief.

The plaintiffs Roe and Doe and the intervenor Hallford, pursuant to 28 U.S.C. 1253, have appealed to this Court from that part of the District Court's judgment denying the injunction. The defendant District Attorney has purported to cross-appeal, pursuant to the same statute, from the court's grant of declaratory relief to Roe and Hallford. Both sides also have taken protective appeals to the United States Court of Appeals for the Fifth Circuit. That court ordered the appeals held in abeyance pending decision here. We postponed decision on jurisdiction to the hearing on the merits.

It might have been preferable if the defendant, pursuant to our Rule 20, had presented to us a petition for certiorari before judgment in the Court of Appeals with respect to the granting of the plaintiffs' prayer for declaratory relief. Our decisions in *Mitchell v. Donovan* (1970), and *Gunn v. University Committee* (1970), are to the effect that 1253 does not authorize an appeal to this Court from the grant or denial of declaratory relief alone. We conclude, nevertheless, that those decisions do not foreclose our review of both the injunctive and the declaratory aspects of a case of this kind when it is properly here, as this one is, on appeal under 1253 from specific denial of injunctive relief, and the arguments as to both aspects are necessarily identical. See *Carter v. Jury Comm'n* (1970); *Florida Lime Growers v. Jacobsen* (1960). It would be destructive of time and energy for all concerned were we to rule otherwise. Cf. *Doe v. Bolton.*

We are next confronted with issues of justiciability, standing, and abstention. Have Roe and the Does established that "personal stake in the outcome of the controversy" . . . that insures that "the dispute sought to be adjudicated will be presented in an adversary context and in a form historically viewed as capable of judicial resolution" . . . ? And what effect did the pendency of criminal abortion charges against Dr. Hallford in state court have upon the propriety of the federal court's granting relief to him as a plaintiff-intervenor?

A. Jane Roe. Despite the use of the pseudonym, no suggestion is made that Roe is a fictitious person. For purposes of her case, we accept as true, and as established, her existence; her pregnant state, as of the inception of her suit in March 1970 and as late as May 21 of that year when she filed an alias affidavit with the District Court; and her inability to obtain a legal abortion in Texas.

Viewing Roe's case as of the time of its filing and thereafter until as late as May, there can be little dispute that it then presented a case or controversy and that, wholly apart from the class aspects, she, as a pregnant single woman thwarted by the Texas criminal abortion laws, had standing to challenge those statutes. . . . Indeed, we do not read the appellee's brief as really asserting anything to the contrary. The "logical nexus between the status asserted and the claim sought to be adjudicated,". . . and the necessary degree of contentiousness . . . are both present.

The appellee notes, however, that the record does not disclose that Roe was pregnant at the time of the District Court hearing on May 22, 1970, or on the following June 17 when the court's opinion and judgment were filed. And he suggests that Roe's case must now be moot because she and all other members of her class are no longer subject to any 1970 pregnancy.

The usual rule in federal cases is that an actual controversy must exist at stages of appellate or certiorari review, and not simply at the date the action is initiated. . . .

But when, as here, pregnancy is a significant fact in the litigation, the normal 266-day human gestation period is so short that the pregnancy will come to term before the usual appellate process is complete. If that termination makes a case moot, pregnancy litigation seldom will survive much beyond the trial stage, and appellate review will be effectively denied. Our law should not be that rigid. Pregnancy often comes more than once to the same woman, and in the general population, if man is to survive, it will always be with us. Pregnancy provides a classic justification for a conclusion of nonmootness. It truly could be "capable of repetition, yet evading review." . . .

We, therefore, agree with the District Court that Jane Roe had standing to undertake this litigation, that she presented a justiciable controversy, and that the termination of her 1970 pregnancy has not rendered her case moot.

B. Dr. Hallford. The doctor's position is different. He entered Roe's litigation as a plaintiff-intervenor, alleging in his complaint that he:

[I]n the past has been arrested for violating the Texas Abortion Laws and at the present time stands charged by indictment with violating said laws in the Criminal District Court of Dallas County, Texas to-wit: (1) The State of Texas vs. James H. Hallford, No. C-69-5307-IH, and (2) The State of Texas vs. James H. Hallford, No. C-69-2524-H. In both cases the defendant is charged with abortion. . . .

In his application for leave to intervene, the doctor made like representations as to the abortion charges pending in the state court. These representations were also repeated in the affidavit he executed and filed in support of his motion for summary judgment.

Dr. Hallford is, therefore, in the position of seeking, in a federal court, declaratory and injunctive relief with respect to the same statutes under which he stands charged in criminal prosecutions simultaneously pending in state court. Although he stated that he has been arrested in the past for violating the State's abortion laws, he makes no allegation of any substantial and immediate threat to any federally protected right that cannot be asserted in his defense against the state prosecutions. Neither is there any allegation of harassment or bad-faith prosecution. In order to escape the rule articulated in the cases cited in the next paragraph of this opinion that, absent harassment and bad faith, a defendant in a pending state criminal case cannot affirmatively challenge in federal court the statutes under which the State is prosecuting him, Dr. Hallford seeks to distinguish his status as a present state defendant from his status as a "potential future defendant" and to assert only the latter for standing purposes here.

We see no merit in that distinction. Our decision in *Samuels v. Mackell* (1971), compels the conclusion that the District Court erred when it granted declaratory relief to Dr. Hallford instead of refraining from so doing. The court, of course, was correct in refusing to grant injunctive relief to the doctor. The reasons supportive of that action, however, are those expressed in *Samuels v. Mackell,* and in *Younger v. Harris* (1971); *Boyle v. Landry* (1971); *Perez v. Ledesma* (1971); and *Byrne v. Karalexis* (1971). See also *Dombrowski v. Pfister* (1965). We note, in passing, that *Younger* and its companion cases were decided after the three-judge District Court decision in this case.

Dr. Hallford's complaint in intervention, therefore, is to be dismissed. He is remitted to his defenses in the state criminal proceedings against him. We reverse the judgment of the District Court insofar as it granted Dr. Hallford relief and failed to dismiss his complaint in intervention.

C. The Does. In view of our ruling as to Roe's standing in her case, the issue of the Does' standing in their case has little significance. The claims they assert are essentially the same as those of Roe, and they attack the same statutes. Nevertheless, we briefly note the Does' posture.

Their pleadings present them as a childless married couple, the woman not being pregnant, who have no desire to have children at this time because of their having received medical advice that Mrs. Doe should avoid pregnancy, and for "other highly personal reasons." But they "fear ... they may face the prospect of becoming parents." And if pregnancy ensues, they "would want to terminate" it by an abortion. They assert an inability to obtain an abortion legally in Texas and, consequently, the prospect of obtaining an illegal abortion there or of going outside Texas to some place where the procedure could be obtained legally and competently.

We thus have as plaintiffs a married couple who have, as their asserted immediate and present injury, only an alleged "detrimental effect upon [their] marital happiness" because they are forced to "the choice of refraining from normal sexual relations or of endangering Mary Doe's health through a possible pregnancy." Their claim is that sometime in the future Mrs. Doe might become pregnant because of possible failure of contraceptive measures, and at that time in the future she might want an abortion that might then be illegal under the Texas statutes.

This very phrasing of the Does' position reveals its speculative character. Their alleged injury rests on possible future contraceptive failure, possible future pregnancy, possible future unpreparedness for parenthood, and possible future impairment of health. Any one or more of these several possibilities may not take place and all may not combine. In the Does' estimation, these possibilities might have some real or imagined impact upon their marital happiness. But we are not prepared to say that the bare allegation of so indirect an injury is sufficient to present an actual case or controversy.... The Does' claim falls far short of those resolved otherwise in the cases that the Does urge upon us, namely, *Investment Co. Institute v. Camp* (1971); *Data Processing Service v. Camp* (1970); and *Epperson v. Arkansas* (1968). See also *Truax v. Raich* (1915).

The Does therefore are not appropriate plaintiffs in this litigation. Their complaint was properly dismissed by the District Court, and we affirm that dismissal.

The principal thrust of appellant's attack on the Texas statutes is that they improperly invade a right, said to be possessed by the pregnant woman, to choose to terminate her pregnancy. Appellant would discover this right in the concept of personal "liberty" embodied in the Fourteenth Amendment's Due Process Clause; or in personal, marital, familial, and sexual privacy said to be protected by the Bill of Rights or its penumbras, see *Griswold v. Connecticut* (1965); *Eisenstadt v. Baird* (1972); ... or among those rights reserved to the people by the Ninth Amendment, *Griswold v. Connecticut* (Goldberg, J., concurring). Before addressing this claim, we feel it desirable briefly to survey, in several aspects, the history of abortion, for such insight as that history may afford us, and then to examine the state purposes and interests behind the criminal abortion laws.

It perhaps is not generally appreciated that the restrictive criminal abortion laws in effect in a majority of States today are of relatively recent vintage. Those laws, generally proscribing abortion or its attempt at any time during pregnancy except when necessary to preserve the pregnant woman's life, are not of ancient or even of common-law origin. Instead, they derive from statutory changes effected, for the most part, in the latter half of the 19th century.

1. Ancient attitudes. These are not capable of precise determination. We are told that at the time of the Persian Empire abortifacients were known and that criminal abortions were severely punished. We are also told, however, that abortion was practiced in Greek times as well as in the Roman Era, and that "it was resorted to without scruple." The Ephesian, Soranos, often described as the greatest of the ancient gynecologists, appears to have been generally opposed to Rome's prevailing free-abortion practices. He found it necessary to think first of the life of the mother, and he resorted to abortion when, upon this standard, he felt the procedure advisable. Greek and Roman law afforded little protection to the unborn. If abortion was prosecuted in some places, it seems to have been based on a concept of a violation of the father's right to his offspring. Ancient religion did not bar abortion.

2. The Hippocratic Oath. What then of the famous Oath that has stood so long as the ethical guide of the medical profession and that bears the name of the great Greek (460(?)-377(?) B.C.), who has been described as the Father of Medicine, the "wisest and the greatest practitioner of his art," and the "most important and most complete medical personality of antiquity," who dominated the medical schools of his time, and who typified the sum of the medical knowledge of the past? The Oath varies somewhat according to the particular translation, but in any translation the content is clear: "I will give no deadly medicine to anyone if asked, nor suggest any such counsel; and in like manner I will not give to a woman a pessary to produce abortion," or "I will neither give a deadly drug to anybody if asked for it, nor will I make a suggestion to this effect. Similarly, I will not give to a woman an abortive remedy."

Although the Oath is not mentioned in any of the principal briefs in this case or in *Doe v. Bolton*, it represents the apex of the development of strict ethical concepts in medicine, and its influence endures to this day. Why did not the authority of Hippocrates dissuade abortion practice in his time and that of Rome? The late Dr. Edelstein provides us with a theory: The Oath was not uncontested even in Hippocrates' day; only the Pythagorean school of philosophers frowned upon the related act of suicide. Most Greek thinkers, on the other hand, commended abortion, at least prior to viability. See Plato, *Republic*; Aristotle, *Politics*. For the Pythagoreans, however, it was a matter of dogma. For them the embryo was animate from the moment of conception, and abortion meant destruction of a living being. The abortion clause of the Oath, therefore, "echoes Pythagorean doctrines," and "[i]n no other stratum of Greek opinion were such views held or proposed in the same spirit of uncompromising austerity."

Dr. Edelstein then concludes that the Oath originated in a group representing only a small segment of Greek opinion and that it certainly was not accepted by all ancient physicians. He points out that medical writings down to Galen (A.D. 130–200) "give evidence of the violation of almost every one of its injunctions." But with the end of antiquity a decided change took place. Resistance against suicide and against abortion became common. The Oath came to be popular. The emerging teachings of Christianity were in agreement with the Pythagorean ethic. The Oath "became the nucleus of all medical ethics" and "was applauded as the embodiment of truth." Thus, suggests Dr. Edelstein, it is "a Pythagorean manifesto and not the expression of an absolute standard of medical conduct."

This, it seems to us, is a satisfactory and acceptable explanation of the Hippocratic Oath's apparent rigidity. It enables us to understand, in historical context, a long-accepted and revered statement of medical ethics.

3. The common law. It is undisputed that at common law, abortion performed before "quickening"—the first recognizable movement of the fetus in utero, appearing usually from the 16th to the 18th week of pregnancy—was not an indictable offense. The absence of a common-law crime for prequickening abortion appears to have developed from a confluence of earlier philosophical, theological, and civil and canon law concepts of when life begins. These disciplines variously approached the question in terms of the point at which the embryo or fetus became "formed" or recognizably human, or in terms of when a "person" came into being, that is, infused with a "soul" or "animated." A loose consensus evolved in early English law that these events occurred at some point between conception and live birth. This was "mediate animation." Although Christian theology and the canon law came to fix the point of animation at 40 days for a male and 80 days for a female, a view that persisted until the 19th century, there was otherwise little agreement about the precise time of formation or animation. There was agreement, however, that prior to this point the fetus was to be regarded as part of the mother, and its destruction, therefore, was not homicide. Due to continued uncertainty about the precise time when animation occurred, to the lack of any empirical basis for the 40-80-day view, and perhaps to Aquinas' definition of movement as one of the two first principles of life, Bracton focused upon quickening as the critical point. The significance of quickening was echoed by later common-law scholars and found its way into the received common law in this country.

Whether abortion of a quick fetus was a felony at common law, or even a lesser crime, is still disputed. Bracton, writing early in the 13th century, thought it homicide. But the later and predominant view, following the great common-law scholars, has been that it was, at most, a lesser offense. In a frequently cited passage, Coke took the position that abortion of a woman "quick with childe" is "a great misprision, and no murder." Blackstone followed, saying that while abortion after quickening had once been considered manslaughter (though not murder), "modern law" took a less severe view. A recent review of the common-law precedents argues, however, that those precedents contradict Coke and that even post-quickening abortion was never established as a common-law crime. This is of some importance because while most American courts ruled, in holding or dictum, that abortion of an unquickened fetus was not criminal under their received common law, others followed Coke in stating that abortion of a quick fetus was a "misprision," a term they translated to mean "misdemeanor." That their reliance on Coke on this aspect of the law was uncritical and, apparently in all the reported cases, dictum (due probably to the paucity of common-law prosecutions for post-quickening abortion), makes it now appear doubtful that abortion was ever firmly established as a common-law crime even with respect to the destruction of a quick fetus.

4. The English statutory law. England's first criminal abortion statute, Lord Ellenborough's Act, came in 1803. It made abortion of a quick fetus, 1, a capital crime, but in 2 it provided lesser penalties for the felony of abortion before quickening, and thus preserved the "quickening" distinction. This contrast was continued in the general revision of 1828. It disappeared, however, together with the death penalty, in 1837, and did not reappear in the Offenses Against the Person Act of 1861, that formed the core of English anti-abortion law until the liberalizing reforms of 1967. In 1929, the Infant Life (Preservation) Act, came into being. Its emphasis was upon the destruction of "the life of a child capable of being born alive." It made a willful act performed with the necessary intent a felony. It contained a proviso that one was not to be found guilty of the offense "unless it is proved that the act which caused the death of the child was not done in good faith for the purpose only of preserving the life of the mother."

A seemingly notable development in the English law was the case of *Rex v. Bourne*, 1939. This case apparently answered in the affirmative the question whether an abortion necessary to preserve the life of the pregnant woman was excepted from the criminal penalties of the 1861 Act. In his instructions to the jury, Judge Macnaghten referred to the 1929 Act, and observed that that Act related to "the case where a child is killed by a wilful act at the time when it is being delivered in the ordinary course of nature." He concluded that the 1861 Act's use of the word "unlawfully," imported the same meaning expressed by the specific proviso in the 1929

Act, even though there was no mention of preserving the mother's life in the 1861 Act. He then construed the phrase "preserving the life of the mother" broadly, that is, "in a reasonable sense," to include a serious and permanent threat to the mother's health, and instructed the jury to acquit Dr. Bourne if it found he had acted in a good-faith belief that the abortion was necessary for this purpose. The jury did acquit.

Recently, Parliament enacted a new abortion law. This is the Abortion Act of 1967. The Act permits a licensed physician to perform an abortion where two other licensed physicians agree (a) "that the continuance of the pregnancy would involve risk to the life of the pregnant woman, or of injury to the physical or mental health of the pregnant woman or any existing children of her family, greater than if the pregnancy were terminated," or (b) "that there is a substantial risk that if the child were born it would suffer from such physical or mental abnormalities as to be seriously handicapped." The Act also provides that, in making this determination, "account may be taken of the pregnant woman's actual or reasonably foreseeable environment." It also permits a physician, without the concurrence of others, to terminate a pregnancy where he is of the good-faith opinion that the abortion "is immediately necessary to save the life or to prevent grave permanent injury to the physical or mental health of the pregnant woman."

5. The American law. In this country, the law in effect in all but a few States until mid-19th century was the pre-existing English common law. Connecticut, the first State to enact abortion legislation, adopted in 1821 that part of Lord Ellenborough's Act that related to a woman "quick with child." The death penalty was not imposed. Abortion before quickening was made a crime in that State only in 1860. In 1828, New York enacted legislation that, in two respects, was to serve as a model for early antiabortion statutes. First, while barring destruction of an unquickened fetus as well as a quick fetus, it made the former only a misdemeanor, but the latter second-degree manslaughter. Second, it incorporated a concept of therapeutic abortion by providing that an abortion was excused if it "shall have been necessary to preserve the life of such mother, or shall have been advised by two physicians to be necessary for such purpose." By 1840, when Texas had received the common law, only eight American States had statutes dealing with abortion. It was not until after the War Between the States that legislation began generally to replace the common law. Most of these initial statutes dealt severely with abortion after quickening but were lenient with it before quickening. Most punished attempts equally with completed abortions. While many statutes included the exception for an abortion thought by one or more physicians to be necessary to save the mother's life, that provision soon disappeared and the typical law required that the procedure actually be necessary for that purpose.

Gradually, in the middle and late 19th century the quickening distinction disappeared from the statutory law of most States and the degree of the offense and the penalties were increased. By the end of the 1950's, a large majority of the jurisdictions banned abortion, however and whenever performed, unless done to save or preserve the life of the mother. The exceptions, Alabama and the District of Columbia, permitted abortion to preserve the mother's health. Three States permitted abortions that were not "unlawfully" performed or that were not "without lawful justification," leaving interpretation of those standards to the courts. In the past several years, however, a trend toward liberalization of abortion statutes has resulted in adoption, by about one-third of the States, of less stringent laws, most of them patterned after the ALI Model Penal Code set forth as Appendix B to the opinion in *Doe v. Bolton.*

It is thus apparent that at common law, at the time of the adoption of our Constitution, and throughout the major portion of the 19th century, abortion was viewed with less disfavor than under most American statutes currently in effect. Phrasing it another way, a woman enjoyed a substantially broader right to terminate a pregnancy than she does in most States today. At least with respect to the early stage of pregnancy, and very possibly without such a limitation, the opportunity to make this choice was present in this country well into the 19th century. Even later, the law continued for some time to treat less punitively an abortion procured in early pregnancy.

6. The position of the American Medical Association. The anti-abortion mood prevalent in this country in the late 19th century was shared by the medical profession. Indeed, the attitude of the profession may have played a significant role in the enactment of stringent criminal abortion legislation during that period.

An AMA Committee on Criminal Abortion was appointed in May 1857. It presented its report to the Twelfth Annual Meeting. That report observed that the Committee had been appointed to investigate criminal abortion "with a view to its general suppression." It deplored abortion and its frequency and it listed three causes of "this general demoralization":

The first of these causes is a wide-spread popular ignorance of the true character of the crime—a belief, even among mothers themselves, that the foetus is not alive till after the period of quickening.

The second of the agents alluded to is the fact that the profession themselves are frequently supposed careless of foetal life. . . .

The third reason of the frightful extent of this crime is found in the grave defects of our laws, both common and statute, as regards the independent and actual existence of the child before birth, as a living being. These errors, which are sufficient in most instances to prevent conviction, are based, and only based, upon mistaken and exploded medical dogmas. With strange inconsistency, the law fully acknowledges the foetus in utero and its inherent rights, for civil purposes; while personally and as criminally affected, it fails to recognize it, and to its life as yet denies all protection.

The Committee then offered, and the Association adopted, resolutions protesting "against such unwarrantable destruction of human life," calling upon state legislatures to revise their abortion laws, and requesting the cooperation of state medical societies "in pressing the subject."

In 1871 a long and vivid report was submitted by the Committee on Criminal Abortion. It ended with the observation, "We had to deal with human life. In a matter of less importance we could entertain no compromise. An honest judge on the bench would call things by their proper names. We could do no less." It proffered resolutions, adopted by the Association, recommending, among other things, that it "be unlawful and unprofessional for any physician to induce abortion or premature labor, without the concurrent opinion of at least one respectable consulting physician, and then always with a view to the safety of the child—if that be possible," and calling "the attention of the clergy of all denominations to the perverted views of morality entertained by a large class of females—aye, and men also, on this important question."

Except for periodic condemnation of the criminal abortionist, no further formal AMA action took place until 1967. In that year, the Committee on Human Reproduction urged the adoption of a stated policy of opposition to induced abortion, except when there is "documented medical evidence" of a threat to the health or life of the mother, or that the child "may be born with incapacitating physical deformity or mental deficiency," or that a pregnancy "resulting from legally established statutory or forcible rape or incest may constitute a threat to the mental or physical health of the patient," two other physicians "chosen because of their recognized professional competence have examined the patient and have concurred in writing," and the procedure "is performed in a hospital accredited by the Joint Commission on Accreditation of Hospitals." The providing of medical information by physicians to state legislatures in their consideration of legislation regarding therapeutic abortion was "to be considered consistent with the principles of ethics of the American Medical Association." This recommendation was adopted by the House of Delegates.

In 1970, after the introduction of a variety of proposed resolutions, and of a report from its Board of Trustees, a reference committee noted "polarization of the medical profession on this controversial issue"; division among those who had testified; a difference of opinion among AMA councils and committees; "the remarkable shift in testimony" in six months, felt to be influenced "by the rapid changes in state laws and by the judicial decisions which tend to make abortion more freely available;" and a feeling "that this trend will continue." On June 25, 1970, the House of Delegates adopted preambles and most of the resolutions proposed by the reference committee. The preambles emphasized "the best interests of the patient," "sound clinical judgment," and "informed patient consent," in contrast to "mere acquiescence to the patient's demand." The resolutions asserted that abortion is a medical procedure that should be performed by a licensed physician in an accredited hospital only after consultation with two other physicians and in conformity with state law, and that no party to the procedure should be required to violate personally held moral principles. The AMA Judicial Council rendered a complementary opinion.

7. The position of the American Public Health Association. In October 1970, the Executive Board of the APHA adopted Standards for Abortion Services. These were five in number:

a. Rapid and simple abortion referral must be readily available through state and local public health departments, medical societies, or other nonprofit organizations.

b. An important function of counselling should be to simplify and expedite the provision of abortion services; it should not delay the obtaining of these services.

c. Psychiatric consultation should not be mandatory. As in the case of other specialized medical services, psychiatric consultation should be sought for definite indications and not on a routine basis.

d. A wide range of individuals from appropriately trained, sympathetic volunteers to highly skilled physicians may qualify as abortion counselors.

e. Contraception and/or sterilization should be discussed with each abortion patient.

Among factors pertinent to life and health risks associated with abortion were three that "are recognized as important":

a. the skill of the physician,

b. the environment in which the abortion is performed, and above all

c. the duration of pregnancy, as determined by uterine size and confirmed by menstrual history.

It was said that "a well-equipped hospital" offers more protection "to cope with unforeseen difficulties than an office or clinic without such resources. . . . The factor of gestational age is of overriding importance." Thus, it was recommended that abortions in the second trimester and early abortions in the presence of existing medical complications be performed in hospitals as inpatient procedures. For pregnancies in the first trimester, abortion in the hospital with or without overnight stay "is probably the safest practice." An abortion in an extramural facility, however, is an acceptable alternative "provided arrangements exist in advance to admit patients promptly if unforeseen complications develop." Standards for an abortion facility were listed. It was said that at present abortions should be performed by physicians or osteopaths who are licensed to practice and who have "adequate training."

8. The position of the American Bar Association. At its meeting in February 1972 the ABA House of Delegates approved, with 17 opposing votes, the Uniform Abortion Act that had been drafted and approved the preceding August by the Conference of Commissioners on Uniform State Laws. We set forth the Act in full in the margin. The Conference has appended an enlightening Prefatory Note.

Three reasons have been advanced to explain historically the enactment of criminal abortion laws in the 19th century and to justify their continued existence.

It has been argued occasionally that these laws were the product of a Victorian social concern to discourage illicit sexual conduct. Texas, however, does not advance this justification in the present case, and it appears that no court or commentator has taken the argument seriously. The appellants and amici contend, moreover, that this is not a proper state purpose at all and suggest that, if it were, the Texas statutes are overbroad in protecting it since the law fails to distinguish between married and unwed mothers.

A second reason is concerned with abortion as a medical procedure. When most criminal abortion laws were first enacted, the procedure was a hazardous one for the woman. This was particularly true prior to the development of antisepsis. Antiseptic techniques, of course, were based on discoveries by Lister, Pasteur, and others first announced in 1867, but were not generally accepted and employed until about the turn of the century. Abortion mortality was high. Even after 1900, and perhaps until as late as the development of antibiotics in the 1940's, standard modern techniques such as dilation and curettage were not nearly so safe as they are today. Thus, it has been argued that a State's real concern in enacting a criminal abortion law was to protect the pregnant woman, that is, to restrain her from submitting to a procedure that placed her life in serious jeopardy.

Modern medical techniques have altered this situation. Appellants and various amici refer to medical data indicating that abortion in early pregnancy, that is, prior to the end of the first trimester, although not without its risk, is now relatively safe. Mortality rates for women undergoing early abortions, where the procedure is legal, appear to be as low as or lower than the rates for normal childbirth. Consequently, any interest of the State in protecting the woman from an inherently hazardous procedure, except when it would be equally dangerous for her to forgo it, has largely disappeared. Of course, important state interests in the areas of health and medical standards do remain. The State has a legitimate interest in seeing to it that abortion, like any other medical procedure, is performed under circumstances that insure maximum safety for the patient. This interest obviously extends at least to the performing physician and his staff, to the facilities involved, to the availability of after-care, and to adequate provision for any complication or emergency that might arise. The prevalence of high mortality rates at illegal "abortion mills" strengthens, rather than weakens, the State's interest in regulating the conditions under which abortions are performed. Moreover, the risk to the woman increases as her pregnancy continues. Thus, the State retains a definite interest in protecting the woman's own health and safety when an abortion is proposed at a late stage of pregnancy.

The third reason is the State's interest—some phrase it in terms of duty—in protecting prenatal life. Some of the argument for this justification rests on the theory that a new human life is present from the moment of conception. The State's interest and general obligation to protect life then extends, it is argued, to prenatal life. Only when the life of the pregnant mother herself is at stake, balanced against the life she carries within her, should the interest of the embryo or fetus not prevail. Logically, of course, a legitimate state interest in this area need not stand or fall on acceptance of the belief that life begins at conception or at some other point prior to live birth. In assessing the State's interest, recognition may be given to the less rigid claim that as long as at least potential life is involved, the State may assert interests beyond the protection of the pregnant woman alone.

Parties challenging state abortion laws have sharply disputed in some courts the contention that a purpose of these laws, when enacted, was to protect prenatal life. Pointing to the absence of legislative history to support the contention, they claim that most state laws were designed solely to protect the woman. Because medical advances have lessened this concern, at least with respect to abortion in early pregnancy, they argue that with respect to such abortions the laws can no longer be justified by any state interest. There is some scholarly support for this view of original purpose. The few state courts called upon to interpret their laws in the late 19th and early 20th centuries did focus on the State's interest in protecting the woman's health rather than in preserving the embryo and fetus. Proponents of this view point out that in many States, including Texas, by statute or judicial interpretation, the pregnant woman herself could not be prosecuted for self-abortion or for cooperating in an abortion performed upon her by another. They claim that adoption of the "quickening" distinction through received common law and state statutes tacitly recognizes the greater health hazards inherent in late abortion and impliedly repudiates the theory that life begins at conception.

It is with these interests, and the weight to be attached to them, that this case is concerned.

The Constitution does not explicitly mention any right of privacy. In a line of decisions, however, going back perhaps as far as *Union Pacific R. Co. v. Botsford* (1891), the Court has recognized that a right of personal privacy, or a guarantee of certain areas or zones of privacy, does exist under the Constitution. In varying contexts, the Court or individual Justices have, indeed, found at least the roots of that right in the First Amendment, *Stanley v. Georgia* (1969); in the Fourth and Fifth Amendments, *Terry v. Ohio* (1968), *Katz v. United States* (1967), *Boyd v. United States* (1886), see *Olmstead v. United States* (1928) (Brandeis, J., dissenting); in the penumbras of the Bill of Rights, *Griswold v. Connecticut*; in the Ninth Amendment, or in the concept of liberty guaranteed by the first section of the Fourteenth Amendment, see *Meyer v. Nebraska* (1923). These decisions make it clear that only personal rights that can be deemed "fundamental" or "implicit in the concept of ordered liberty," are included in this guarantee of personal privacy. They also make it clear that the right has some extension to activities relating to marriage, *Loving v. Virginia* (1967); procreation, *Skinner v. Oklahoma* (1942); contraception, *Eisenstadt v. Baird* (WHITE, J., concurring in result); family relationships, *Prince v. Massachusetts* (1944); and child rearing and education, *Pierce v. Society of Sisters* (1925), *Meyer v. Nebraska*.

This right of privacy, whether it be founded in the Fourteenth Amendment's concept of personal liberty and restrictions upon state action, as we feel it is, or, as the District Court determined, in the Ninth Amendment's reservation of rights to the people, is broad enough to encompass a woman's decision whether or not to terminate her pregnancy. The detriment that the State would impose upon the pregnant woman by denying this choice altogether is apparent. Specific and direct harm medically diagnosable even in early pregnancy may be involved. Maternity, or additional offspring, may force upon the woman a distressful life and future. Psychological harm may be imminent. Mental and physical health may be taxed by child care. There is also the distress, for all concerned, associated with the unwanted child, and there is the problem of bringing a child into a family already unable, psychologically and otherwise, to care for it. In other cases, as in this one, the additional difficulties and continuing stigma of unwed motherhood may be involved. All these are factors the woman and her responsible physician necessarily will consider in consultation.

On the basis of elements such as these, appellant and some amici argue that the woman's right is absolute and that she is entitled to terminate her pregnancy at whatever time, in whatever way, and for whatever reason she alone chooses. With this we do not agree. Appellant's arguments that Texas either has no valid interest at all in regulating the abortion decision, or no interest strong enough to support any limitation upon the woman's sole determination, are unpersuasive. The Court's decisions recognizing a right of privacy also acknowledge that some state regulation in areas protected by that right is appropriate. As noted above, a State may properly assert important interests in safeguarding health, in maintaining medical standards, and in protecting potential life. At some point in pregnancy, these respective interests become sufficiently compelling to sustain regulation of the factors that govern the abortion decision. The privacy right involved, therefore, cannot be said to be absolute. In fact, it is not clear to us that the claim asserted by some amici that one has an unlimited right to do with one's body as one pleases bears a close relationship to the right of privacy previously articulated in the Court's decisions. The Court has refused to recognize an unlimited right of this kind in the past. *Jacobson v. Massachusetts* (1905) (vaccination); *Buck v. Bell* (1927) (sterilization).

We, therefore, conclude that the right of personal privacy includes the abortion decision, but that this right is not unqualified and must be considered against important state interests in regulation.

We note that those federal and state courts that have recently considered abortion law challenges have reached the same conclusion. A majority, in addition to the District Court in the present case, have held state laws unconstitutional, at least in part, because of vagueness or because of overbreadth and abridgment of rights. . . .

Others have sustained state statutes. . . .

Although the results are divided, most of these courts have agreed that the right of privacy, however based, is broad enough to cover the abortion decision; that the right, nonetheless, is not absolute and is subject to some limitations; and that at some point the state interests as to protection of health, medical standards, and prenatal life, become dominant. We agree with this approach.

Where certain "fundamental rights" are involved, the Court has held that regulation limiting these rights may be justified only by a "compelling state interest," *Kramer v. Union Free School District* (1969); *Shapiro v. Thompson* (1969), *Sherbert v. Verner* (1963), and that legislative enactments must be narrowly drawn to express only the legitimate state interests at stake. . . .

In the recent abortion cases, cited above, courts have recognized these principles. Those striking down state laws have generally scrutinized the State's interests in protecting health and potential life, and have concluded that neither interest justified broad limitations on the reasons for which a physician and his pregnant patient might decide that she should have an abortion in the early stages of pregnancy. Courts sustaining state laws have held that the State's determinations to protect health or prenatal life are dominant and constitutionally justifiable.

The District Court held that the appellee failed to meet his burden of demonstrating that the Texas statute's infringement upon Roe's rights was necessary to support a compelling state interest, and that, although the appellee presented "several compelling justifications for state presence in the area of abortions," the statutes outstripped these justifications and swept "far beyond any areas of compelling state interest." Appellant and appellee both contest that holding. Appellant, as has been indicated, claims an absolute right that bars any state imposition of criminal penalties in the area. Appellee argues that the State's determination to recognize and protect prenatal life from and after conception constitutes a compelling state interest. As noted above, we do not agree fully with either formulation.

A. The appellee and certain amici argue that the fetus is a "person" within the language and meaning of the Fourteenth Amendment. In support of this, they outline at length and in detail the well-known facts of fetal development. If this suggestion of personhood is established, the appellant's case, of course, collapses, for the fetus' right to life would then be guaranteed specifically by the Amendment. The appellant conceded as much on reargument. On the other hand, the appellee conceded on reargument that no case could be cited that holds that a fetus is a person within the meaning of the Fourteenth Amendment.

The Constitution does not define "person" in so many words. Section 1 of the Fourteenth Amendment contains three references to "person." The first, in defining "citizens," speaks of "persons born or naturalized in the United States." The word also appears both in the Due Process Clause and in the Equal Protection Clause. "Person" is used in other places in the Constitution: in the listing of qualifications for Representatives and Senators, Art. I, 2, cl. 2, and 3, cl. 3; in the Apportionment Clause, Art. I, 2, cl. 3; in the Migration and Importation provision, Art. I, 9, cl. 1; in the Emolument Clause, Art. I, 9, cl. 8; in the Electors provisions, Art. II, 1, cl. 2, and the superseded cl. 3; in the provision outlining qualifications for the office of President, Art. II, 1, cl. 5; in the Extradition provisions, Art. IV, 2, cl. 2, and the superseded Fugitive Slave Clause 3; and in the Fifth, Twelfth, and Twenty-second Amendments, as well as in 2 and 3 of the Fourteenth Amendment. But in nearly all these instances, the use of the word is such that it has application only postnatally. None indicates, with any assurance, that it has any possible pre-natal application.

All this, together with our observation, that throughout the major portion of the 19th century prevailing legal abortion practices were far freer than they are today, persuades us that the word "person," as used in the Fourteenth Amendment, does not include the unborn. This is in accord with the results reached in those few cases where the issue has been squarely presented. . . . Indeed, our decision in *United States v. Vuitch* (1971), inferentially is to the same effect, for we there would not have indulged in statutory interpretation favorable to abortion in specified circumstances if the necessary consequence was the termination of life entitled to Fourteenth Amendment protection.

This conclusion, however, does not of itself fully answer the contentions raised by Texas, and we pass on to other considerations.

B. The pregnant woman cannot be isolated in her privacy. She carries an embryo and, later, a fetus, if one accepts the medical definitions of the developing young in the human uterus. See *Dorland's Illustrated Medical Dictionary* (24th ed. 1965). The situation therefore is inherently different from marital intimacy, or bedroom possession of obscene material, or marriage, or procreation, or education, with which *Eisenstadt* and *Griswold, Stanley, Loving, Skinner,* and *Pierce* and *Meyer* were respectively concerned. As we have intimated above, it is reasonable and appropriate for a State to decide that at some point in time another interest, that of health of the mother or that of potential human life, becomes significantly involved. The woman's privacy is no longer sole and any right of privacy she possesses must be measured accordingly.

Texas urges that, apart from the Fourteenth Amendment, life begins at conception and is present throughout pregnancy, and that, therefore, the State has a compelling interest in protecting that life from and after conception. We need not resolve the difficult question of when life begins. When those trained in the respective disciplines of medicine, philosophy, and theology are unable to arrive at any consensus, the judiciary, at this point in the development of man's knowledge, is not in a position to speculate as to the answer.

It should be sufficient to note briefly the wide divergence of thinking on this most sensitive and difficult question. There has always been strong support for the view that life does not begin until live birth. This was the belief of the Stoics. It appears to be the predominant, though not the unanimous, attitude of the Jewish faith. It may be taken to represent also the position of a large segment of the Protestant community, insofar as that can be ascertained; organized groups that have taken a formal position on the abortion issue have generally regarded abortion as a matter for the conscience of the individual and her family. As we have noted, the common law found greater significance in quickening. Physicians and their scientific colleagues have regarded that event with less interest and have tended to focus either upon conception, upon live birth, or upon the interim point at which the fetus becomes "viable," that is, potentially able to live outside the mother's womb, albeit with artificial aid. Viability is usually placed at about seven months (28 weeks) but may occur earlier, even at 24 weeks. The Aristotelian theory of "mediate animation," that held sway throughout the Middle Ages and the Renaissance in Europe, continued to be official Roman Catholic dogma until the 19th century, despite opposition to this "ensoulment" theory from those in the Church who would recognize the existence of life from the moment of conception. The latter is now, of course, the official belief of the Catholic Church. As one brief amicus discloses, this is a view strongly held by many non-Catholics as well, and by many physicians. Substantial problems for precise definition of this view are posed, however, by new embryological data that purport to indicate that conception is a "process" over time, rather than an event, and by new medical techniques such as menstrual extraction, the "morning-after" pill, implantation of embryos, artificial insemination, and even artificial wombs.

In areas other than criminal abortion, the law has been reluctant to endorse any theory that life, as we recognize it, begins before live birth or to accord legal rights to the unborn except in narrowly defined situations and except when the rights are contingent upon live birth. For example, the traditional rule of tort law denied recovery for prenatal injuries even though the child was born alive. That rule has been changed in almost every jurisdiction. In most States, recovery is said to be permitted only if the fetus was viable, or at least quick, when the injuries were sustained, though few courts have squarely so held. In a recent development, generally opposed by the commentators, some States permit the parents of a stillborn child to maintain an action for wrongful death because of prenatal injuries. Such an action, however, would appear to be one to vindicate the parents' interest and is thus consistent with the view that the fetus, at most, represents only the potentiality of life. Similarly, unborn children have been recognized as acquiring rights or interests by way of inheritance or other devolution of property, and have been represented by guardians ad litem. Perfection of the interests involved, again, has generally been contingent upon live birth. In short, the unborn have never been recognized in the law as persons in the whole sense.

In view of all this, we do not agree that, by adopting one theory of life, Texas may override the rights of the pregnant woman that are at stake. We repeat, however, that the State does have an important and legitimate interest in preserving and protecting the health of the pregnant woman, whether she be a resident of the State or a nonresident who seeks medical consultation and treatment there, and that it has still another important and legitimate interest in protecting the potentiality of human life. These interests are separate and distinct. Each grows in substantiality as the woman approaches term and, at a point during pregnancy, each becomes "compelling."

With respect to the State's important and legitimate interest in the health of the mother, the "compelling" point, in the light of present medical knowledge, is at approximately the end of the first trimester. This is so because of the now-established medical fact, referred to above at 149, that until the end of the first trimester mortality in abortion may be less than mortality in normal childbirth. It follows that, from and after this point, a State may regulate the abortion procedure to the extent that the regulation reasonably relates to the preservation and protection of maternal health. Examples of permissible state regulation in this area are requirements as to the qualifications of the person who is to perform the abortion; as to the licensure of that person; as to the facility in which the procedure is to be performed, that is, whether it must be a hospital or may be a clinic or some other place of less-than-hospital status; as to the licensing of the facility; and the like.

This means, on the other hand, that, for the period of pregnancy prior to this "compelling" point, the attending physician, in consultation with his patient, is free to determine, without regulation by the State, that, in his medical judgment, the patient's pregnancy should be terminated. If that decision is reached, the judgment may be effectuated by an abortion free of interference by the State.

With respect to the State's important and legitimate interest in potential life, the "compelling" point is at viability. This is so because the fetus then presumably has the capability of meaningful life outside the mother's womb. State regulation protective of fetal life after viability thus has both logical and biological justifications. If the State is interested in protecting fetal life after viability, it may go so far as to proscribe abortion during that period, except when it is necessary to preserve the life or health of the mother.

Measured against these standards, Art. 1196 of the Texas Penal Code, in restricting legal abortions to those "procured or attempted by medical advice for the purpose of saving the life of the mother," sweeps too broadly. The statute makes no distinction between abortions performed early in pregnancy and those performed later, and it limits to a single reason, "saving" the mother's life, the legal justification for the procedure. The statute, therefore, cannot survive the constitutional attack made upon it here.

This conclusion makes it unnecessary for us to consider the additional challenge to the Texas statute asserted on grounds of vagueness. See *United States v. Vuitch.*

To summarize and to repeat:

1. A state criminal abortion statute of the current Texas type, that excepts from criminality only a life-saving procedure on behalf of the mother, without regard to pregnancy stage and without recognition of the other interests involved, is violative of the Due Process Clause of the Fourteenth Amendment.

(a) For the stage prior to approximately the end of the first trimester, the abortion decision and its effectuation must be left to the medical judgment of the pregnant woman's attending physician.

(b) For the stage subsequent to approximately the end of the first trimester, the State, in promoting its interest in the health of the mother, may, if it chooses, regulate the abortion procedure in ways that are reasonably related to maternal health.

(c) For the stage subsequent to viability, the State in promoting its interest in the potentiality of human life may, if it chooses, regulate, and even proscribe, abortion except where it is necessary, in appropriate medical judgment, for the preservation of the life or health of the mother.

2. The State may define the term "physician," as it has been employed in the preceding paragraphs of this Part XI of this opinion, to mean only a physician currently licensed by the State, and may proscribe any abortion by a person who is not a physician as so defined.

In *Doe v. Bolton*, procedural requirements contained in one of the modern abortion statutes are considered. That opinion and this one, of course, are to be read together.

This holding, we feel, is consistent with the relative weights of the respective interests involved, with the lessons and examples of medical and legal history, with the lenity of the common law, and with the demands of the profound problems of the present day. The decision leaves the State free to place increasing restrictions on abortion as the period of pregnancy lengthens, so long as those restrictions are tailored to the recognized state interests. The decision vindicates the right of the physician to administer medical treatment according to his professional judgment up to the points where important state interests provide compelling justifications for intervention. Up to those points, the abortion decision in all its aspects is inherently, and primarily, a medical decision, and basic responsibility for it must rest with the physician. If an individual practitioner abuses the privilege of exercising proper medical judgment, the usual remedies, judicial and intra-professional, are available.

Our conclusion that Art. 1196 is unconstitutional means, of course, that the Texas abortion statutes, as a unit, must fall. The exception of Art. 1196 cannot be struck down separately, for then the State would be left with a statute proscribing all abortion procedures no matter how medically urgent the case.

Although the District Court granted appellant Roe declaratory relief, it stopped short of issuing an injunction against enforcement of the Texas statutes. The Court has recognized that different considerations enter into a federal court's decision as to declaratory relief, on the one hand, and injunctive relief, on the other. We are not dealing with a statute that, on its face, appears to abridge free expression, an area of particular concern under *Dombrowski* and refined in *Younger v. Harris*.

We find it unnecessary to decide whether the District Court erred in withholding injunctive relief, for we assume the Texas prosecutorial authorities will give full credence to this decision that the present criminal abortion statutes of that State are unconstitutional.

The judgment of the District Court as to intervenor Hallford is reversed, and Dr. Hallford's complaint in intervention is dismissed. In all other respects, the judgment of the District Court is affirmed. Costs are allowed to the appellee.

It is so ordered.

Source: Roe v. Wade, 410 U.S. 113 (1973).

Freedom of Access to Clinic Entrances Act (1994)

From her own experience in London in 1957, Gloria knew the feelings of loneliness and isolation that individuals could experience as they sought an abortion, and she was deeply committed to removing any obstacles to those who had made that decision. Laws that sought to limit a woman's ability to get an abortion were a constant over the decades after the Supreme Court's decision in Roe v. Wade. *Gloria was vigilant in her efforts to prevent the legal system and society from backsliding on the individual choice central to this issue, which she saw as central to a woman's autonomy. Whether it was the physical access to clinics or financial barriers reflected in efforts to limit Medicaid's coverage of abortion, Gloria worked unceasingly to protect women's right to reproductive choice in the face of an ongoing effort by conservatives to scale back the guarantees of* Roe.

An Act to amend title 18, United States Code, to assure freedom of access to reproductive services.

Be it enacted by the Senate and House of Representatives of the United States of America in Congress assembled,

Section 1. SHORT TITLE.

This act may be cited as the "Freedom of Access to Clinic Entrances Act of 1994."

Section 2. PURPOSE.

Pursuant to the affirmative power of Congress to enact this legislation under section 8 of article I of the U.S. Constitution, as well as under section 5 of the fourteenth amendment to the Constitution, it is the purpose of this Act to protect and promote the public safety and health and activities affecting interstate commerce by establishing Federal criminal penalties and civil remedies for certain violent, threatening, obstructive and destructive conduct that is intended to injure, intimidate or interfere with persons seeking to obtain or provide reproductive health services.

Section 3. FREEDOM OF ACCESS TO CLINIC ENTRANCES.

Chapter 13 of title 18, United States Code, is amended by adding at the end thereof the following new section:

"Sec. 248 Freedom of Access to Clinic Entrances.

"(a) Prohibited Activities. Whoever—

"(1) by force or threat of force or by physical obstruction, intentionally injures, intimidates or interferes with or attempts to injure, intimidate or interfere with any person because that person is or has been, or in order to intimidate such person or any other person or any class of persons from, obtaining or providing reproductive health services;

"(2) by force or threat of force or by physical obstruction, intentionally injures, intimidates or interferes with or attempts to injure, intimidate or interfere with any person lawfully exercising or seeking to exercise the First Amendment right of religious freedom at a place of religious worship; or

"(3) intentionally damages or destroys the property of a facility, or attempts to do so, because such facility provides reproductive health services, or intentionally damages or destroys the property of a place of religious worship, shall be subject to the penalties provided in subsection (b) and the civil remedies provided in subsection (c), except that a parent or legal guardian of a minor shall not be subject to any penalties or civil remedies under this section for such activities insofar as they are directed exclusively at that minor.

"(b) Penalties. Whoever violates this section shall—

"(1) in the case of a first offense, be fined in accordance with this title, or imprisoned not more than one year, or both; and

"(2) in the case of a second or subsequent offense after a prior conviction under this section, be fined in accordance with this title, or imprisoned not more than 3 years, or both; except that for an offense involving exclusively a nonviolent physical obstruction, the fine shall be not more than $10,000 and the length of imprisonment shall be not more than 6 months, or both, for the first offense; and the fine shall be not more than $25,000 and the length of imprisonment shall be not more than 18 months, or both, for a subsequent offense; and except that if bodily injury results, the length of imprisonment shall be not more than 10 years, and if death results, it shall be for any term of years or for life.

"(c) Civil Remedies.

"(1) Right of Action.

"(A) In general. Any person aggrieved by reason of the conduct prohibited by subsection (a) may commence a civil action for the relief set forth in subparagraph (B), except that such an action may be brought under subsection (a)(1) only by a person involved in providing or seeking to provide, or obtaining or seeking to obtain, services in a facility that provides reproductive health services, and such an action may be brought under subsection (a)(2) only by a person lawfully exercising or seeking to exercise the

First Amendment right of religious freedom at a place of religious worship or by the entity that owns or operates such place of religious worship.

"(B) Relief. In any action under subparagraph (A), the court may award appropriate relief, including temporary, preliminary or permanent injunctive relief and compensatory and punitive damages, as well as the costs of suit and reasonable fees for attorneys and expert witnesses. With respect to compensatory damages, the plaintiff may elect, at any time prior to the rendering of final judgment, to recover, in lieu of actual damages, an award of statutory damages in the amount of $5,000 per violation.

"(2) Action by Attorney General of the United States.

"(A) In general. If the Attorney General of the United States has reasonable cause to believe that any person or group of persons is being, has been, or may be injured by conduct constituting a violation of this section, the Attorney General may commence a civil action in any appropriate United States District Court.

"(B) Relief. In any action under subparagraph (A), the court may award appropriate relief, including temporary, preliminary or permanent injunctive relief, and compensatory damages to persons aggrieved as described in paragraph (1)(B). The court, to vindicate the public interest, may also assess a civil penalty against each respondent—

"(i) in an amount not exceeding $10,000 for a nonviolent physical obstruction and $15,000 for other first violations; and

"(ii) in an amount not exceeding $15,000 for a nonviolent physical obstruction and $25,000 for any subsequent violation.

"(3) Actions by State Attorneys General.

"(A) In general. If the Attorney General of a State has reasonable cause to believe that any person or group of persons is being, has been, or may be injured by conduct constituting a violation of this section, such Attorney General may commence a civil action in the name of such State, as parens patriae on behalf of natural persons residing in such State, in any appropriate United States District Court.

"(B) Relief. In any action under subparagraph (A), the court may award appropriate relief, including temporary, preliminary or permanent injunctive relief, compensatory damages, and civil penalties as described in paragraph (2)(B).

"(d) Rules of Construction. Nothing in this section shall be construed—

"(1) to prohibit any expressive conduct (including peaceful picketing or other peaceful demonstration) protected from legal prohibition by the First Amendment to the Constitution;

"(2) to create new remedies for interference with activities protected by the free speech or free exercise clauses of the First Amendment to the Constitution, occurring outside a facility, regardless of the point of view expressed, or to limit any existing legal remedies for such interference;

"(3) to provide exclusive criminal penalties or civil remedies with respect to the conduct prohibited by this section, or to preempt State or local laws that may provide such penalties or remedies; or

"(4) to interfere with the enforcement of State or local laws regulating the performance of abortions or other reproductive health services.

"(e) Definitions. As used in this section:

"(1) Facility. The term "facility" includes a hospital, clinic, physician's office, or other facility that provides reproductive health services, and includes the building or structure in which the facility is located.

"(2) Interfere with. The term "interfere with" means to restrict a person's freedom of movement.

"(3) Intimidate. The term "intimidate" means to place a person in reasonable apprehension of bodily harm to him- or herself or to another.

"(4) Physical Obstruction. The term "physical obstruction" means rendering impassable ingress to or egress from a facility that provides reproductive health services or to or from a place of religious worship, or rendering passage to or from such a facility or place of religious worship unreasonably difficult or hazardous.

"(5) Reproductive Health Services. The term "reproductive health services" means reproductive health services provided in a hospital, clinic, physician's office, or other facility, and includes medical, surgical, counseling, or referral services relating to the human reproductive system, including services relating to pregnancy or the termination of a pregnancy.

"(6) State. The term "State" includes a State of the United States, the District of Columbia, and any commonwealth, territory, or possession of the United States.

SEC. 4. CLERICAL AMENDMENT.

The table of sections at the beginning of chapter 13 of title 18, United States Codes, is amended by adding at the end the following new item:

"248. Blocking access to reproductive health services.

SEC. 5. SEVERABILITY.

If any provision of this Act, an amendment made by this Act, or the application of such provision or amendment to any person or circumstance is held to be unconstitutional, the remainder of this Act, the amendments made by this Act, and the application of the provisions of such to any other person or circumstance shall not be affected thereby.

SEC. 6. EFFECTIVE DATE.

This Act takes effect on the date of the enactment of this Act, and shall apply only with respect to conduct occurring on or after such date.

Source: Freedom of Access to Clinic Entrances Act of 1994. U.S. Code 18: 248.

Bibliography

Any bibliography for a biography of Gloria Steinem must include the many works that chronicle her life as well as those that reflect her reform efforts and the broader context in which she lived and worked. Consequently, I have included numerous additional works to which a reader can turn in an effort to understand the people and events that were at the heart of her work and life. There are also works that help frame the period and will provide a reader additional valuable context for Gloria's decades long reform efforts.

Gloria has never stopped being a journalist and a writer, and thus a central part of this bibliography is her own work, both individual articles and books, some of which include versions of her earlier efforts. Finally, given the age in which Gloria has lived and worked, modern media also offer us some important sources from which to draw. The video entries included here serve as valuable supplements to the standard print works. These multimedia resources are further supplemented by some internet-based information, including Gloria's own website.

Given her five decades of activism and the decade of reporting that preceded it, there are innumerable articles and interviews, long and short, especially in newspapers and the popular press, of which the ones included here are only a fraction. But in the end, this wide-ranging collection of materials provides resources from which one can get an ever-deeper understanding and appreciation of Gloria Steinem, the person and the activist, as well as of the life she led and the society she helped change.

BOOKS

Berry, Mary Frances. 1986. *Why Era Failed: Politics, Women's Rights, and the Amending Process of the Constitution.* Bloomington: Indiana University Press.

Blackwell, Geoff, and Ruth Hobday. 2020. *I Know This to Be True: Gloria Steinem*. San Francisco: Chronicle Books.

Boles, Janet K. 1979. *The Politics of the Equal Rights Amendment: Conflict and the Decision Process*. Boston: Addison-Wesley Longman.

Bradley, Patricia. 2004. *Mass Media and the Shaping of American Feminism, 1963–1975*. Jackson: University Press of Mississippi.

Brownmiller, Susan. 1999. *In Our Time: Memoir of a Revolution*. New York: Dial Press.

Chisholm, Shirley. 1970. *Unbought and Unbossed*. Boston: Houghton Mifflin Harcourt.

Chisholm, Shirley. 1973. *The Good Fight*. New York: HarperCollins.

Cobble, Dorothy Sue, Linda Gordon, and Astrid Henry. 2014. *Feminism Unfinished: A Short, Surprising History of American Women's Movements*. New York: Liveright.

Cohen, Marcia. 1988. *The Sisterhood: The True Story of the Women Who Changed the World*. New York: Simon & Schuster.

Collins, Gail. 2003. *America's Women: 400 Years of Dolls, Drudges, Helpmates, and Heroines*. New York: William Morrow.

Collins, Gail. 2009. *When Everything Changed: The Amazing Journey of American Women from 1960 to the Present*. New York: Little, Brown.

Critchlow, Donald T. 2005. *Phyllis Schlafly and Grassroots Conservatism: A Woman's Crusade*. Princeton, NJ: Princeton University Press.

Davis, Flora. 1991. *Moving the Mountain: The Women's Movement in America since 1960*. New York: Simon & Schuster.

Dow, Bonnie. 1996. *Prime-Time Feminism: Television, Media Culture, and the Women's Movement since 1970*. Philadelphia: University of Pennsylvania Press.

Dreier, Peter. 2012. "Gloria Steinem." In *The 100 Greatest Americans of the 20th Century*, 381–85. New York: Bold Type Books.

Farrell, Amy Erdman. 1998. *Yours in Sisterhood: Ms. Magazine and the Promise of Popular Feminism*. Chapel Hill: University of North Carolina Press.

Faux, Marian. 1988. Roe v. Wade: *The Untold Story of the Landmark Supreme Court Decision That Made Abortion Legal*. New York: Scribner.

Felsenthal, Carol. 1982. *Phyllis Schlafly: The Sweetheart of the Silent Majority*. Washington, DC: Regnery Gateway.

Feminist Family Value Forum. 1996. *Foundation for a Compassionate Society*. Fitchburg, MA: QuakerBooks of FGC.

Friedan, Betty. 1963. *The Feminine Mystique*. New York: Norton.

Friedan, Betty. 2000. *Life So Far: A Memoir*. New York: Simon & Schuster.

Gupta, Ruchira, ed. 2014. *As If Women Matter: The Essential Gloria Steinem Reader*. New Delhi: Rupa Publications India.

Heilbrun, Carolyn G. 1995. *Education of a Woman: The Life of Gloria Steinem.* New York: Dial Press.

Hull, N. E. H., and Peter Charles Hoffer. 2010. *Roe v. Wade: The Abortion Rights Controversy in American History.* 2nd rev. edition. Lawrence: University Press of Kansas.

Hymowitz, Carol, and Michaele Weissman. 1984. *A History of Women in America.* New York: Bantam.

Karbo, Karen. 2018. "Gloria Steinem." In *In Praise of Difficult Women: Life Lessons From 29 Heroines Who Dared to Break the Rules,* 42–51. Washington, DC: National Geographic.

Klagsbrun, Francine, ed. 1973. *The First Ms. Reader.* New York: Warner Paperback.

Lazo, Caroline Evensen. 1998. *Steinem: Feminist Extraordinaire.* Minneapolis, MN: Lerner Publishing Group.

Levine, Suzanne Braun, and Mary Thom, eds. 2007. *Bella Abzug: How One Tough Broad from the Bronx Fought Jim Crow and Joe McCarthy, Pissed Off Jimmy Carter, Battled for the Rights of Women and Workers, Rallied against War and for the Planet, and Shook Up Politics along the Way.* New York: Farrar, Straus and Giroux.

MacLean, Nancy. 2008. *The American Women's Movement, 1945–2000: A Brief History with Documents.* Boston: Bedford/St. Martin's.

Mankiller, Wilma Pearl. 1993. *Mankiller: A Chief and Her People.* New York: St. Martin's.

Mansbridge, Jane J. 1986. *Why We Lost the ERA.* Chicago: University of Chicago Press.

Manso, Peter, ed. 1969. *Running against the Machine: The Mailer-Breslin Campaign.* Garden City, NY: Doubleday.

Marcello, Patricia Cronin. 2004. *Gloria Steinem: A Biography.* Westport, CT: Greenwood Press.

Morgan, Robin, ed. 1970. *Sisterhood Is Powerful: An Anthology of Writings from the Women's Liberation Movement.* New York: Vintage Books.

Morgan, Robin, ed. 1984. *Sisterhood Is Global: The International Women's Movement Anthology.* New York: Anchor.

Morgan, Robin, ed. 2003. *Sisterhood Is Forever: The Women's Anthology for a New Millennium.* New York: Washington Square Press.

National Commission on the Observance of International Women's Year. 1978. *The Spirit of Houston: The First National Women's Conference: An Official Report to the President, the Congress and the People of the United States.* Washington, DC: Government Printing Office.

Oliver, Susan. 2007. *Betty Friedan: The Personal Is Political.* New York: Pearson.

Randolph, Sherie M. 2015. *Florynce "Flo" Kennedy: The Life of a Black Feminist Radical.* Chapel Hill: University of North Carolina Press.

Rinker, Jess. 2019. *Gloria Takes a Stand: How Gloria Steinem Listened, Wrote and Changed the World*. Illustrated by Daria Peoples Riley. New York: Bloomsbury Children's Books.

Seidman, Rachel F. 2019. *Speaking of Feminism: Today's Activists on the Past, Present, and Future of the U.S. Women's Movement*. Chapel Hill: University of North Carolina Press.

Spruill, Marjorie J. 2017. *Divided We Stand: The Battle over Women's Rights and Family Values That Polarized American Politics*. New York: Bloomsbury USA.

Steinem, Gloria. 1963. *The Beach Book*. New York: Viking.

Steinem, Gloria. 1983. *Outrageous Acts and Everyday Rebellions*. New York: Henry Holt.

Steinem, Gloria. 1988. *Marilyn*. New York: Henry Holt.

Steinem, Gloria. 1993. *Revolution from Within: A Book of Self-Esteem*. Boston: Little, Brown.

Steinem, Gloria. 1995. *Moving beyond Words: Age, Rage, Sex, Power, Money, Muscles: Breaking the Boundaries of Gender*. New York: Touchstone.

Steinem, Gloria. 2006. *Doing Sixty and Seventy*. Oakland, CA: Elders Academy Press.

Steinem. Gloria. 2013. *On Self-Esteem and Scholars, Witches and Other Freedom Fighters*. Brooklyn, NY: BetterListen!

Steinem, Gloria. 2015. *My Life on the Road*. New York: Random House.

Steinem, Gloria. 2019. *The Truth Will Set You Free, But First It Will Piss You Off!: Thoughts on Life, Love, and Rebellion*. New York: Random House.

Stern, Sydney Ladensohn. 1997. *Gloria Steinem: Her Passions, Politics, and Mystique*. New York: Birch Lane Press.

Thom, Mary. 1997. *Inside* Ms.: *25 Years of the Magazine and the Feminist Movement*. New York: Henry Holt.

Thom, Mary, ed. 1987. *Letters to* Ms., *1972–1987*. New York: Henry Holt.

Tobias, Sheila. 1998. *Faces of Feminism: An Activist's Reflections on the Women's Movement*. New York: Perseus.

Wandersee, Winifred D. 1988. *On the Move: American Women in the 1970s*. Boston: Twayne.

Zarnow, Leandra Ruth. 2019. *Battling Bella: The Protest Politics of Bella Abzug*. Cambridge, MA: Harvard University Press.

NEWSPAPERS, PERIODICALS, JOURNALS

Bennetts, Leslie. 1992. "Deconstructing Gloria." *Vanity Fair*, January 1992.

Bumiller, Elisabeth. 1983. "Gloria Steinem, the Everyday Rebel: Two Decades of Feminism, and the Fire Burns as Bright." *Washington Post*, October 12, 1983.

Carroll, Rebecca. 2018. "What I See: Gloria Steinem, Shoulder to Shoulder with Women of Color." *New York Times*, December 10, 2018.

Collins-Hughes, Laura. 2018. "Gloria Steinem, Watching Herself Onstage, Knows She's in Good Hands." *New York Times*, September 13, 2018.

Dwyer, Kate. 2018. "How I Get It Done: Gloria Steinem," *New York*, August 21, 2018.

Farb, Carolyn. 2017. "New Again: Gloria Steinem." *Interview*, March 8, 2017.

Gwinn, Mary Ann, 2015. "Q&A with Gloria Steinem: Still Enjoying 'Life on the Road' at 81." *Seattle Times*, November 6, 2015.

Hepola, Sarah. 2012. "Gloria Steinem, a Woman Like No Other," *New York Times*, March 16, 2012.

Hess, Amanda, 2017. "How a Fractious Women's Movement Came to Lead the Left." *New York Times Magazine*, February 7, 2017.

Izzo, Amanda. 2002. "Outrageous and Everyday: The Papers of Gloria Steinem," *Journal of Women's History* 14 (2): 151–53.

Kramer, Jane. 2015. "Road Warrior," *New Yorker*, October 19, 2015.

Leland, John. 2016. "Showgirls, Pastrami and Candor: Gloria Steinem's New York," *New York Times*, October 7, 2016.

Levitt, Leonard. 1971. "SHE: The Awesome Power of Gloria Steinem." *Esquire*, October 1971.

Murphy, Tim. 2016. "The Time Gloria Steinem Made Bernie Sanders an 'Honorary Woman.'" *Mother Jones*, January 20, 2016.

Paquette, Danielle. 2015. "A Late-Night, Backseat Cadillac Ride with Gloria Steinem." *Washington Post*, November 3, 2015.

Pogrebin, Abigail. 2011. "How Do You Spell Ms.?" *New York*, October 28, 2011.

Raab, Scott. 2015. "The ESQ&A: Gloria Steinem on Feminism's Third Wave and the Unhelpful Bill Gates." *Esquire*, October 23, 2015.

Redden, Molly. 2017. "Gloria Steinem on Her Bill Clinton Essay: 'I Wouldn't Write the Same Thing Now.'" *The Guardian*, November 30, 2017.

Ryzik, Melena. 2017. "A Look at Global Feminism, with Two of Its Inventors," *New York Times*, November 3, 2017.

Shriver, Maria. 2011. "Gloria Steinem." *Interview*, July 11, 2011.

Steinem, Gloria. 1963a. "A Bunny's Tale, Part 1." *Show*, May 1963.

Steinem, Gloria. 1963b. "A Bunny's Tale, Part 2." *Show*, June 1963.

Steinem, Gloria. 1965. "Gloria Steinem Spends a Day in Chicago with Saul Bellow." *Glamour*, July 1965.

Steinem, Gloria. 1967. "The Party: Truman Capote Receives 500 'People I Like.'" *Vogue*, January 1967.

Steinem, Gloria. 1968a. "The Black John Wayne." *New York*, November 11, 1968.

Steinem, Gloria. 1968b. "Ho Chi Minh in New York." *New York*, April 8, 1968.

Steinem, Gloria. 1968c. "In Your Heart You Know He's Nixon," *New York*, October 28, 1968.
Steinem, Gloria. 1968d. "Paul Newman: The Trouble with Being Too Good-Looking." *Woman's Own*, May 25, 1968.
Steinem, Gloria. 1968e. "Trying to Love Eugene." *New York*, August 5, 1968.
Steinem, Gloria. 1968f. "Women and Power." *New York*, December 23, 1968.
Steinem, Gloria. 1969a. "After Black Power, Women's Liberation." *New York*, April 7, 1969.
Steinem, Gloria. 1969b. "The Making (and Unmaking) of a Controller." *New York*, May 5, 1969.
Steinem, Gloria. 2005. "Shirley Chisholm: Front-Runner." *New York*, January 19, 2005.
Steinem, Gloria, and Linda Scott. 2003. "Imagining Feminism in the Marketplace: Linda Scott (University of Illinois) Interviews Gloria Steinem." *Advertising & Society Review* 4 (4). https://muse.jhu.edu/article/50201/figure/img03.
"Text of the Report Submitted by President's Commission on National Goals." *New York Times*, November 28, 1960.
Weller, Sheila. 2016. "In Defense of Gloria Steinem (Who Really Needs No Defending)." *Observer*, February 8, 2016.
Winkler, Elizabeth. 2015. "Gloria Steinem's Feminist Road Trip." *New Republic*, October 28, 2015.

MULTIMEDIA

ABC News. 2010. *Nightline: UpClose with Gloria Steinem*. Released April 6, 2010. DVD.
Arthur, Karen, dir. 1985. *A Bunny's Tale*. Aired February 25, 1985, on ABC. VHS.
hooks, bell, and Gloria Steinem. 2014. "bell hooks and Gloria Steinem at Eugene Lang College." YouTube, October 8, 2014. https://www.youtube.com/watch?v=tkzOFvfWRn4.
Lopez, Kamala, dir. 2016. *Equal Means Equal*. Documentary film released March 2016. Los Angeles: Heroica Films.
Mann, Emily. 2018. *Gloria: A Life*. Originally directed by Diane Paulus, off-Broadway.
PBS. 2013–. *Makers: Women Who Make America*. Documentary series, premiered February 26, 2013.
Steinem, Gloria, and Peter Kunhardt, dir. 2011. *Gloria: In Her Own Words*. Aired August 15, 2011, on HBO.
Taymor, Julie, dir. 2020. *The Glorias*. Feature film released September 30, 2020. Los Angeles: Page Fifty-Four Pictures.

INTERNET SOURCES

Cunningham, Clare. n.d. "Gloria Steinem's Life on the Road." Sutori. https://www.sutori.com/story/gloria-steinem-s-childhood-on-the-road--be8eBmJVxaTdASiqhm7VgV6w.

Dreier, Peter. 2019. "Celebrating Gloria Steinem: We All Stand on Her Shoulders." Public Seminar, January 2, 2019. https://publicseminar.org/2019/01/celebrating-gloria-steinem.

Office of Gloria Steinem. n.d. Gloria Steinem. http://www.gloriasteinem.com.

Midkoff, Sarah. 2019. "This Is What Gloria Steinem Was Doing at Your Age." Refinery 29, March 25, 2019. https://www.refinery29.com/en-us/2019/03/227816/what-gloria-steinem-was-doing-at-your-age.

Stan, Adele M. 2013. "'If We Each Have a Torch, There's a Lot More Light': Gloria Steinem Accepts the Presidential Medal of Freedom." Rewire.com, November 20, 2013. https://rewirenewsgroup.com/article/2013/11/20/if-we-each-have-a-torch-theres-a-lot-more-light-gloria-steinem-accepts-the-presidential-medal-of-freedom.

Index

Abzug, Bella, xviii, xx, xxi, 49, 67–69, 77, 92–98, 132, 140
Achter, Kayla, 30, 31
Aesop's Fables, 175
"After Black Power Comes Women's Liberation," xx, 60, 181
Albright, Madeline, 157, 163, 182
Alcott, Louisa May, 15, 130
Alda, Alan, 114, 127
Alinsky, Saul, 175
Allen, Woody, 49
American Cancer Society, 46
American Psychiatric Association, 174
Amherst, Massachusetts, 5, 6
Anderson, John, 159
Anka, Paul, 83, 84
Antupit, Sam, 46
Aquino, Cory, 114
Atlantic Monthly, 132
Aviator glasses, 22
"Awesome Power of Gloria Steinem, The," 88, 89

Bachman, Michelle, 160
Bale, David, 133, 134, 182
Barefoot in the Park, 127
Barnes sisters, 9
Barris, George, 150
Basie, Count, 3
"Battle of the Sexes," 113

Beach Book, The, 46, 47, 59, 86, 125, 149, 180
Bedford-Stuyvesant Restoration Corporation, 129
Belafonte, Harry, 169
Bell, Griffin, 131
Bellow, Saul, 50
Belton, Sharon Sayles, 161
Bender, Marylin, 92
Benoit, Joan, 111
Benton, Robert, 39, 46, 82, 124, 125, 130
Berle, Milton, 39
Bernstein, Leonard, 25
Beyoncé, 114
Bible, 46
Biden, Joseph R., 183
Big Band era, 3
Bigelow, Kathryn, 176
Bingham, Sallie, 111
Bombay, India, 33
Bonnie and Clyde, 39, 125
Bork, Robert, 150
Boston Public Gardens, 132
Bower, Ruth, 111, 117
Bowles, Chester, 30
Brandeis, Louis, 2
Braun, Carol Moseley, 165
Breslin, Jimmy, 57, 58, 59
Brooke, Edward, 85
Brown, Jim, 128

226 Index

Brownmiller, Susan, xxi, 86
Brzezinski, Zbigniew, 37, 38
Buckley, William F., Jr., 125
"Bunny's Tale, A," 42–48, 86, 167, 182
Burma, 33
Burr, Richard, 163
Burstein, Karen, 161
Bush, George H.W., 147, 151, 165, 182
Bush, George W., 160, 169, 182
Byrne, Jane, 165

Caldwell, Sarah, 120
Cambridge, Massachusetts, 36
Capote, Truman, 128
Carbine, Patricia, 90, 101–105, 110, 113, 116, 119, 137
Carpenter, Liz, 69, 74
Carter, Hodding, III, 74
Carter, Jimmy, 95–98, 131, 143, 146, 159, 181
Carter, Rosalyn, 94, 96
CBS Morning News, 84
Center for Constitutional Rights, 170
Central Intelligence Agency (CIA), 35, 81
Chavez, Cesar, 48, 49, 54, 102
Cher, 153
Chester Bowles Fellowship, 27, 28, 30, 33, 179
Chisholm, Shirley, xix, 64, 68, 69, 72, 73, 77
Choice Not an Echo, A (Schlafly), 78
Choice USA, 85
Chotzinoff, Blair, 25, 26, 28, 125, 127, 179
Chotzinoff, Pauline, 25, 26, 125
Chotzinoff, Samuel, 25, 26, 125
Civil Rights Act of 1964, 52, 64, 156, 166
Clarenbach, Kay, 64, 65
Clarklake, 3, 4, 7, 9, 12, 21, 129, 139
Clinton, Bill, 156, 157, 167, 168, 182
Clinton, Hillary, xv, xix, 114, 157, 161, 162, 163, 164, 169, 183
Coates, Odia, 84
Code Pink, 170

Columbia Broadcasting System (CBS), 36, 37
Columbia University, 129, 131, 177
Comden, Betty, 125
Commission on Gender Equity, 165
Conant, James B., 64
Conrad, Joseph, 46
Conroy, Catherine, 64
Consumer Reports, 110
Conversation with..., A, 153
Cooks, Rachel, 164
Cosmopolitan, 107
Costanza, Midge, 94, 96
Count Basie, 3
Cronkite, Walter, 132, 153
Culture Project, 170

Damned Whores and God's Police, 116
Dancing, 3, 10, 11
Danforth, John, 160
David's Clothing Store, 11, 16
Davis, Angela, 114
Davis, Ossie, 169
De Beauvoir, Simone, 65, 169
de Blasio, Bill, 165
Dee, Ruby, 169
Deep Throat, 152
Democratic National Convention, 1968, xvii, 55, 56, 128, 165
Democratic National Convention, 1972, 73
Desmond, Paul, 125
Devlin, Bernadette, 70
Dietrich, Marlene, 128
Direct Impact Africa (DIA), 169
Doing Sixty and Seventy, xxii, 174, 182
Donahue, Phil, 111, 138, 152
Donor Direct Action, 169
"Dr. Howard's Medicine," 7, 9, 14
Dworkin, Andrea, 70, 86, 152, 166

Eastwood, Mary, 64
Edgar, Joanne, 103
Egan, Father Harvey, 84, 85
Ehrenreich, Barbara, 114, 169
Eisenhower, Dwight, 179

Eliot, T.S., 46
Ellington, Duke, 3
Emily's List, 161
Equal Employment Opportunity Commission (EEOC), 64, 65
Equal Pay Act (1963), 185–90
Equal Rights Amendment (ERA), xvi, 68, 69, 77, 78, 79, 87, 93, 143, 144, 146, 147, 155, 156, 162, 174, 181, 190
Equality Now, 170
Esquire, 39, 40, 42, 46, 51, 52, 88, 124, 125
Eve Ensler, 170
Evers, Myrlie, 74

Faludi, Susan, 114
Falwell, Jerry, 143
Farenthold, Sissy, 73
Farrell, Mike, 169
Fasteau, Brenda Feigen, xix, 92, 131, 139, 101
Faust, Drew Gilpin, 138
Fedor, Teresa, 164
Felker, Clay, 40, 42, 51, 54, 83, 102, 104, 111
Feminine Mystique, The (Friedan), xv, xvi, xxiv, 59, 60, 62, 65, 86, 90, 91, 92, 180
Feminist Majority Foundation, 119
Feminist Revolution, 82
Ferraro, Geraldine, xv, 111, 144, 145, 153, 182
Fight, The, 90
Finch, Robert, 131
Finkelstein, Nina, 103
Fiorina, Carly, 118
First Ms. Reader, The, 121
Flynt, Larry, 165
Fonda, Jane, 114, 137, 170, 182
Ford Foundation, 30, 110, 129
Ford, Betty, 94, 96
Ford, Gerald, 93, 94, 181
Fortune, 36
Fourth Procedure, The (Pottinger), 131
Francis, Bev, 174
Frank, Leo, 2

Franken, Al, 167, 168
Free Europe Committee, 36
Free to Be...You and Me, 121, 138
Freedom of Access to Clinic Entrances Act (1994), 213–216
Friedan, Betty, xvi, xviii, xx, xxi, 59, 60, 62, 64, 65, 66, 69, 77, 82, 86, 90–92, 114, 140, 180
Friedenberg, Walter, 39
Front Page Award, 113

Galbraith, John Kenneth, 47, 70, 71, 126
Gandhi, 32, 48
Geneva, Switzerland, 24, 25, 179
Georg Jenson, 5
Gilliam, Terry, 39
Gillibrand, Kristen, 165
Gilligan, Carol, 111
Ginsburg, Ruth Bader, xix, xxiv, 27, 131, 157, 171, 182
Glamour, 47, 50, 70
Gloria in Her Own Words, 176, 183
Gloria: A Life, 176
Glorias, The, 177
Glover, Danny, 169
Goldwater, Barry, 78, 144
Good Housekeeping, 107
Gore, Albert, Jr., 160, 171
Gould, Lois, 152
Graduate, The, 127
Graham, Katherine, 79, 104, 109, 128
Grasso, Ella, xv, 71
Gray, Clive, 35, 36
Greece, 30
Green, Adolph, 125
Greenwalt, Crawford, 64
Greer, Germaine, 58, 86
Gruenthe, Alfred M., 64
Guinzburg, Tom, 51, 83, 125, 126

Haener, Dorothy. 64
Hand, Learned, 64
Harrington, Michael, 37
Harris, Elizabeth (Betty), 101–105
Harris, Kamala, xvi

Harris, LaDonna, 69
Harvard Crimson, 167
Harvard Law Review, 92
Harvard Law School, 131, 172
Harvard University, 132, 138
"Having My Baby," 83
Hayes, Harold, 39
Hayes, Randy, 169
Hayes, Susan, 39
Hedgebrook, 175
Heifitz, Jascha, 25
Help! For Tired Minds, 39, 180
Helsinki Youth Festival, 40
Henry, Aaron, 74
Henry, Buck, 127
Hepburn, Katherine, 114
Hill, Anita, 151, 168
Hite, Shere, 152
Ho Chi Minh, 51
"Ho Chi Minh in New York," 50, 51, 175
Hobart and William Smith College, 177
Hofstra University, 177
Horbal, Koryne, 85
Howard, Dr. Kenneth, 7
Huerta, Dolores, 48, 49
Hughes, Dorothy Pitman, 61, 74, 75, 139, 148
Humphrey, Hubert, 53
Hunter College, 93

Independent Research Service (IRS), 40, 81
Independent Service for Information (ISI), 36–40, 48, 169, 180
India, 28, 30–34, 35, 41, 48, 68, 76, 77, 130, 169
International Women's Year (IWY), 93
International Women's Year (IWY) Commission, 94

Jackson, C.D., 36, 37, 38
Jackson, Glenda, 114
Jagger, Bianca, 153
James, Harry, 3

John Birch Society, 95
John Fairfax Ltd., 115, 116
Johnson, Lyndon, 52, 53, 64, 69, 83, 101, 180
Johnson, Rafer, 128, 129
Jolie, Angelina, 114
Jones, Paula, 168
Jordan, Crystal Lee, 121
Jordan, Hamilton, 98
Joyce, Jean, 30
Joyner, Florence Griffith, 112
Joyner-Kersee, Jackie, 112

Kagan, Elena, 172
Kaiser, Robert, 40
Kalb, Marvin, 40
Kavanaugh, Brett, 168
Kellogg's, 108
Kennedy, Edward M., 98
Kennedy, Florynce (Flo), 74, 139
Kennedy, John F., xxiv, 46, 64, 126, 180
Kennedy, Robert, 52–54, 72, 128, 129
Kerr, Clark, 64
Kerry, John, 169
King, Billie Jean, 113
King, Martin Luther, Jr., xix, 54, 66
Kirkpatrick, Jeane, 147
Kissinger, Henry, 132
Koestler, Arthur, 25
Kopechne, Mary Jo, 98
Kramer vs. Kramer, 39, 125
Krupsak, Mary Ann, 94
Ku Klux Klan (KKK), 2, 95
Kunin, Madeline, 162
Kurtzman, Harvey, 39
Kwong, Y.H., 33

Ladies' Home Journal, 107
Lady Bic Shaver, 119
Lahti, Christine, 176, 177
Lang, Dale, 116–118
Las Vegas, Nevada, 34
Lauper, Cyndi, 111
Laura Scales House, 19, 23, 24
Leaf, Jonathan, 90
Lerner, Michael, 169

Levine, Bob, 173
Levitt, Leonard, 87, 88
Lewinsky, Monica, 157, 167, 168
Lewis, John, 171
Liberty Media, 118, 119
Library Journal, 117
Life, 48
Lightfoot, Lori, 165
Lindsay, John, 54
Lindsay, Mary, 47
Lombardo, Guy, 3
London, England, 28, 29, 179
Longworth, Alice Roosevelt, 128
Look, 48, 70, 101
Loring, Rosalind, 64
Lovelace, 166
Lovelace, Linda, 151, 152

MacDonald, Jay, 118
MacKinnon, Catharine, 166
MAD, 39
Mailer, Norman, 57–59, 61, 181
Majority Enterprise, 102
Makers (PBS Documentary), 176, 183
Mankiller, Wilma, 133, 138
Mann, Emily, 176
Manning, Robert, 132
Marchiano, Linda Boreman, 152, 165, 166
Marilyn: Norma Jean, xxi, 150, 155, 182
Marshall, Thurgood, 151, 171
Matilda Publications, 116
McCall's, 91, 101–104
McCarthy, Eugene, 47, 52–56, 72
McGinnis, Joe, 57
McGovern, George, xix, 53, 55, 56, 70–74, 76, 93, 112
McGovern, Terry, 74
McLeish, Archibald, 25
#MeToo movement, 151, 163, 166–168
Miller, Arthur, 126
Millett, Kate, 86, 93
Mink, Patsy, 93
Miranda House, 30
Mitchell, John, 131
Monroe Elementary School, 8

Monty Python, 39
Morgan, Robin, 86, 93, 113, 117, 137, 152, 169, 170, 182
Moses, Marion, 48
Mother Jones, 110
Moving beyond Words: Age, Rage, Sex, Power, Money, Muscles: Breaking the Boundaries of Gender (Steinem), 136, 174, 173, 182
Ms., xviii, xx, xxii, 69, 77, 86, 87, 90, 97, 99–121, 137, 139, 145, 146, 149, 150–152, 155, 168, 173, 174, 181
Ms. Foundation for Education and Communication, 110, 116
Ms. Foundation for Women, 110, 115, 119, 120, 138, 170, 173
Ms. *Guide to Health*, 121
Murray, Pauli, 64
"My Father's Footsteps," 41
My Life on the Road (Steinem), 29, 41, 175, 177, 183

Nabisco, 108
Nader, Ralph, 159
National Domestic Workers Alliance, 165
National Farmworkers Association (NFWA), 48, 49
National Memorial for Peace and Justice, 171
National Organization for Women (NOW), xv, xvi, 59, 64–65, 90, 150, 180
National Student Association (NSA), 35, 36, 40, 180
National Women's Conference (Houston, 1977), xviii, 90, 93–96, 143, 144, 181
National Women's Hall of Fame, 177
National Women's Political Caucus (NWPC), xviii, xx, 67–69, 72, 76, 77, 90, 92, 100, 160, 181
New Woman, 91
New York, 47, 50, 51, 56, 58, 59, 60, 70, 72, 74, 76, 102, 103, 111, 119, 128, 144, 175, 180, 181
New York Daily News, 58, 132

New York Herald Tribune, 52
New York Times, xix, 38, 47, 55, 69, 81, 84, 90, 93, 98, 99, 125, 141, 159, 161, 167, 168
New York Times Book Review, 92
Newman, Paul, 47, 49
Newsweek, 69, 70, 91, 100, 115
Newswomen's Club of New York, 113
Nichols, Mike, 127
Nixon, Pat, 54, 55, 102, 142
Nixon, Richard, 54–57, 73, 77, 83, 93, 112, 131, 180, 181
Not in Our Name, 170
Nuneviller, Janey, 2, 10
Nuneviller, Joseph, 1, 10
Nuneviller, Marie, 1, 10, 31

Obama, Barack, xix, 161–163, 177, 182
Oberlin College, 2
Ocean Beach Pier, 3, 4, 5
O'Connor, Sandra Day, 27, 144, 147, 181
O'Hanrahan, Inka, 64
Onassis, Jacqueline, 49, 128, 132
Ordeal (Lovelace), 152
Orwell, George, 25
Outrageous Acts and Everyday Rebellions, xxv, 137, 149, 150, 181
Oxford University, 25

Paley, Grace, 152
Palin, Sarah, 160, 162
Patch, Robert, 24
Patch, Susanne Steinem, 1–3, 5–7, 15, 16, 17, 22, 24, 27, 40, 83, 140–142, 173, 179
Pauley, Jane, 153
Paulus, Diane, 176
Peacock, Mary, 103
Pelosi, Nancy, xv, 114, 182
People v. Larry Flynt, The, 165
Pincus, Walter, 38
Pitman, Dorothy. *See* Hughes, Dorothy Pitman
Place in the Heart, 125
Playboy, 42
Playboy Bunny, 43–45

Playboy Club, 42, 44, 180
Pogrebin, Letty Cottin, 93, 103, 104, 110, 119, 135, 137, 152
Poo, Ai-Jen, 171
Pottinger, Stan, 124, 130, 132, 155
Powell, Lewis, 150
President Cleveland, 33
Presidential Medal of Freedom, 49, 177, 183
President's Commission on National Goals, 64
Proctor & Gamble, 108
Psychiatrists for Equal Rights, 174

Quinn, Christine, 165

Radcliffe College, 78
Radio Corporation of American (RCA), 44
Radio Free Europe, 36
Raitt, Bonnie, 169
Ramparts, 81
Rayburn, Sam, 101
Raymer Junior High School, 10
Reagan, Ronald, xvi, 98, 143–145, 147, 150, 159, 165, 181
Reasoner, Harry, 109
Red Stockings, 59, 81–83, 180
Redford, Robert, 153
Reno, Janet, 157, 182
Reuben's Delicatessen, 126
Revlon, 108, 113
Revolution from Within: A Book of Self-Esteem (Steinem), xxi, 136, 154, 173, 182
Ribicoff, Abraham, 71, 72
Rich, Adrienne, 152
Ride, Sally, 114, 153
Roach, Archbishop John, 84
Robb, Lynda Johnson, 96
Rockefeller, Nelson, 78
Roe v. Wade, 83, 150, 168, 169, 171, 181, 190–213
Rosen, Kenneth, 105
Rosenthal, Abe, 38
Ross, Deborah, 163

Roth, Renee, 161
Ruckelshaus, Jill, 69
Rules for Radicals (Alinsky), 175
"Ruth's Song (Because She Could Not Sing It)," 41, 149
Ryan, Cornelius, 46

Said, Edward, 169
Sanders, Bernie, 162, 163
Sargent, Herb, 127, 128
Sarnoff, Robert, 44
Sassy, 115, 116
Scarsdale, New York, 5
Scheuer, James, 61
Schlafly, Phyllis, 78, 95, 143, 144, 146, 160
Schlesinger, Arthur, Jr., 71, 74
Schneiderman, Eric, 168
Schorr, Daniel, 40
Scotland, 25
Selling of the President, The (McGinnis), 57
Seven Sisters colleges, xxv, 18, 20, 26, 30, 33, 36, 70, 124
Sharpe, John E., Dr., 29
Shaul, Dennis, 40
Sheehy, Gail, 95
Sheen, Martin, 169
Show, 40, 42, 43, 45, 46, 180, 182
Shriver, Sargent, 101
Sigmund, Paul, 36, 39
Simmons College, 177
Simon & Schuster, 173
Sinatra, Frank, 128
Sisterhood Is Global Institute, 169, 170
Sisterhood Is Powerful (Morgan), 137
Sloan, Margaret, 74, 139
Smith, Margaret Chase, xv
Smith College, xxiv, 5, 6, 18, 19–27, 48, 59, 62, 68, 77, 91, 127, 130, 176, 177, 179
Smithsonian, 110
Sondheim, Stephen, 52
Sorenson, Ted, 126, 127
Sotomayor, Sonia, 171, 172, 182
Southern, Terry, 167
Southern Methodist University, 177
Soviet Union, 113

Spirit of Houston, The: The First National Women's Conference, 96
Stanton, Frank, 37, 38
Steinbeck, John, 126
Steinem, Ed, 10
Steinem, Gloria: abortion in London, 28–30; adult relationship with her mother, 148–149; birth and early childhood, 1–6; cancer, 154–155; Carter, Jimmy Carter, 96–98; Chotzinoff, Blair, 25–28; circle of female friends, 137–139; college, 19–25; critics, 81–83, 88–89; emergence as movement leader, 65–66, 69; Equal Rights Amendment (ERA), 68, 77–79, 146; fellowship year in India, 30–34; feminist advocate and organizer, 147–49, 155–56; freelance writing career, 39, 42–48, 50–51, 70; honors, awards, and recognitions, 176–177; Leo, father, dies, 40; Mailer mayoral campaign, 57–59, 61; marriage to David Bale, 133–134; *Ms.*, 99–119; Ms. Foundation, 119–121; National Women's Conference (1977), 93–96; *New York*, 51–57; political campaign efforts, 159–65; pornography, 152, 165–66; presidential campaign, 1968, 52–57; presidential campaign, 1972, 70–74; protecting *Roe v. Wade*, 150–151; Red Stockings abortion speak out, 59–60; relationship with her father, 41–42; reproductive rights, 83–85, romantic relationships, 124–33; Ruth, mother, dies, 145–146; sexual harassment/#MeToo movement, 151, 166–169; speaking tours, 74–77, 146–148; Sue, sister, relationship with, 16–18, 140–141; tensions with Friedan, 90–92; Toledo years caring for mother, Ruth, 6–16; United Farmworkers, 48–49, 54; Vienna Youth Festival, 35–38, Woodrow Wilson Fellowship, 86–87

Steinem, Joseph, 1, 7
Steinem, Leo, 1–7, 24, 25, 27, 34, 35, 40, 41, 130, 146, 179, 180
Steinem, Pauline, 1, 2, 3, 4
Steinem, Ruth Nuneviller, 1–16, 24, 27, 31, 90, 130, 140, 141, 145, 146, 149, 179, 181
Steinem, Susanne. *See* Patch, Susanne Steinem
Stevenson, Adlai, 27, 48, 52, 53
St. Joan of Arc Catholic Church, 84, 85
Stop ERA, 78, 93, 95
Sulzbergers, 125
Summers, Anne, 115, 116
Sundance Film Festival, 177
Sweetser, Susan, 162
Switzerland, 24

"Take Your Daughter to Work Day," 120, 170
Tale of Two Cities, A (Dickens), 14
Talese, Gay, 50
Talese, Nan, 50
Taymor, Julie, 177
Ted Mack & the Original Amateur Hour, 10
That Was the Week That Was, 127
Theosophy, 31
Theron, Charlize, 114
Thomas, Clarence, 151, 160, 166, 167
Thomas, Franklin, 129, 131, 134
Thomas, Marlo, 110, 111, 119, 121, 138, 153, 173
Time, 27, 48, 55, 111
Title IX, 112, 145
Today, 48, 111, 153, 154
Toledo Blade, 3
Toledo, OH Board of Education, 1
Toledo, Ohio, 1, 3, 6, 7, 8, 9, 10–16, 54, 130, 133, 134, 139, 149, 179
Toledo News Bee, 3
Tomlin, Lily, 114
Town beyond the Wall (Wiesel), 127
Trump, Donald, xix, xxiii, 164, 167–169, 171, 183
Truth Will Set You Free, but First It Will Piss You Off!: Thoughts on Life, Love, and Rebellion, The (Steinem), 183
Tufts University, 177

Ueberroth, Peter, 111
United Farm Workers (UFW), 48, 49
United for Peace and Justice, 170
United Nations, 147, 169
United States House Representatives, xv, 151
United States Senate, xv, 68, 151
United States Supreme Court, 65, 83, 145, 147, 157, 181
University of Geneva, 24
University of Pennsylvania, 132
University of Toledo, 2
URGE: Unite for Reproductive & Gender Equity, 85
U.S. Information Agency, 45
U.S. News & World Report, 132
U.S. State Department, 35, 36
U.S. Women's National Soccer Team, The (USWNT), 112
Utne, 118

Van Dyke, Dick, 39
Vanderbilt, Amy, 46
Vassar College, 33
Vienna Youth Festival, 35, 36, 180
Vietnam War, 49, 52, 146
Viking Press, 46, 51, 125
Vogue, 128
Votaw, Carmen Delgado, 95, 97, 98
Voters for Choice, 85, 133

Waite High School (Toledo, OH), 10, 11, 179
Walker, Alice, 114
Walters, Barbara, 154
Warner Communication, 104, 105
Washington, DC, 19
Washington Post, 40, 79, 81, 104, 109, 128
Washington University, 78, 177
Watergate scandal, 81, 98, 146
Waters, Maxine, 95

Webb, Charles, 127
Weddington, Sarah, 98
Western High School (Washington, DC), 17, 18, 179
Wheaton College, 177
Who's Afraid of Virginia Woolf?, 127
Wiesel, Eli, 127
Woman, 183
Woman Alive!, 121
Women Against Pornography, 152
Women's Action Alliance (WAA), 76, 100, 101
Women's March on Washington (2017), 164
Women's Media Center, 137, 170, 182
Women's Own, 47

Women's Strike for Peace, 49
Woodrow Wilson Center, 86, 87, 131, 175
Woodrow Wilson Fellowship, 86, 87, 137
Woods, Harriett, 160, 161
Woodville Road house, 8, 9
Woodward, Joanne, 49
Woodward, Lynette, 112
Working Mother, 116, 118
Working Woman, 116, 118

Yale University, 132, 177
Yates, Sandra, 115, 116

Zuckerman, Mort, 132, 133, 155

About the Author

William H. Pruden III is the director of civic engagement, a college counselor, and an instructor in history and social studies at Ravenscroft School in Raleigh, North Carolina. He earned an AB in history from Princeton University, a JD from Case Western Reserve University, and master's degrees from Wesleyan University and Indiana University. In addition to numerous presentations at conferences, he has contributed chapters to books on a number of American history topics and has had hundreds of articles published in historical encyclopedias and reference works.

www.ingramcontent.com/pod-product-compliance
Lightning Source LLC
Chambersburg PA
CBHW060947230426
43665CB00015B/2100